FOUR NEW YALE PLAYWRIGHTS

FOUR NEW

YALE PLAYWRIGHTS

JOHN GASSNER, *Editor*

Crown Publishers, Inc., New York

In memory of

Yale's President A. Whitney Griswold

(1906–1963)

A STAUNCH FRIEND OF THE SCHOOL OF DRAMA

CONTENTS

FOREWORD

This second volume of recent Yale plays follows hard on the heels of the first, which appeared last fall.* Like its predecessor, it has been edited by John Gassner, in whose playwriting classes at Yale these works were brought into being.

It will be obvious to the reader that the diversity in subject matter in these selections and the variations in intention and style are proof, if proof be needed, that the Drama School does not champion writing according to formula. Each student-playwright is given the freedom to develop his ideas as he will, but in classes and seminars his work is brought under careful scrutiny and submitted to exhaustive discussion and analysis by both teachers and students. It is attacked, defended, dissected, and in many cases reconstructed and rewritten as a result of these sessions.

Three of these plays have been produced in the Yale University Theatre. Their creators were thus provided with an invaluable experience, the opportunity to learn at first hand what happens when a manuscript is translated into a performance by a director, actors, and designers. Such stu-

* *Three Plays from the Yale School of Drama,* New York, E. P. Dutton & Co., 1964.

dents, it seems to me, have the best of both worlds. First, they have the unique kind of expert critical guidance that only a rare teacher like Professor Gassner can provide, and second they have the stimulus and challenge of weighing the public response to their efforts.

This process of combining classroom theory and academic discussion with realistic practice by demonstration in the theatre has been the keystone in the educational philosophy of the Yale Drama School. That it has met with some success may be seen in the achievements of some of our graduates and alumni who have been subjected to it. Among these are Frank Gilroy (*The Subject Was Roses*), Michael Stewart (*Bye-Bye Birdie, Carnival, Hello, Dolly!*), and Tad Mosel (*All the Way Home*)—to mention only a few.

In the present drought, when scripts of some originality and integrity are at a premium, it is hoped that educational and community theatre directors may find these plays to their liking and give them production.

F. CURTIS CANFIELD
Dean of the School of Drama
Yale University
New Haven

"NEW PLAYS":
AN INTRODUCTION

The facts are simple, the interpretations complex. I have assembled here four plays by young writers. Their plays were written and produced or scheduled for production at Yale University's School of Drama, founded as a "department of drama" by the famed George Pierce Baker forty years ago and expanded into a full-fledged "school" by its first dean, F. Curtis Canfield, a decade ago.

Something can be noted about each of the writers, which may be of interest to us as to the origins, for better or worse, of new American playwrights in recent years. There was a time when it was part of our cultural "redskin" folklore that playwrights were diamonds in the rough. It was believed ever so democratically that they emerged from the loam of untutored mankind and brought with them raw experience which they transferred to the stage. Our native "cult of experience" required this view. It was fostered in the 1920's by insurgent Greenwich Village and left-bank bohemianism; in the 1930's by the economic dislocation of the Depression and the idolatry of so-called proletarian art which located spiritual health and millennial vision primarily in a deprived working-class milieu; and in the 1940's by a young generation's confrontation of the acrid realities of global war. More recently it was, of course, the "beatnik" movement, chiefly on the West Coast, that once more glorified the "redskins" as the prime source of creative vitality and challenge to the complacencies of an allegedly affluent society. The cult of crude experience (call it, if you will, elemental realism) has also been associated, rather paradoxically, with the cult of showbusiness. We have assumed that the necessary condition for becoming a successful playwright was baptism by "showbusiness," the special *métier* of titillating the public. Before 1920, it depended upon the stage rather than upon the movies and currently upon television for facile farcical and melodramatic entertainment. Since then, this public has depended, even in some musicals, upon a factitious realism and growing coarsening of sensibility considered contiguous with experience and alien to formal education.

It would not be difficult to prove that the facts give the lie to the folklore, and that virtually all the estimable American playwrights who emerged after World War I were anything but "redskins." But many seemed apologetic that they weren't and made a great show of swinging tomahawks from their Park Avenue tepees. The few playwrights who had not completed a formal education tried to complete it informally and privately, as O'Neill did with assiduous reading of Strindberg and the Greeks. And many of them picked up the odds and ends of Freudian and, later, Marxian patter. Nevertheless, myth sustained by belief becomes reality in effect, and it is only in recent years, when a college or even post-graduate education became the commonest of properties, that our "redskin" mythology ceased to be a sacrosanct assumption. All the young authors represented in the present small collection of plays are attending or have attended a graduate school at Yale, and were at one time or another sustained in part or whole by scholarships and fellowships. In the ensuing paragraphs I provide data concerning the four new playwrights supplied by themselves; they unblushingly reported considerable association with a formal education. Taking them in alphabetical order there is this to say:

MARK EISENSTEIN attended Wesleyan University and then taught at the University of Connecticut, as well as freelanced by writing scripts for WABD-TV before attending the Yale graduate drama school, where he received a Theatre Guild Fellowship and also won the Merrill award for playwriting with the wryly original race play *The Fighter,* twice under option for New York production since its presentation at Yale. Mr. Eisenstein is now an instructor in English at Hofstra University, where he is in charge of a workshop in Creative Writing. It is to be presumed that he saw life "in the raw" when he served in the U.S. Navy, but his "redskin" reputation is blemished by the revelation that he graduated from Wesleyan University with a Phi Beta Kappa key among his effects.

ROBERT E. INGHAM'S *vita* must be given in his own words for the flavor they communicate and for his favorable report on a university:

"I was born the 27th of January, 1934, some 30 miles east of the Blue Ridge Mountains in Bedford County, Virginia. There were six children, and we lived on a farm. My father worked for the Post Office too, so we didn't have to farm very hard, and as a result, I had a lot of time to dangle my feet in the creek and be spooky. I was named after Robert E. Lee. There was an old set of *Battles and Leaders of the Civil War* in the attic, and I used to look through it, before I was old enough to read the text, at all those beards and captions, 'Killed at Gettysburg,' 'Mortally Wounded at Frayser's Farm,' 'Captured in the Bloodly Angle,' and I grew up with a great desire to know what had happened.

"Both my parents were great talkers, and for a time I was the family listener. My mother could make a story out of anything: courthouse Virginia and her childhood, her seven great-aunts who still wept for their only and baby brother killed at Appomattox Courthouse on the day General Lee surrendered, my other great-grandfather, who walked to Richmond on a game knee to prove he could be an infantryman, and my great-uncle Tom Dick McCraw, the most contrary man in central Virginia, who died protesting right-of-way with a trolley car. My father knows the King James version from beginning to amen, and read us a chapter every night. He used to entertain me in the hayfields with Cromwell's words to Wolsey, complete to tears and gestures. He grew up in Wales and Manchester, came to this country when he was 15, alone, and was, among other things, a cavalryman on the Mexican Border in 1918. And I heard about it all.

"Thus, it was inevitable that I would grow up to be a performer and a word-merchant. I never liked schools, and spent much of my time fighting them, with the result that I am still in school at an age when most people who like them are finished and long gone. I went to Berea College for two years, and a small school in my home town for one semester, and spent most of my time being an actor and reading things I didn't have time for, and generally being shiftless. I volunteered for the draft in 1954, and tried school again in 1956 at the University of Virginia. I owe a great debt to the University of Virginia, which let me be a nut; it surrounded me with intelligent people and let me act and read and roam around and grow up without having to jump up and down every thirty seconds and say 'Yea, yea, I love you,' and in the end gave me both an education and a plumber's license. By this time I had to finish growing up; I had a wife and the first of what is now a family of three sons. I didn't want to be just an actor; I had seen too many of my friends scattering photographs of themselves and résumés through casting offices like dogs at lamp posts. So I decided to try something with all this free material I had picked up along the way, and wrote a one-act play. That was more like it, so I wrote a long play and went off to teach school and get out of debt. Two years later, I came to the Yale Drama School, and the long play became *A Simple Life*."

Mr. Ingham was the holder of a John Golden Fund Fellowship when this play was staged with extraordinary vigor in the Yale University Theatre by the dean of the School of Drama, F. Curtis Canfield. He holds the RCA-NBC Fellowship at this writing.

BILL KLEB was born in Kansas City, Missouri, on December 19, 1939. He majored in English Literature, and took a B.A. at Yale College in 1961. The following year he taught Freshman English at Yale under the terms of a Carnegie Fellowship, and that year he was also awarded an honorary Woodrow Wilson Fellowship. Mr. Kleb wrote his first play, a long one-acter, in the spring of 1963 and entered the Yale School of Drama the following fall. He had spent the year prior to that (1962–1963) at the University of Paris, where he was awarded a diploma in "French Civilization." *Honeymoon in Haiti* was written during his first year at the drama school, and at the end of that year Mr. Kleb was awarded the Eugene O'Neill Fellowship in playwriting. In his second year of the Doctor of Fine Arts program at Yale, Mr. Kleb is at this writing getting a production for three of his one-act plays at the University Theatre, one of which is *Honeymoon in Haiti*. The plays are being staged by Professor Frank McMullan, head of the School's play directing department.

ROBERT MURRAY, the author of *The Good Lieutenant*, for which production has been pending for some time, started winning prizes for his competence in the fine arts while he was still in elementary school in his native state, Wisconsin. He also started writing stories and plays at an early age. Two of his stories were published in *The Paris Review* in 1954–55. While majoring in English and Comparative Literature at the University of Wisconsin under Professor Haskell Block and others, he became actively engaged with the theatre when he

joined The Wisconsin Players, receiving awards for acting
and directing as well as a special citation for a play, *A Stroll
in Hexagon,* produced by the group. He appeared in a season
of repertory with The Wisconsin Players. He was commis-
sioned a Second Lieutenant in the U.S. Army in 1954, when
he was only twenty-two years old, and served in Germany.
In 1960 he held a Theatre Guild Fellowship in Playwriting
at the Yale School of Drama made available by the late
Lawrence Langner, and it was in one of my playwriting
seminars there that Mr. Murray first exhibited drafts of *The
Good Lieutenant.* He also wrote other plays during his stay at
Yale, and one of these, *High Cockalorum,* a romantic comedy set in the West of 1875, was staged at the School of
Drama for the University Theatre's subscription audiences
by Professor McMullan. At this writing, a production is pending for still another play, entitled *Flickers.* Mr. Murray now
lives in Aspen, Colorado, with his wife and three children,
and is Program Director for the Aspen Institute for Human-
istic Studies.

Playwrights are apt to welcome an opportunity to explain
their intentions or their experiences with their work. Arthur
Miller and Tennessee Williams have done so frequently and at
considerable length. Some of the new playwrights in the
present volume have also availed themselves of the opportunity to do so, although with a becoming modesty or modera-
tion. What they say may contribute to a proper appraisal of
their plays and problems by their readers and producers.

Mr. Murray's statement reads as follows:

"*The Good Lieutenant* was the first full-length play that I
wrote. In a sense, it's really a two-act play with an epilogue.
While this may diminish its professional production oppor-
tunities it seems to me the right arrangement. I'm as interested
in the form of this play as I am in its content because I think
they complement one another. The 'plot' is, I think, almost
geometrically predictable. I tried something along sparer

lines than melodrama—although I hope that the dramatic or
the theatrical has not been sacrificed, for that would be
erasing the effort to write a play. The theme of wisdom gained
and innocence lost is a traditional theme of course, and a
particularly American one. And while a 'theme' was not
uppermost in my mind while writing the play (I was more
interested in the situation and the dilemma) I see that there
it is. To this traditional theme I hope that I have added a
twist to another traditional theme, the theme that brutality
and refinement are of themselves guilty or innocent of evil.
It's a much more complicated world than that and the theatre
is the place to hint at and remind us of it."

Mr. Eisenstein reports the following:

"*The Fighter* was first produced in April, 1958, on Yale
University's experimental stage. Actually, it was first heard in
a playwriting seminar the preceding year at which time John
Gassner expressed considerable enthusiasm and offered important suggestions which were subsequently incorporated
into a second draft. Next fall, the second draft was given a
reading at a playwright's lab and shortly thereafter it was
chosen for thesis production by George Mallonee, who
worked with the author on further revisions prior to production in April.

"At first it seemed the major problem in producing the
play would be in the casting. At the time, there were no Negro
male actors enrolled at the school. Surprisingly enough, once
it was decided to cast two white actors in the (Negro) leading
roles, the problem of race disappeared. Black face make-up
seemed hardly appropriate and nothing was done to physically
suggest the fact that the two brothers were Negroes. It was
decided to let the lines themselves suggest the color of skin
and I remember revising the opening scene only two or three
days in advance of the opening night's performance with just
this in mind. Nor was any attempt made at getting the actors
to deliver their lines with a regional accent.

"At the time, I was surprised by the number of people who read the script without being impressed but who spoke of being deeply moved by the play when it was staged. This is not offered as an excuse for a script which may be difficult to read, but it does suggest one of the reasons potential producers in New York have had difficulty raising money. Also, I was amazed by the number of people who liked the play but failed to see the 'fighter' and his situation as part of the extended metaphor it was meant to be.

"Staging of the play offered problems because of the numerous short scenes and the shifting of time from past to present and back again. The problem was solved by Mr. Mallonee who used bits and pieces of sets to suggest more than was apparent. He also depended heavily on lighting to achieve the desired results. Aside from the technical problems which he readily solved, I best remember Mr. Mallonee's direction and the cast's performance as being deeply and personally involved, especially after the second night's performance. Before the third night's performance Mr. Mallonee told his cast how much the play meant to him and that night Jim Inman, playing the lead, received seven curtain calls and the next day told me that for him the play was a religious experience.

"Although the play's mood and its sense of time and place are essentially realistic, the realism was achieved by such diverse and occasionally non-realistic means as sets made up of fragments and internal monologues delivered directly to the audience. As an example of the latter, I refer you to a few speeches Adele delivers in the second act. When the play demanded a kind of stylization, the performance was stylized. When a scene called for realism, it was played realistically. No time was wasted worrying about the niceties of particular schools of playwriting. Techniques from perhaps any and all schools were used. The only consideration was whether or not a particular technique or device would work. This was true of both the writing of the play and its production."

Mr. Ingham offers other insights. He writes:

"My experience with the Yale production of *A Simple Life,* staged by Dean F. Curtis Canfield, was somewhat peculiar, because I was an actor in it as well as the playwright. This came about because we had a very strong actor for Tippin, Mr. Jon Jory, and no one old enough for Purcell. We felt that it would be disastrous to cast a very young or very young-looking man against a strong Tippin and thus force him to fight for age as well as for stage, and there I was, with my receding hairline. This was a blessing, in one way, for it saved me the painful experience playwrights most often recount, of writhing through rehearsals wondering what on earth those people are doing up there. I kept busy.

"And I benefitted from the production; I saw many things that I had not seen before. Whether or not I would have seen more from a seat in the house, I shall never know, but I have a pretty good idea of what's wrong with the play and what works in it. I found out, for one thing, that Purcell couldn't be played the way I had imagined him. I found out that Tippin could be played exactly opposite from anything I had in mind and could still work, perhaps even better than what I had had in mind. I was able to feel the show, to discover that some scenes had too many lines or too few. The other things that can be learned about a play—questions of clarity or confusion, that too much has been said or not enough, can only be answered really by performance, through the re-action of an audience, and I think I could feel that from the stage as well as I could have picked it up from loitering around the lobby during intermissions.

"In such circumstances, of course, the playwright is even more dependent upon his advisers, Mr. Gassner in the seminar and Dean Canfield in the production. This was a much different play when it came to Yale, and much weaker. It has been my experience—in my brief experience—that a playwright becomes an overindulgent parent, and a point is reached where every word his darlings say has as much worth as any other word, and the play becomes cluttered with an awful lot of odds and ends. My classmates and Mr. Gassner were most helpful in pointing this out, and identifying the more offensive instances. Mr. Canfield continued this process, and was kind enough, at the same time, to let me keep a few things that my heart was set on, and test them against an audience. As a result, I think I am in a better position to revise this play—if I ever get around to it—and to control the new scripts that I am working on now. I think I have learned from this production more than any amount of friendly advice could have ever taught me."

Mr. Kleb's observations are also worth noting as impressions least affected by time, since his play was the most recently produced of the plays in our volume. Mr. Kleb states:

"*Honeymoon in Haiti* was written in the spring of my first year at the Yale Drama School (1964) and produced by Professor Frank McMullan as a major production in January, 1965. We were six weeks in rehearsal and, unfortunately, the manuscript had gone to the printers before it had had the benefit of a production. Thus, during rehearsals, certain changes were made, primarily in the last part of the play, which are not in the present text. For the most part these involved cutting repetitious passages and clarifying certain details in the plot. Dr. Gassner's help and advice, especially in the later stages of the script's growth, were invaluable, supplying an objective viewpoint which made the changes consistent and stageworthy. There is, of course, no substitute for the agony of a rehearsal period and eventual production. A play which has not had the benefit of either is not yet a play; it is merely the outline of one."

After these reports nothing of moment need be noted, and judgment must be left to the readers of these plays. At most a *caveat* is in order for those whose experience with the reading of plays and with actual playgoing is not extensive. It is not as easy as it may seem to read a play, and judgment passed on a playwright's effort and achievement cannot be formed without missing the target unless one is prepared to take into consideration the medium in which plays are expected to become effective.

One of my distinguished predecessors at Yale, the late playwright, critic, and teacher Walter Prichard Eaton, devoted a lucid little essay to the subject, *On Reading Plays.* Here he maintained that no published play (especially a modern prose work) can be read properly or judged justly until it was understood that "there is a radical difference between the plan and purpose of a play and of any other form of literature put into print." The difference is perhaps too obvious to be labored in the introduction to a book that is unlikely to fall into the hands of a reader or reviewer unacquainted with the theatre of his times or indifferent to it. The play is written to be performed on the stage rather than merely read in the library. Mr. Eaton would have preferred us to say not "written" but chiefly "planned and built," but I prefer "written" since the quality of the dialogue is hardly an inessential consideration even in the case of prose drama. But he is correct in reminding us that the stage play is intended to be *seen* as well as heard, as well as indeed to be visualized for us by living actors impersonating the author's characters. The audience apprehends the play directly, as in the actual world, whereas the reader of a novel reads words which he translates into an experience of images and ideas associated in his mind with the word-symbols on the page. The novel, by its very nature, is *indirectly apprehended* in accordance with the associations the reader makes with the words. These must surely vary from person to person or remain in flux, acquiring objectivity or fixity chiefly from what the novelist overtly explains, defines, and exhorts the reader to understand.

What is objective and fixed about a play comes from the stage representation apprehended directly and simultaneously by all members of the audience presumably awake and sober. For that very reason the playwright, unless he takes the risk of cluttering and impeding the stage action, renounces a good deal, if not all, of the literary material, whether descriptive or explanatory, that makes most novel-reading easier and richer than play-reading. Except, of course, in the work of the world's supreme poet-dramatists, which if it is not "easier" reading is certainly rich and rewarding as literature in addition to being stageworthy. Except in the case of a few writers of modern prose drama (Bernard Shaw is the most notable exception in English), the playwright writes without conspicuous literary embellishment and is compelled to rely almost entirely on the dialogue and on the stage action he assigns to his characters. His descriptions of the latter and his stage directions are normally intended solely for the guidance of the actor, the stage director, the scene and costume designer, and other artists associated with the theatrical production, such as the man who lights the show, attends to the sound effects (if any), and provides any music and choreography that the play may require. The play "script," in other words, is often likely to seem barren to the reader unaccustomed or unwilling to visualize the work for himself or to translate what he reads into some approximation of what he should actually be *seeing* and *hearing* in an auditorium. (Experiencing and responding, moreover, not alone but as a member of an audience—that is, not as an emotionally and intellectually isolated individual.) The play's public is subject to contagion for better or worse; it is susceptible to all kinds of non-literary and non-intellectual circumstances and conditions, irritations and seductions. I doubt that it has ever been possible for any playwright or stage producer to anticipate and control all these factors. "Theatre" would be risky business even if playwrights and producers were less vulnerable than other artists, or businessmen, or even scientists, to error and folly.

Dialogue, the reader must conclude, is an especially important consideration if he is the sort of literary gourmet (and I have known some admirable ones) who must have piquant writing before he can tolerate ordinary dramatic writing. He is bound to be disappointed, especially in the modern realistic theatre, by the very plays that audiences have accepted as the dramatic masterpieces of a particular year or decade.

The reader, let alone the stage producer or director, should not allow himself to be put off by a playwright's deliberate commonplaces and repetitions, if they are patently expressive, or by his conscious resort to dialect, argot, or cliché, if his intentions of characterizing and localizing an action are achieved by these means appropriately and credibly. This may limit the life-span of a play, may date it within a generation or even a decade. But we can look to contrary examples provided by Sophocles, Euripides, Shakespeare, Ibsen, Chekhov, O'Casey, O'Neill and Brecht. In any case, no one can guarantee the life-span of so perishable a commodity as a play, and the first important requirement is that it possess life or even mere liveliness for its own times and in its own milieu. If it doesn't, it is not likely to have a second chance at life. (We know, of course, some fortunate exceptions to this probability, such as a few plays by the romantic geniuses Georg Büchner and Alfred de Musset.) After all, the playwright cannot often speak in his own person as novelists have done, and he cannot normally resort to overt literary style without paying heed to the characters to whom he assigns his dialogue and aiming for an impression of naturalness or convincing expressiveness.

This means, of course, that his actors must be able to maintain the illusion of human speech (I say the illusion, not the actuality), and this requires not only speakable prose or verse, but some of the informality, casualness, or even awkwardness suitable to the characters. (Here Shakespeare's most dramatic blank verse is the supreme example.) As Walter Prichard Eaton put it, perhaps a trifle more simply than I would, "When you read a printed play, therefore, you are reading literature (and by no means is all effective dramatic writing actually 'literature') written under rigid restrictions and for a definite end—as speech delivered by actors to advance the story, to reveal character, and to create the illusion of life. It must primarily be appraised for its success in doing these things, and may therefore attain a high rating as dramatic literature when, judged by more ordinary literary standards, it would merit little praise."

Bearing in mind that it is primarily the actor speaking the dialogue and making the movements required of him who brings the play to life on the stage, the good dramatic writer supplies the actors with the most suitable and expressive patterns and tonalities of speech and non-speech, sharps *and flats,* and emotional lability. To dialogue, especially dialogue intended for "realistic" or "representational" theatre, we may well apply what John Stuart Mill said about verse in his *Thoughts on Poetry* in 1859: "If we may be excused the antithesis, we should say that eloquence is *heard,* poetry is *overheard.*" Except for deliberate, appropriately styled direct address to the audience, dialogue is *overheard* even more than poetry. It is usually idle to require of characters in a dramatic situation the efficiency Israel Putnam required of his men at Bunker Hill when he told them, "You are all marksmen—don't one of you fire until you see the whites of their eyes." Except in special circumstances and in very "high" comedy, the characters, far from expressing themselves in polished and accurate phrases, are more apt to be bumblers than marksmen.

Regardless of the degree of education and literary commitment one may posit for the Yale playwrights included in the present volume, this, then, is certain: The work with which their novitiate is represented here is intended to be writing

for the stage. It does not consist of style for the sake of
style, no matter how distinctive the writing in each individual
play; and each play represents various degrees of success in
sacrificing many an indulgence in comment or verbal embellishment that threatened to impede forward action and
visualization on the stage, the growth of one part of a situation out of another part, and progression toward some climax
of action or realization arising from the characters and their
critical pressures. Both with respect to merits and defects or
limitations, the plays offer possibilities of study and of positive
and negative example. Naturally, it is also to be hoped that
each author has something to show and say, something that
justifies the play as more than a mere action and as something
that Matthew Arnold, less deterred from using rhetorically
charged terms by his times than we are by our own, aptly
called a "criticism of life." And whatever style, in any sig-
nificant sense of the term, appears in the work of the new
authors must ultimately derive from what they have to declare
with their action, characterization, and speech. As Shaw puts
it in *Major Barbara,* "He who has nothing to assert has no
style and can have none."

JOHN GASSNER
*Sterling Professor of Playwriting
and Dramatic Literature*
Yale University
New Haven

THE FIGHTER

MARK EISENSTEIN

Presented April 9, 1958, at the School of Drama,
Yale University, with the following cast:

ADELE ('DELL) GRIFFIN	James Inman
WINDY	Richard Forsyth
FIRST BOY	Ray Panighetti
SECOND BOY	John Thomas
WILLIE GRIFFIN	John Callahan
HARRY	Harvey Keith
JACK	Michael Rutenberg
FRED	Dan Potter
JACK'S DATE	Dorothy Jarman
FRED'S DATE	Carolyn Gaiser
THE LITTLE WHITE GIRL	Sami Sramek
THE DEPUTY	Gordon Taylor
THE BARKER	Fletcher Coleman
MARGIE	Zelma Weisfeld
THE PIMPLY-FACED YOUTH	John Sillings
JIMMY	Hector Mendoza
FRANK	Tom Cooke
GIRL	Mary Jane Herndon

THE PHOTOGRAPHER	George Tuttle
THE REPORTER	Russ Moro
DOROTHY	Betty Engel
THE POLICE CAPTAIN	Michael Rutenberg
THE SERGEANT	George Tuttle
BOYS AT CARNIVAL	Ray Panighetti,
	John Thomas

Directed by George E. Mallonee

Settings by Philip Eck

Costumes by Cynthia Taylor   Lighting by Joan Larkey

TIME: Present and past.

PLACE: A small city in the South.

ACT ONE. *A room in a Negro boarding house.*

ACT TWO. *A carnival midway.*

ACT THREE. SCENE 1: *A room in a Negro boarding house.*
SCENE 2: *A jail.* SCENE 3: *The same as Scene 1.*

ACT ONE

SCENE: *A room in a Negro boarding house. A dresser on which an alarm clock ticks, stands to one side. The shade, full drawn over the open window, billows up occasionally with the first breeze of the afternoon. A single brass tap drips water down the side of a dirty wash basin by the door and an iron bedstead, its paint splotched and peeling, lies against the far wall. Two straight-back chairs and a wastepaper basket complete the room's furnishings.*

AT RISE: *Before the curtain goes up, a calliope playing a melody as sad and lonely as a young boy's first discovery of something corrupt in the world can be heard off in the distance. As the curtain goes up a big Negro is discovered lying stripped to his waist on the bed. He stares*

*at the ceiling, his hands clasped across his chest and his head resting
on a soiled pillow. As the calliope continues to play, the melody is
suddenly cut by the voice of a barker . . . "All right, folks! Tonight and
tonight only . . . the house of illusion! Now you see it and now you
don't! Makes the old feel young and the young feel foolish!" The big
Negro suddenly rolls over, buries his head in his arms as though trying
to ward off a blow, then begins to rock slowly back and forth. A knock
on the door and the noise begins to subside. Another knock on the
door and the noise stops altogether and the big Negro stops rocking
back and forth. Finally, the door opens and a dirty little man with the
butt of a cigar stuck in his mouth enters. He wears blue suede shoes,
his tie is undone, and he wipes his face with a soiled handkerchief as
he comes into the room.*

WINDY. You asleep?

'DELL. No.

WINDY. You better get some sleep. You didn't sleep last night and
you go on in another four hours.

'DELL. I guess maybe I dozed off a little.

WINDY. Hey, look. How long you think a guy's gonna put up with
someone, he's a fighter only he don't want to fight?

'DELL. You don't like it, why don't you get someone else?

WINDY. Sure. Go on. Insult me. I tell you something for your own
good and all you want to do is insult me. It's been two years since
you been anything but a bum. So I'll tell you something. You lose this
one and I'll have a hard time matching you with a kangaroo.

'DELL. It don't make no difference. East. North. South. West. Back
on down where I started from. One tank town after another until the
whole world looks like a bus stop on a Saturday afternoon.

WINDY. Then do something about it if you don't like it! You go on
tonight like you been going on and in six months' time the only people
who'll remember your name will be me and the landlady.

'DELL. Then let them forget. I don't care.

WINDY (*stung*). What do you mean, let 'em forget? You used to
be somebody. All right. So your brother threw you a fast one. But I
remember how it used to be.

'DELL. Leave my brother out of it, Windy!

WINDY. . . . your brother wasn't such a bum you could have been
something today. . . .

'DELL. I said leave my brother out of it!

WINDY. All right. All right. I'm sorry. (*After a pause*) Did you eat yet?

'DELL. A little.

WINDY. You shouldn't eat an hour before you go on. It's no good.

'DELL. Did they catch him yet?

WINDY. No. At least I didn't hear anything. You think he'd do what they say?

'DELL. Maybe something. But not what they say. He's my brother and he wouldn't do what they say he did.

WINDY. Yeah. You can't believe anything you hear down here. The heat must get them. You go outside and they're like bugs looking for the shade.

'DELL. You believe he did what they say?

WINDY. No. They all lie like I never heard anyone lie before. If they haven't caught him yet, he should be across the state line by now. It's only forty miles.

'DELL. Who do I fight tonight?

WINDY. What difference does it make? You put on a good show, that's all you have to worry about.

'DELL. Tell me who I fight tonight, Windy.

WINDY. Some guy. I forget his name. It don't make any difference.

'DELL. What color is he, Windy?

WINDY. He's kind of old. It's not much but it might lead to something if you look good.

'DELL. What is he, black?

WINDY. Yeah. A colored kid. It's out at the carnival. Seventy-five bucks if you win and fifty bucks if you lose. It's better than nothing.

'DELL. How long is it they been looking for him, Windy?

WINDY. Two days. They got lousy cops down here. I'll lay money he's across the state line already.

'DELL. I hear they're gonna use bloodhounds.

WINDY. You believe everything you hear down here and you'll go crazy. Besides, they don't even know where to start looking. I wouldn't worry if I was you.

'DELL. They catch him down here, a lawyer wouldn't do much good, would it?

WINDY. Depends on the lawyer. You have to figure he got across the state line. Just figure he made it across the line to where you can help him.

'DELL. Sometimes I wonder.

WINDY. Yeah? What about?

'DELL. About a lot of things. You know what makes people do what they do?

WINDY. You think too much. You ought to try and get some sleep.

'DELL. You think maybe I'm getting too old, Windy?

WINDY. Who told you that? That's all I need, a fighter who thinks he's too old so he can't fight no more.

'DELL. Sometimes I get nightmares, Windy.

WINDY. Everybody gets nightmares once in a while. Try to forget your brother and get some sleep.

'DELL. Sometimes I see faces when I sleep. I see faces like I see at the fights.

WINDY. How about going for a walk? A walk might do you good.

'DELL. I keep getting this dream. I'm getting beat up bad. My face is all cut up and I keep missing and I want to take a count, but I can't. The other guy, he's a little guy with arms down to his knees and the crowd, they keep yelling for him to give me more and I keep crying for him to stop but he won't.

WINDY. Look. You got to forget what happened. You go in the ring someone is liable to get hurt. That's what the crowd come to see, so someone gets hurt, it isn't your fault. You understand?

'DELL. But I didn't have to punch a man crazy to win, did I? I didn't have to jab him till he couldn't see and him hanging on me, crying, and the blood running down his face and the crowd screaming for me to give him more and the referee not doing anything and me just trying to break away so I wouldn't have to see his face.

WINDY. What are you talking about? You won fair and square and just because someone got hurt don't mean it's your fault. Beside, the crowd loved it and if you wasn't so dumb you could be somebody today.

'DELL. I punched a man crazy, Windy.

WINDY. Go on. Get off it. He was punchy to begin with. You just like to think it was your fault because that was the last time you seen your brother.

'DELL. Windy?

WINDY. Yeah?

'DELL. He gets across the state line, how much would a good lawyer cost?

WINDY. What you could make in a month if you look good tonight.

'DELL. You want me to mess him up, Windy? That what you want me to do?

WINDY. Just a little. Not much. You know what the crowd likes. Why? You think you might come out on top for a change?

'DELL. I don't like it, Windy. He's probably just a kid.

WINDY. Never mind you don't like it. What you like don't pay your bills. Remember that. Just tell yourself it's for your brother.

'DELL. How many rounds, Windy?

WINDY. Play with him for three rounds. Put him away in the fourth if you can. Want me to let the shade up?

'DELL. No. I like it better with the shade down.

WINDY. Just remember. You look good tonight and maybe you still got a future. All you got to do is win a couple and you'll be all right.

'DELL. I don't like it.

WINDY. You think too much.

'DELL. You ever play baseball when you were a kid?

WINDY. Sure. All kids play baseball.

'DELL. My brother used to play baseball.

WINDY. Sure. Your brother used to be a real hot-shot. The land-lady treat you all right?

'DELL. She treats me all right.

WINDY. Anybody say anything to you?

'DELL. No.

WINDY. You want me to ask her if you can have a bigger room?

'DELL. No. I don't want a bigger room.

WINDY (*getting up*). I better get going. I got things to do. Just remember. You look good tonight and maybe we can get back to Chicago.

'DELL. Yeah.

WINDY. I'll see you out at the carnival grounds at nine. You better try and get some sleep. (*leaves*)

(*For a while, 'DELL remains motionless on the floor. But then the flutter of the shade catches his attention and he sits up as the sound of the calliope is heard once more.*)

'DELL (*to audience*). Mess a guy up. Cut him up for the crowd. Maybe punch a guy crazy again. But you punch a guy crazy 'cause you don't know what you're doing—it's not the same thing. But he wouldn't do what they say. Maybe something, but not what they say. . . .

(*As* 'DELL *sits up and begins to question himself, the light shifts to the forepart of the stage and the following scene is played in memory.* WILLIE, *dressed as a boy, appears swinging a baseball bat. Following him on stage are a couple of his admirers.*)

FIRST BOY. Come on, Willie! Hit me a short one!

SECOND BOY. Here we go, Willie! A nice easy one!

FIRST BOY. You the best we got, Willie! Let's see how far you can hit it!

(WILLIE *stands back and takes a tremendous swing at the ball and the ball arches up and out of sight as the boys stare after it.*)

WILLIE. Hey, how's that for a hit! Old Willie, he sure knows how to drive them home, don't he?

SECOND BOY. Nobody gonna beat us while you got something to say, huh, Willie?

FIRST BOY. Old Willie got the best swing around.

SECOND BOY. When you going away, Willie?

WILLIE. Going away Saturday. Yes sireee. Chicago, here I come!

SECOND BOY. We sure gonna miss you, Willie.

FIRST BOY. Your brother, he going too?

WILLIE (*still swinging his bat*). Not now. He's not old enough. Maybe next year.

FIRST BOY. You really going to Chicago, Willie?

WILLIE. That's right. My aunt, she says it's better for us boys to go to Chicago. She says we have more opportunity in Chicago.

SECOND BOY. Willie's going to Chicago and stay with his uncle. Ain't that right, Willie?

WILLIE. That's right.

FIRST BOY. Is it far?

WILLIE. Three or four thousand miles, that's all.

FIRST BOY. But how you gonna get there, Willie?

WILLIE. Take a train.

SECOND BOY. All by yourself?

WILLIE. Sure.

FIRST BOY. They talk the same in Chicago like they do here?

WILLIE. 'Course they do.

SECOND BOY. Willie's gonna be real important in Chicago. They got opportunity in Chicago. Ain't that right, Willie?

WILLIE. Gonna play baseball and make a lot of money.

FIRST BOY. I wish I was going to Chicago.

SECOND BOY. Maybe we can come visit you some day, huh, Willie?

WILLIE. Sure. Why not?

SECOND BOY. You should see the clothes his aunt bought him. Ain't that right, Willie?

WILLIE. Real nice clothes.

SECOND BOY. A nice new pair of pants, a white shirt with a stiff collar and a brand new pair of shoes with all leather heels.

FIRST BOY. With all leather heels, Willie?

WILLIE. 'Course. In Chicago, everybody wears shoes with all leather heels.

FIRST BOY. Wish I had a new pair of shoes.

SECOND BOY. My mother, she promised she gonna buy me a new pair of shoes for my birthday.

FIRST BOY. Hey, there goes old man Moe!

SECOND BOY. Where?

FIRST BOY. Right over there!

SECOND BOY (*beginning to chant*).
    Moe, Moe, broke his toe
    riding on a buffalo!
    Moe, Moe, broke his toe
    riding on a buffalo!

(*The* FIRST BOY *picks up the chant and the two of them scatter after their prey, leaving* WILLIE *suddenly alone. He turns slowly and then sits down beside his kid brother who has been watching from the porch steps.*)

'DELL. They shouldn't do that, should they, Willie?

WILLIE. No.

'DELL. They're mean, aren't they, Willie?

WILLIE. They just think they're smart.

'DELL. You wouldn't make fun of someone just because he walks funny, would you, Willie?

WILLIE. No.

'DELL. Just because someone can't walk right don't mean you should laugh at him, does it?

WILLIE. No.

'DELL. Willie?

WILLIE. What?

'DELL. Can I go to Chicago with you?

WILLIE. Not this year, maybe next year.

'DELL. But I want to go with you, Willie.

WILLIE. You be a good boy and as soon as I get some money you can come up and live with me.

'DELL. You promise, Willie?

WILLIE. Sure. But you got to promise to do what Aunt Mae wants because Aunt Mae, she works hard to do right for us.

'DELL. I promise, Willie. It won't take long, will it, Willie?

WILLIE. 'Course not. I go to Chicago I'm gonna be the best baseball player in the whole big world. Gonna make a lot of money and buy me a great big car, all chrome and foam rubber and do nothing except maybe drive around all the time and go fishing or on a picnic maybe. You be a good boy and listen to what Aunt Mae says and next year I'll let you come up and stay with me.

'DELL. And you and me, we could go to the movies every Saturday afternoon. Couldn't we, Willie? And you wouldn't have to support me, Willie, because I could get a job in Chicago and make a lot of money myself and when you play ball I could watch, couldn't I, Willie?

WILLIE. Sure you could.

'DELL. And when you hit the ball real hard, so hard nobody can see it and everybody stands up to cheer, I can tell them I'm your brother, can't I?

WILLIE. Sure you can.

'DELL. I never been on a picnic, Willie.

WILLIE. 'Course you haven't. But I get rich we'll go on so many picnics after a while you won't pay no more mind to going on a picnic than you do to getting up in the morning.

'DELL. You really think so, Willie?

WILLIE. Sure I do.

'DELL (*worried*). Willie?

WILLIE. What?

'DELL. If you're the best baseball player in the world will I still be your brother?

WILLIE. 'Course you'll still be my brother. What kind of silly talk is that?

'DELL. You sure, Willie?

WILLIE. Sure I'm sure. A brother is something you either have or you don't have and nothing's gonna happen can change it.

'DELL (*relieved*). You want to see how good I can throw, Willie?

WILLIE (*getting up*). Here! You throw and I'll hit!

'DELL. Don't hit it too far, Willie!

WILLIE (*hitting ball back to* 'DELL). One for you and one for me!

'DELL (*happy*). One for you and one for me!

WILLIE. You want to see a good one?

'DELL (*ecstatic*). Let's see how far you can hit it, Willie!

(*Again* 'DELL *throws the ball to his brother and this time* WILLIE *stands back and hits the ball with all his might. Then the two of them watch as the ball sails up and out of sight.*)

(*Full of admiration*) You gonna be the greatest baseball player in the world, Willie!

WILLIE. That's right, boy, and when Willie gets rich, he won't forget his friends!

(*But the spell is broken as the door of* 'DELL'*s room opens and* HARRY *enters.*)

'DELL. What do you want? I told you yesterday I didn't want no company.

HARRY. But you just had some company and I don't see why you should talk to him and not to me.

'DELL. What do you mean, I just had some company? How do you know what I just had?

HARRY. I like to share my cocktail hour, don't you? I think you're afraid of me.

'DELL. Why? Why should I be afraid of you?

HARRY. I don't know. Maybe you're afraid of me because I might know something.

'DELL. Know what? What are you, a cop?

HARRY. A policeman? I think that's funny.

'DELL. You got the wrong room, mister. I don't want to talk to someone I don't have to.

HARRY. The name is Harry and it's a sign of poor breeding to throw someone out of your room when all he wants is a little conversation. Aren't you ever lonely?

'DELL. Maybe I don't like you. You ever think of that? Maybe I just don't want to talk to you.

HARRY. But you interest me. As a matter of fact, you've interested me ever since I saw you get off the bus last week.

'DELL. You saw me get off the bus?

HARRY. Of course. But tell me, do you really hate everybody? Isn't there anyone that you like?

'DELL. Who told you I hate everybody? There's lots of people I like. I got a lot of friends.

HARRY. It must be nice to have a lot of friends, but if you have so many friends, then why can't you find room for one more?

'DELL. Because I don't want no more friends, that's why!

HARRY. You're hiding from the police, aren't you?

'DELL. Hiding from the police? Why should I be hiding from the police? I didn't do nothing wrong.

HARRY. I just wondered. I never see you leave your room and you keep the shade drawn over the window all the time.

'DELL. How do you know I never let the shade up? How do you know what I do?

HARRY. I'm sorry. I thought you knew.

'DELL. Knew what?

HARRY. Knew that I've taken the room across the hall.

'DELL. You? What's someone like you want a room in a place like this for?

HARRY. Of course, I really don't hate everybody as you do. I'm beyond that stage. Instead of hating, I'm amused.

'DELL. Talk sense, man. What do you mean "amused"?

HARRY. Amused by the things that still bother you. I smile. You hate. It's almost the same thing.

'DELL. I don't know what you're talking about.

HARRY. It's been a perfectly lovely day. But you didn't go out today, did you? You didn't go out because you were afraid all you'd see would be the candy wrappers on the sidewalks and the hair in men's nostrils as they cheat each other out of money and women.

'DELL. How do you know what I see when I go out?

HARRY. I can tell. I used to be the same way. But it's even worse after sundown, isn't it? What's left of the sun is like a wound in the sky and the sick and crippled begin to stir and come out for a breath of air. They're looking for a Negro, you know.

'DELL. What about it? They're not looking for me, are they?

HARRY. I don't know. They could be. If they catch him down here he won't get a fair trial. You know that, don't you?

'DELL. So what?

HARRY. Doesn't that bother you?

'DELL. No.

HARRY. Even if he didn't do what they say he did?

'DELL. No.

HARRY. I don't believe you.

'DELL. Nothing bothers me. It don't bother me what they do.

HARRY. That's not true. You're afraid, aren't you?

'DELL. Afraid of what?

HARRY. Afraid everything in the world is ugly . . . that nothing has any meaning. . . .

'DELL. That's a lie!

HARRY. . . . afraid nothing makes any sense . . . afraid you might be as ugly and empty yourself. You're really just like me. You just haven't learned to laugh yet, that's all.

'DELL. I was like you I'd go shoot myself.

HARRY. Do you really think so?

'DELL. That's right. I'd go shoot myself.

HARRY. I doubt it.

'DELL. Tell me something.

HARRY. What?

'DELL. You laugh at everything?

HARRY. Yes, everything. Why do you ask?

'DELL. You laugh at the law? You laugh when they hang the poor man and let the rich man go free? That make you laugh?

HARRY. Of course.

'DELL. You laugh when a dog gets run over and everybody hurries by like they didn't even see it? That make you laugh?

HARRY. Usually.

'DELL. How about you? You ever laugh at yourself?

HARRY. Why yes, don't you?

'DELL. No.

HARRY. You will.

'DELL. Why do you say that? Do you think I'm funny?

HARRY. Of course you're funny. You're funny because you hate the world and everything that's in it, but you won't even admit it to yourself.

'DELL. That's a lie!

HARRY. Is it?

'DELL. You think I'm like you? That I got nobody? Is that what you think?

HARRY. Then you do have someone?

'DELL. Sure I got someone.

HARRY. A woman?

'DELL. No. Not a woman.

HARRY. A friend?

'DELL. No.

HARRY. Then who have you got?

'DELL. I got a brother.

HARRY. A brother? And you're fond of your brother?

'DELL. Sure I like my brother. Why shouldn't I like my brother?

HARRY. I didn't say you shouldn't like him.

'DELL. You make it sound like there's something wrong if I like my brother.

HARRY. I'm sorry.

'DELL. My brother's all right.

HARRY. May I ask when it was that you saw your brother last?

'DELL. Two years ago. Why? What difference does that make?

HARRY. No difference, I was just wondering.

'DELL. Wondering about what?

HARRY. Wondering about your brother.

'DELL. What about my brother? You know something about my brother you better tell me.

HARRY. It's nothing really. It's silly.

'DELL. What about my brother?

HARRY. It was just a thought I had.

'DELL. What was it you thought? You tell me what you think.

HARRY. Supposing you found something out.

'DELL. Find out what?

HARRY. I'm not sure. Something.

'DELL. You think he did what they say he did? Is that what you think?

HARRY. No. Why? What's he supposed to have done?

'DELL. Don't you know?

HARRY. No. Should I?

'DELL. Supposing I find out what?

HARRY. Supposing you found out that you could no longer like your brother, that's all.

'DELL. You think anything could make me hate my brother?

HARRY. I don't know. It's possible, isn't it?

'DELL. No! Nothing could make me hate my brother!

HARRY. But if something did, you'd be like me, wouldn't you?

'DELL. What do you mean, I'd be like you? Tell me what you mean?

HARRY. It's obvious, isn't it? Lose your brother and you'd laugh at everything too.

'DELL. No! I won't be like you! Do you hear me? I won't be like you!

HARRY (*like a pleased little schoolboy*). You'd like to hit me, wouldn't you?

'DELL (*sitting down on the edge of bed and almost pleading*). Why don't you go back to your own room, mister?

HARRY. I will pretty soon.

'DELL (*quietly and to himself*). He wouldn't do what they say.

HARRY (*beginning to lose himself in his own thoughts*). I'm sorry. I didn't hear you.

'DELL. He wouldn't do what they say he did. Maybe something, but not what they say.

HARRY. Who?

'DELL. My brother.

HARRY. Is he the one they're looking for?

(*As the two of them become more and more engrossed in their own thoughts, the sound of the calliope is heard once more.*)

'DELL. That's right. He's the one they're looking for.

HARRY. I have a friend who'd love to sketch your face. She has a passion for Negro faces. Great big oval eyes, high cheek bones, sensuous lips.

'DELL. Sometimes I'd like to go to some place where I could sleep and not see no faces.

HARRY. She'll probably be over later on.

'DELL. Who?

HARRY. I just told you. A friend of mine.

'DELL. A girl friend?

HARRY. Something like that. How would you like to go to a party later on?

'DELL. Party? Where?

HARRY. In my room. I'm having some people over.

'DELL. I don't want to go to no party.

HARRY. Do you have a job?

'DELL. You mean what do I do?

HARRY. Yes.

'DELL. I'm a prizefighter.

HARRY. Really? Do you enjoy it? Is it fun?

'DELL. Why? What do you want to know for?

HARRY. Just curious. Are you fighting tonight?

'DELL. Yeah. I got a fight tonight.

HARRY. Where?

'DELL. Out at the carnival.

HARRY. Hot today, wasn't it?

'DELL. There's a breeze coming up.

HARRY. It's funny the way a breeze can break the spell of a day.

'DELL. The sun will be going down pretty soon.

HARRY. I took a walk before. You should have gone with me. I watched some girls eating lunch in the park. I bought them each an ice-cream cone and we had a lovely talk.

'DELL. I once went to a park. Me and my brother.

(*A woman's laugh comes from somewhere offstage and the flickering light of a cooking fire flares up in the shadows.*)

JACK (*offstage*). Anybody want another beer?

FRED (*offstage*). Not me. I'm so stuffed I can hardly move.

JACK. Might as well finish what we've got.

FRED'S DATE. Let's sit down over here, Fred.

(FRED *and* FRED'S DATE *enter and make themselves comfortable.*) Don't you just love the way the honeysuckle smells?

FRED. Think I'll lay down and take a nap.

FRED'S DATE. Not now, Fred.

(*In the shadows, watching, stand* WILLIE *and* 'DELL.)

'DELL (*whispering*). What are they doing now, Willie?

WILLIE. Drinking beer.

'DELL. Let me see, Willie.

(JACK *and* JACK'S DATE *enter.*)

JACK. Hey, you know something? We didn't even touch the ice cream.

FRED. Let it melt. Who cares?

JACK. Hey, Fred. Why don't you tell the girls what happened in the bank this morning?

FRED. You tell them. I'm too full.

JACK. Okay. I'll tell them. Seems come closing time Fred was two cents short for the day and when he told Mr. Whimple, Mr. Whimple got all shook up, so Fred . . . . Hello? What's this? (*getting up*) Looks like we got company. Come on over here, boy. We won't bite.

(WILLIE *and* 'DELL *step cautiously forward.*)

WILLIE. We're sorry if we did something wrong.

JACK. Something wrong? (*To* FRED) They didn't do nothing wrong, did they, Fred?

FRED. 'Course not. It's a free country, isn't it?

JACK. You boys want to join us for a while?

WILLIE. Don't you want us to go?

JACK. Go? Why should I want you boys to go? If there's anything I can't stand it's for someone to be real mean and nasty. Why don't you boys come a little closer? We won't hurt you.

WILLIE. We just wanted to see.

FRED. Sure. That makes sense.

JACK. See what?

'DELL. See if people ate off the grass like Willie said.

JACK. You mean you never been to a picnic before?

WILLIE. No sir. We never been to a picnic.

JACK. Really? Tell you what. How would you boys like to go on a picnic right now?

WILLIE. Yes sir. We'd like that.

FRED'S DATE. Make them go away, Jack.

JACK. What for? They seem like a couple of nice little nigra boys, don't they, Fred? It's just that they never been to a picnic before, that's all.

FRED. Sure. Tell them to sit down and we'll all have a party.

JACK (*to* WILLIE). That's a real nice pair of shoes you got on, boy.

WILLIE. Yes sir. But I think we ought to go home.

JACK. Go home? You kidding, boy? What kind of gratitude you call that? Someone invites you to go to a picnic, the polite thing to do is say "Yes sir. Thank you, sir."

WILLIE. Yes sir.

JACK. That's better. Just don't pay no attention to Janice. She don't mean any harm.

JACK'S DATE. Wouldn't you boys like some ice cream?

WILLIE. Yes ma'am. We'd like that fine.

JACK. Of course they'd like some ice cream. What kind of foolish question is that? Tell you boys what I'm gonna do. You boys behave yourself and I'm gonna let you sit right down with us just like it was the most natural thing in the world and we'll all have some ice cream. How would you like that?

WILLIE. Yes sir. We'd like that fine.

JACK. You got hospitality, the thing to do is use it, right, Fred?

FRED. Right. You got some ice cream and somebody else don't, the thing to do is to share it.

JACK'S DATE. I just thought of something.

JACK. You did? What?

JACK'S DATE. The ice cream is all melted.

JACK. No. It can't be. Not when we just got some company. You sure? You hear that, boys? The ice cream is all melted. Isn't that a shame?

FRED'S DATE. Make them go away, Fred.

WILLIE. I think 'Dell and me ought to go home.

JACK. Now what kind of manners you call that, boy? Someone invites you to eat some ice cream, it isn't polite to say you're going home just because the ice cream is all melted.

FRED. It's very impolite.

JACK'S DATE. Awfully impolite.

JACK. Especially when we been so nice to you and you don't even deserve it. Aren't you at least gonna try to entertain us before you go home?

WILLIE. Yes sir. I'd like to. But I don't know what you mean.

JACK. I mean can you sing or dance? That's what I mean.

WILLIE. No sir. 'Dell and me, we don't know how to sing or dance.

JACK. What do you mean, you don't know how to sing or dance?

WILLIE. No sir. We don't know how to sing or dance. Nobody ever taught us.

JACK. Boy, I want you to come over here.

(WILLIE *walks to where* JACK *stands.*)

Boy, we been real nice to you. How come you aren't gonna be real nice to us?

WILLIE. Yes sir.

JACK. What do you mean, yes sir? Is that all you can say?

WILLIE. No sir.

JACK. Boy, you know we been extra nice to you, that's right, isn't it? And you aren't even supposed to be here. How come you think you're so good?

WILLIE. I don't think I'm so good.

JACK. Don't lie to me, boy! Of course you think you're good. You think you're so good you got a right to go where you're not supposed to go. That's right, isn't it, boy?

WILLIE. No sir. But I'm sorry if I done something wrong.

JACK. No. You aren't sorry. Don't give me that. Tell me something, boy. You know why you think you're so good?

WILLIE. No sir. I don't know.

JACK (*to his friends*). See? He's got on a new pair of shoes, that's why he thinks he's so good.

FRED. Sure. That's why he thinks he's so good.

JACK. Where'd you get them new shoes, boy?

WILLIE. My aunt. She give 'em to me because I'm going to Chicago.

JACK. You hear that? He thinks he's so good because he's going to

Chicago. You know something, boy? It isn't right for someone like you to have a new pair of shoes. Someone like you gets a new pair of shoes and he gets all kinds of biggety ideas. . . .

FRED. Sure. You give 'em a new pair of shoes and they think they own the world.

JACK. Now, boys, I want you to take them shoes off and give 'em to me real quiet like or I'll call the police and tell 'em you were where you weren't supposed to be.

FRED. Give him the shoes, boy.

(WILLIE *takes his shoes off and gives them to* JACK.)

JACK. That's it, boy. And just so you won't get no more biggety ideas, I think we'll just burn these shoes in the fire. . . .

HARRY. It's all pretty stupid.

'DELL. What's pretty stupid?

HARRY (*getting lost in his own thoughts*). Everything. My being here, for example. Being bored. Reducing the world to a word that's been used over and over again and has no meaning. Nothing's meant anything to the lot of us for so long, maybe she's right for wanting to pretend her husband cares.

'DELL (*lost in his own thoughts*). Willie must have forgiven me because he knows I tried to make them listen. Only they wouldn't. But he doesn't have to worry because if they catch him, I'll get a good lawyer and everything will be all right. It's not gonna be like it's been. I'll get some good fights and make some real money and Willie won't have nothing to worry about. We can go back to Chicago. Anybody can talk and dress or throw a ball like Willie, they don't have to worry about nothing in Chicago.

HARRY. I'm sure that meeting in a place like this gives her a sense of sin she hasn't enjoyed in years. Still it's cruel to have been born during the month of May and be reminded of the years at the very same time that the lilac is just beginning to bloom. Things put off for fear they wouldn't fulfill the promise of their conception, one year following another and each more quickly than the one before, until all that's left is the jealousy of those who remember how it might have been. . . .

'DELL. I told them but they wouldn't listen. I tried to make them listen, but they wouldn't. But it's my fault because I did it. Only they wouldn't listen to me and Willie took the blame. . . .

(*The light dims on* HARRY *and a* LITTLE WHITE GIRL *of about ten enters jumping rope. She stops when she catches sight of* 'DELL *sitting by himself on the porch steps, and the following scene is played in memory.*)

LITTLE GIRL. I know something you don't know.

'DELL. About Willie?

LITTLE GIRL. Willie's not going to Chicago.

'DELL. Why? Why isn't Willie going to Chicago?

LITTLE GIRL. Because Mrs. Corbett says Willie stole two dollars and Willie's going to be lucky if they don't hang him.

'DELL. That's not true! Willie didn't steal no money!

LITTLE GIRL. Mrs. Corbett says Willie was playing the pinball machine and there was two dollars on top of the register and when she turned around the money was gone.

'DELL. But that don't mean that Willie took the money! Willie wouldn't do nothin' like that!

LITTLE GIRL. Yes he did! Mrs. Corbett says he did!

'DELL. Willie's going to Chicago! They got opportunity in Chicago and Willie's gonna play baseball and make a lot of money and next year I'm gonna go to Chicago too, and stay with him!

LITTLE GIRL. No, you're not. Mrs. Corbett says Willie's going to jail for four or five years and that'll teach him not to steal from white people.

'DELL. But Willie didn't steal no money!

LITTLE GIRL (*skipping rope again*).
Eeney, meeney, miney, moe!
Catch a nigger by the toe!
If he hollers let him go!
Eeney, meeney, miney, moe!

'DELL. Willie's going to Chicago! They got opportunity in Chicago! My aunt, she says Willie's going to Chicago tomorrow!

LITTLE GIRL (*sing-song fashion*). Willie's going to jail! Willie's going to jail!

'DELL. My aunt, she bought Willie a whole lot of new clothes to go to Chicago!

LITTLE GIRL. Mrs. Corbett says Willie doesn't know his place and it's time he went to jail! Everybody knows Willie is a bad little nigger boy!

'DELL. Willie didn't do what she say he done!

LITTLE GIRL. Of course he did.

'DELL. No he didn't!

LITTLE GIRL. Yes he did. I saw him!

'DELL. You're a liar! That's what you are! A big liar!

LITTLE GIRL. You better not call me a liar, you nasty little nigger boy! You hear me? You call me a liar any more and you'll go to jail too!

'DELL. Liar! Liar!

LITTLE GIRL. You better stop that or my father will come beat you with a stick!

'DELL. Liar! Liar!

LITTLE GIRL. All right! You asked for it! I'm going home and tell my father!

(*The* LITTLE GIRL *disappears and* 'DELL *sits down on the porch steps and begins to sob. A tall, thin man with the star of the law pinned to his shirt crosses slowly in front of* 'DELL *and then sits down.*)

DEPUTY. Piece of candy, boy?

'DELL. No. I don't want no candy.

DEPUTY. You better have a piece of candy and you'll feel better.

'DELL. Yes sir.

DEPUTY. That's better. Where's your aunt, boy?

'DELL. She's working. She won't be home till later. Why do you want to see my aunt?

DEPUTY. Your aunt's a good woman, boy. She works hard to do right for you and your brother.

'DELL. Yes sir.

DEPUTY. I got bad news for your aunt.

'DELL. About Willie?

DEPUTY. That's right, boy.

'DELL. You think Willie did what they say he did? Is that what you think?

DEPUTY. Willie's in jail.

'DELL. In jail?

DEPUTY. You steal two dollars and you'll go to jail, too, boy. Jail's a bad place to be. They put you in jail, boy, they lock you up in a cage and they only feed you once a day. You wouldn't want to go to jail, would you, boy?

'DELL. No sir. But Willie didn't steal two dollars, honest he didn't!

DEPUTY. You accusing Mrs. Corbett of telling lies, boy? Mrs. Corbett's got a witness.

'DELL (*scared*). No sir.

DEPUTY. Everybody knows your brother Willie is a troublemaker.

'DELL (*angrily*). That's not true! That's a lie!

DEPUTY. You better watch what you say, boy. You know who I am, don't you?

'DELL (*quietly*). Yes sir.

DEPUTY. Then I think you better apologize.

'DELL. I'm sorry, sir.

DEPUTY. That's better. Were you with your brother this morning?

'DELL. Yes sir.

DEPUTY. And didn't you stop off at Mrs. Corbett's on the way to school?

'DELL. Yes sir.

DEPUTY. And didn't Willie play the pinball machine like Mrs. Corbett told him she didn't want him to because it wasn't for nigra boys to play with?

'DELL. Yes sir. But he didn't take the money. I took the money.

DEPUTY. You took the money?

'DELL. Yes sir. I took the money. Aren't you gonna put me in jail, too?

DEPUTY. You wouldn't lie to me, would you, boy? Mrs. Corbett had two dollars on top of the register and she turned her back and when she turned around the money was gone. Mrs. Corbett even got a witness.

'DELL. Willie didn't take the money. I took the money.

DEPUTY. But why did you take the money, boy?

'DELL. Because I wanted to buy Willie a new pair of shoes.

DEPUTY. But why would the girl say she saw Willie take the money if he didn't take it? Answer me that, boy.

'DELL. I don't know. Did they have any trouble finding him?

DEPUTY. No. They didn't have no trouble finding him.

'DELL. Didn't he try to run away?

DEPUTY. Run away? He didn't even know we was looking for him. He was waiting for us in the principal's office just like the principal said.

'DELL. You gonna put me in jail, too?

DEPUTY. How old are you, boy?

'DELL. Twelve. Willie, he's fifteen.

DEPUTY. Willie's no good. Everybody knows Willie's gonna come to no good, always talking big and telling folks he's going North where they got opportunity. Didn't he get into trouble only last week going where he wasn't supposed to go?

'DELL. It wasn't his fault.

DEPUTY. What do you mean, it wasn't his fault?

'DELL. We weren't doing nothing.

DEPUTY. You were where you weren't supposed to be, weren't you?

'DELL. Yes sir. But we were just watching. We weren't doing anything.

DEPUTY (*defensively*). You were where you weren't supposed to be, weren't you? Just answer me that.

'DELL. Yes sir.

DEPUTY. Then how do you mean it wasn't his fault? Mrs. Corbett says Willie is always hanging around the store just asking for trouble with that sassy mouth of his, always sticking his nose where it don't belong.

'DELL. They made fun of us.

DEPUTY. Never mind they made fun of you. Boys like you aren't supposed to be in places like that or in stores where you aren't wanted and Willie going around telling folks he's going to Chicago so he can grow up to be a real biggety nigra. Even if he didn't take the money he ought to go to jail.

'DELL. All we wanted to do was to see.

DEPUTY. See? See what, boy? Come on, speak up.

'DELL. Willie said there was a place where people sat on the grass and ate supper. We just wanted to see if it was true.

DEPUTY. That don't give you a right to bust in when people are having a picnic, does it?

'DELL. We didn't bust in.

DEPUTY. Willie got into a fight. Everybody knows Willie got into a fight because he was where he wasn't supposed to be.

'DELL. We didn't bust in. They saw us standing there, looking, and they asked if Willie and me would like to come sit down so we said yes, we'd like that. Then one of them told us if we sat real quiet like on the grass and behaved, they'd give us each some ice cream.

DEPUTY. Did you thank the people?

'DELL. Yes sir. We said thank you.

DEPUTY. You didn't slop all over everything, did you?

'DELL. No sir. We didn't slop over nothing.

DEPUTY. How about when the people asked you to sing or dance? Can't you sing or dance even a little?

'DELL. No sir. Nobody ever taught us.

DEPUTY. So then what happened?

'DELL. They made fun of Willie.

DEPUTY. What do you mean, they made fun of Willie?

'DELL. The man, he got mad and said for Willie to come closer and Willie did. Then the man, he said Willie thought he was so good because he got on a new pair of shoes and it wasn't right for Willie to have a new pair of shoes because it give him big ideas like going where he wasn't supposed to go. Then the man said for Willie to give him the shoes and Willie did that too, and then the man, he threw the shoes in the fire.

DEPUTY. But that don't give Willie the right to go play the pinball machine where he isn't wanted, does it?

'DELL. No sir.

DEPUTY. Of course it don't.

'DELL. You gonna put me in jail, too?

DEPUTY (*getting up, wearily*). Somebody got to go to jail, it's better if it's Willie, boy.

'DELL. But Willie didn't take the money! Honest, Willie didn't take the money!

DEPUTY. Mrs. Corbett got a witness, boy . . . Mrs. Corbett got a witness. . . . (*walking off*)

'DELL. But Willie didn't take the money! Honest, Willie didn't take the money!

(*The* DEPUTY *leaves and* 'DELL *stares after him for a moment without noticing* TWO BOYS, *friends of* WILLIE's, *who have entered.*)

FIRST BOY. Sure it's true. Ask 'Dell if you don't believe me.

SECOND BOY. Hey, 'Dell, is it true Willie stole two dollars from Mrs. Corbett this morning?

'DELL. Willie didn't steal no two dollars!

FIRST BOY. Sure it's true. Willie stole two dollars from Mrs. Corbett so they put him in jail.

'DELL. That's a lie!

SECOND BOY. If Willie isn't in jail, then where is he?

FIRST BOY. Yeah. Where is he if he isn't in jail?

SECOND BOY. You go to jail they put you in a cage and they only feed you once a day!

FIRST BOY. Looks like Willie won't play no baseball for a long time!

'DELL. Willie didn't steal no two dollars!

FIRST BOY. Willie, he don't look so smart right now, always going where he isn't supposed to and strutting around talking about going to Chicago and playing baseball like he was better than anybody else!

SECOND BOY. Sure. Anybody can talk big. (*Imitating* WILLIE) Sure. Going to Chicago and make a lot of money playing baseball. Got a new pair of pants, a white shirt with a stiff collar and a new pair of shoes. (*Swinging an imaginary baseball bat*) Whoeee! Look at that ball fly! But don't you boys worry. I get rich I won't forget my friends! No siree! Anytime you boys want you can come visit me up in the jail house! (*The boys burst out laughing.*)

'DELL. You leave Willie alone!

SECOND BOY. Hey! You looking for a fight or something?

'DELL. You leave Willie alone! Willie didn't do nothing to you!

SECOND BOY (*going into a crouch to the delight of his companion*). This what you mean, boy? This what you got in mind?

(*'DELL suddenly charges his older opponent, but the* FIRST BOY *trips him and he sprawls to the ground and the boys laugh.*)
Hey, boy! You want to fight you gotta learn to stand up on your feet first!

FIRST BOY. That ain't no way to fight, just laying there on the ground!

SECOND BOY. You want to fight? That what you want? C'mon. I'll show you how to fight!

(*'DELL gets to his feet but now his fists are like rocks and something in the look on his face causes the boys to quiet down and giggle nervously.*)

FIRST BOY. I gotta go home.

SECOND BOY. Me, too. C'mon. Let's go.

FIRST BOY. Sure. That's right. Fight fair, that's all right. But I don't want nothing to do with no kid's gonna get mad.

(*The* TWO BOYS *drift away and as* 'DELL *stands motionless,* HARRY *gets up and puts a hand on his shoulder.*)

HARRY. If nothing has any meaning . . .

'DELL. C'mon! Take your hands off me!

HARRY (*backing away*). You shouldn't be so suspicious.

'DELL. Go on! Get out of here!

HARRY. I just want you to remember if you need any help, you can always count on me.

CURTAIN

ACT TWO

SCENE: *The carnival grounds at night. A large ferris wheel revolves endlessly to the lilt of the "Missouri Waltz." A raised platform. Tents, mud, garish lights. Balloons.*

AT RISE: *'DELL sits on an orange crate stuck in the mud of an off corner. He wears a soiled bathrobe and watches as a BARKER with a straw hat and red arm band gets up on the platform and begins to strum an occasional chord on the ukelele he carries. A group of BOYS slowly collects around the platform. The BARKER with the straw hat exchanges a few remarks with them, all the while toying with his ukulele. Finally, the flap of the tent behind is pulled aside and a tired-looking girl in a hula skirt steps forth. The chatter stops and the BARKER gets down to business, strumming his ukulele in earnest and encouraging the crowd.*

BARKER. All right, fellas! Step a little closer! She won't bite! So don't be bashful! Margie isn't.

(*He looks up at MARGIE and smiles. In reply, MARGIE thumbs her nose at the BARKER.*)

Come on, boys! Margie likes boys! Margie likes to show them a thing or two! So step right up and don't be bashful! Only fifty cents a head and we'll all have a good time! When Margie was a little girl, Margie was the teacher's pet! But things do change, so step a little closer and remember tonight and tonight only Margie gives it all she's got for only fifty cents a head!

(*Off to one side, WINDY enters and speaks to 'DELL.*)

WINDY. You know what you got to do, don't you, kid? You go on in ten minutes.

'DELL. Yeah. I know what I got to do.

WINDY. Just remember. I don't want you to tag him till I tell you to. You feel all right?

'DELL. Yeah. I'm okay.

WINDY. Remember. You make it look good and you still got a future. Just tell yourself it's for your brother.

'DELL. I'll remember.

(*WINDY exits and a PIMPLY-FACED YOUTH steps toward the platform.*)

YOUTH (*to the* BARKER). Why don't she smile? Don't she feel good tonight?

BARKER. Margie's been working overtime, son. She's all tuckered out. But you boys pony up your money and you'll see Margie smile again. Isn't that right, Margie? And that ain't all. That ain't all. So step right up and don't be bashful. Margie will be with you in just a little while! Come on, fellas! It's getting a bit chilly out here for Margie! We don't want to keep Margie out here in nothing but a hula skirt all night! Don't be bashful! The tickets are only fifty cents apiece and Margie aims to please us all!

YOUTH. I seen her last night.

BARKER (*paying no attention to the* YOUTH). Don't nobody want to see Margie tonight? Poor Margie is maybe getting a little too old, but she's still got to eat, fellas! So you boys with the strong stomachs line up and she'll be with you in just a little while!

YOUTH. I seen her last night, mister, and it's a gyp.

BARKER (*pretending not to hear the* YOUTH). Makes the old feel young and the young feel foolish! Makes the dead feel live and the live feel funny!

YOUTH. But I seen her last night and she didn't do what she should have done.

(*The* BARKER *suddenly stops his strumming and the* BOYS *fall back with the exception of the* PIMPLY-FACED YOUTH.)

BARKER. Boy, you trying to tell me you didn't enjoy the show last night? You mean you can stand right there in front of me and tell me you didn't enjoy gazing at that vision of feminine beauty? Ain't you got a red blood corpuscle in your whole body, boy? You think Margie's gonna gyp some boy don't even know what a woman is yet and maybe never will? C'mon, boy, a little respect!

'DELL (*to audience*). There'll be a thousand faces looking up at me. They'll be looking up at me like they're looking up at her, like some kind of animal. The other guy. He'll be looking at me, too. He'll be sitting in his corner and when the bell rings he'll try to feel me out to see how smart I am. But I don't have to do nothing. I stay with him four rounds, nobody'd know the difference. Just because Windy says I got to mess him up don't mean I do. But I gotta look good. I look good and it'll be like it used to be . . . like the time Willie came home. . . .

(*The light picks up* WILLIE *fresh out of jail for the first time.*)

'DELL. Say something to me, Willie! Just don't look at me like that.

WILLIE. Hey, boy. How you doing? Everything all right?

'DELL. Sure. I'm all right. How about you? You gonna stay around for a while? Gee, it's nice to see you, Willie. . . .

WILLIE. Kind of nice to be back. Sort of dead in a town like this, though. . . .

'DELL. I could help you get a job, Willie. Mr. Gillis down at the grocery store is looking for someone to help with the orders.

WILLIE. I don't want no job in a grocery store, say, "Yes, ma'am, no ma'am. Beans is two for a quarter, ma'am." What kind of job you call that?

'DELL. I tried to tell them, Willie, but they wouldn't listen to me. Honest I did, Willie.

WILLIE. Sure. That's all right. I believe you. Not much doing in a town like this. Small towns give me the creeps.

'DELL. You want something to eat, Willie? We got plenty to eat.

WILLIE. No. I don't want nothing to eat.

'DELL. If you want to stay I can talk with the Reverend, Willie.

WILLIE. Aunt Mae worry much about me before she died?

'DELL. She didn't say much, but she worried a lot. It would be nice if you could stay, Willie.

WILLIE. Anybody say anything about me while I was gone?

'DELL. They didn't say much.

WILLIE. They better not.

'DELL. Did they do anything mean to you, Willie?

WILLIE. No. They didn't do nothing mean to me.

'DELL. Did you just get out, Willie?

WILLIE. No. I been out about a month. Been looking around. Had a little money I'd go out and buy me a ticket to Chicago and never come back.

'DELL. You want some money, Willie?

WILLIE. Why? You got any money?

'DELL. Sure. I got some money.

WILLIE. How much you got?

'DELL. Made twenty-five dollars last night.

WILLIE. You pulling my leg, boy? Doing what?

'DELL. Boxing at a fireman's benefit.

WILLIE. You kidding? How'd you make out? You win?

'DELL (*proud and ashamed at the same time*). Yeah. I won.

WILLIE. Hey, that's great!

'DELL. You really think so, Willie? You aren't ashamed of me?

WILLIE. Ashamed of you? What for?

'DELL. Fighting.

WILLIE. Why should I be ashamed of you fighting?

'DELL. Last week they got me and another kid an exhibition down at the Elks. Won that one, too.

WILLIE. You did? Say, how many fights you had?

'DELL. I don't know. Eight. No. Nine. Won seven and lost two.

WILLIE. Hey, I got an idea!

'DELL. What?

WILLIE. Let's you and me both go to Chicago! You go to Chicago, you're any good you can make some real money!

'DELL. You think so?

WILLIE. Sure. Why not?

'DELL. No. I don't think it's right. You fight professional you really have to mean it.

WILLIE. Look, we'll go to Chicago together. You want me to play baseball, don't you? All right, but how am I gonna play baseball if all I do is stay down here?

'DELL. You still want to play baseball, Willie?

WILLIE. Sure I do. But I stay down here, I won't get no chance, will I? Come on, what do you say? Days I play ball and nights I make sure you don't waste your time. Together we can really show them who we are!

'DELL. I could support you, couldn't I, Willie? I could make enough for the two of us.

WILLIE. Sure. That's right. You want to play ball you can't do it on an empty stomach. That's for sure.

'DELL. You could get to be real good, couldn't you, Willie?

WILLIE. Sure. Start off with one of those minor league teams or even a good shop team and no time at all, I'll be driving them over the grandstands! You just watch and see! What do you say, kid? You be the meat and potatoes for a while and in a couple of years the gravy'll be all over the place!

'DELL. That's great, Willie! I know you can do it! We'll go to Chicago together!

(*The memory is cut short by the* BARKER.)

BARKER. The thing is Margie is a lady, boy. (*To* MARGIE) Ain't that right, Margie? (*In reply,* MARGIE *thumbs her nose at the* BARKER.)

YOUTH. But she didn't do what she should have done.

BARKER. Of course she didn't, and you know why? Because down deep inside, Margie is a lady, and you treat a lady with respect and there's no telling how much gratitude she'll show, ain't that right, boys?

'DELL (*to the audience*). Seems like everybody got to have something to hang on to. But supposing what you got to hold on to is a lie? Five more minutes and they'll turn the lights on over the ring. Windy'll lace up my gloves and the sweat will start running. I'll look down and see a thousand faces I can't stand no more and then the referee will call us together. . . .

(*Again the sad, lonely music of the calliope is heard and then* WILLIE *saunters in.*)

WILLIE (*to someone who isn't really there*). No. Just looking for my brother, that's all. Thanks, anyway.

'DELL. Willie! What you doing here?

WILLIE. What do you mean what am I doing here? I got a brother's gonna be champ someday I got a right to watch him work out, don't I? (*Momentarily distracted*) Man, look at him punch that bag. (*Turning back*) Hey, boy. You look real professional.

'DELL. What do you mean look real professional? I am real professional. Here. Watch this. (*Backs away and demonstrates a couple of combinations to the delight of his brother.*) There. How's that? Pretty good, huh?

WILLIE. You're all right, boy. You sure don't look like no amateur to me.

'DELL (*happy*). And you're not so bad yourself. (*Suddenly dropping to the position of the shortstop*) Okay, Willie. Here it comes. (WILLIE *takes his stance at the plate.*) Don't let him fool you, Willie! C'mon, Willie! The bases are loaded and the score's tied at the end of the ninth inning! C'mon, Willie! You can do it! Easy! Easy! Don't let him scare you! There it is! Low and inside! C'mon, Willie! You can do it!

(WILLIE *swings his imaginary bat and then the two of them watch as the ball leaves the park.*)

WILLIE. How's that for a hit?

'DELL (*arm in arm with his brother*). Just like the man says, once you got it there's nothing gonna take it away from you!

WILLIE. Right!

'DELL. You hear the news?

WILLIE. No. What news?

'DELL. They got me signed for the main event down at the arena next month.

WILLIE. No kidding? Hey, that's all right.

'DELL. They tell me I win that one and it's time for me to get off the ice truck and give it everything I got.

WILLIE. That's great. 'Course, you get to be a big shot you probably will forget you even got a brother.

'DELL. What kind of talk is that? What kind of two-bit brother's gonna forget someone can hit a ball like you? But how'd you know I was down here, Willie?

WILLIE. Checked in your room and you wasn't there so I figured where else would you be.

'DELL. But I thought you was supposed to be out of town, Willie. I thought you was supposed to be in Detroit.

WILLIE. You mean about that class C team? C'mon, you didn't really think I was gonna try out for some class C team nobody even heard of, did you?

'DELL. But you got to start someplace, Willie. You want to play big time baseball, you can't start out on top. I mean I know you're good, but how you gonna prove it unless you get a chance to show somebody?

WILLIE. You're right.

'DELL. Sure I'm right. What was it, Willie? Was it you got scared?

WILLIE. Scared?

'DELL. You know. Scared maybe you wouldn't look so good.

WILLIE. Yeah, sure. That's it. I got scared. I got thinking I'd get up there and somebody'd give me a bat, then somebody'd throw me a fast one and with everybody looking I'd just freeze. So I figured the best thing to do was not to go.

'DELL. But everybody gets scared once in a while, Willie. Don't you think every time I go in the ring, I get scared?

WILLIE. I'm sorry I let you down, 'Dell.

'DELL. That's okay. Hey, c'mon. Don't take it so hard. You'll get another chance.

WILLIE. You really think so?

'DELL. Sure. But the next time, remember. You're scared, don't let it throw you.

WILLIE. Look, can you do me a favor?

'DELL. Sure. Like what?

WILLIE. Could you loan me twenty-five?

'DELL. But I just gave you twenty-five dollars yesterday, Willie. . . .

WILLIE. Look, you don't want to give it to me, forget it.

'DELL. You know it's not that, Willie . . . you know I got it I'll give it to you. . . .

('DELL *is hurt but the scene is cut short by the* BARKER *once again. . . .*)

BARKER. Boy, what is it's wrong with you? Is it you got bad eyes and can't see or is it you just got bad manners and don't mind insulting a poor defenseless girl what's trying her best to bring you a little comfort and pleasure? Just what is it's wrong with you?

YOUTH. But she doesn't do what she's supposed to do. I seen the show last night and it's a gyp.

BARKER. Make sense, boy! Make sense! What do you mean, boy, she didn't do what she was supposed to do? Come on, boy, speak up! (*To* MARGIE) Come on, Margie. Step a little closer for a minute.

(*To the* YOUTH) You, boy. You come over here a little closer too. That's right. That's better. (*To* MARGIE) A little closer, Margie. That's a good girl. Now, boy, I want you to be truthful. (*To* MARGIE) Raise your skirt, Margie. Higher. Higher. There. That's high enough. (*To the other* BOYS) Any higher and we start charging right here and now. Okay, boy, you still think you got gypped? (*To* MARGIE) Now turn around slow, Margie. That's it.

(*To the* YOUTH) It ain't my fault if you got too much imagination, boy. The trouble with you is you ain't growed up yet. (*To the other* BOYS) Tell you folks out there what I'm gonna do. If it's all right with you folks I'll have Margie put on a free show and I guarantee Margie'll make a liar out of my young friend here. Come on, Margie! Shake it up! C'mon, boys, the line forms to the right!

'DELL (*to the audience*). Seventy-five bucks if I win and fifty bucks if I lose. But I don't want to cut nobody up. You cut somebody up and you do it because you're mad and you don't know what you're doing, maybe that's not so bad. But cut somebody up so maybe you can help your brother? It shouldn't have got me like it did, but when you got something to hold on to you don't want to let it go, not even a little, and if he didn't want to play baseball we still could have opened up a sport store. . . .

(*A light picks up a table for two.* WILLIE, *all dressed up, is seated and* JIMMY *the waiter straightens the linen.*)

JIMMY. Nice to have you back in circulation, Mr. Griffin. Things haven't been the same without you.

WILLIE. Nice to be back, believe me, Jimmy. Everything the same as usual?

JIMMY. People are hungry as ever, if that's what you mean.

WILLIE. If someone comes in asking for me, it's my kid brother, so send him over to my table, okay?

JIMMY. Sure thing, Mr. Griffin.

WILLIE. And next time Mr. Lewis needs a dealer, just make sure he gives me a day's notice.

(*He winks and* JIMMY *smiles.* 'DELL, *glad to see his brother, crosses over to the table.* WILLIE *rises.*)

'DELL. Hey, boy. It's nice to see you.

WILLIE (*shaking his brother's hand.*) Real nice to be back. Here. Sit down. Take a load off your feet.

'DELL. How was it? Everything all right?

WILLIE. 'Course. Old Willie knows how to take care of himself. Takes more than three months in the cooler to take the shine off old Willie.

'DELL. You look real good, Willie.

WILLIE. Sharp. That's the word. You know what I did the first thing I got back to town?

'DELL. No. Tell me what's the first thing you did, Willie.

WILLIE. First thing I did, I went to the best store in town and I said "Open me an account. Willie's back in circulation."

'DELL. That the first thing you did, Willie? You're right on the ball.

WILLIE. Sure. Old Willie, he don't waste no time. Then the next thing I did I figured I'd give you a ring so we could go out and celebrate.

'DELL. Sure is a nice place.

WILLIE. The best. Here, we'll start off with a bottle of wine. What kind of wine do you like?

'DELL. You need any money, Willie? You need any money, you just give the word, Willie.

WILLIE. You kidding, boy? I don't need no money. You don't buy clothes like these just picking your teeth, you know.

'DELL. I thought maybe you'd need some money, Willie.

WILLIE. Not old Willie. Old Willie, he got a lot of friends. You got a lot of friends, you don't need any money.

'DELL. Sure. That's right. You got a lot of friends you don't need any money. (*Sounding a new note*) But why didn't you tell them you didn't have nothing to do with it, Willie?

WILLIE. You pay a lawyer for advice you better take it. That makes sense, don't it? Besides, it didn't look too good, all that money on the table and me, big as life, cutting the cards.

'DELL. You were cutting the cards when the cops came in?

WILLIE. Sure. I thought you knew. How was I supposed to know the game was hot? I just happened to meet one of the fellas and he invited me over and when I got there they asked me wouldn't I deal and I didn't see no harm in it, so I did.

'DELL. But you weren't playing, were you, Willie?

WILLIE. 'Course not. Just dealing. But you can't tell that to no judge.

'DELL. Sure. That's right. A judge is hard to make believe. I been thinking, Willie. Remember how we used to talk about opening a sport store, the two of us, if I ever got enough money together?

WILLIE. Sure. I remember. Why? What about it?

'DELL. I been doing all right. Been getting some real good fights. Saving my money. Some people tell me the way I'm going, in a couple of years I could really be something. A contender for the title even.

WILLIE. Hey, that's great!

'DELL. But I want to quit, Willie. I got a big fight tonight. I win tonight and we'll have the money, Willie, and the two of us could open up a nice little place. What do you say, Willie?

WILLIE. Fighting what's his name, I hear. Sure. Sounds great. But you don't want to just jump into something like that. Something like that takes a lot of planning.

'DELL. I figured it all out. I figured you could be the front man and I could take care of the headaches. We could do it, Willie. Honest we can.

WILLIE. Sure. But let's talk about it on a full stomach. You talk better on a full stomach.

'DELL. Don't order anything for me, Willie. I got to be at the arena in a couple more hours.

WILLIE. Yeah? It's bad when business interferes with pleasure. (*To* JIMMY *the waiter*) Make it a couple of martinis, Jimmy, and a steak medium rare. Just tell the cook Willie's back in town.

JIMMY. Sure thing, Mr. Griffin. (*exits*)

'DELL. They don't mind you coming here?

WILLIE. You kidding? Hey, where you been? You gotta learn to wake up and live.

'DELL. Maybe you're right. But about what I was saying, Willie. I think it would be good for the both of us.

WILLIE. You mean opening up a sport store?

'DELL. Sure. We don't have to go into it big right away. It's just like you used to say, we could start out small. The way I figure it, I win the next one we'll have plenty to open with and if things got a little tight once in a while, I could always pick up a little something for exhibitions and things like that. The way I figure it we could start small and once we learn the ropes we could spread out a little. . . .

WILLIE. Sure. Sounds terrific. (*Momentarily distracted*) Look. Wait here a minute. I gotta see someone.

'DELL (*looking across the room*). Isn't that Mr. Lewis?

WILLIE. Yeah. That's Mr. Lewis.

'DELL (*suspiciously*). Mr. Lewis is a big time gambler, isn't he, Willie?

WILLIE. Mr. Lewis is a real smart man.

'DELL. How come you know Mr. Lewis so good?

WILLIE. Mr. Lewis and me are old friends. That's all.

'DELL. I don't want you to hang around with people like that, you hear me, Willie?

WILLIE. Hey, look, boy. Don't start telling me who I can see and who I can't, okay?

'DELL. I'm telling you I don't want you to hang around with people like that, Willie!

WILLIE (*mocking*). What do you want me to do, run a sport store, is that what you want?

'DELL. What's wrong with running a sport store? That's what you always wanted, wasn't it?

WILLIE. You mean that's what you always wanted. I don't want no sport store, stay cooped up all the time. What kind of life do you call that?

'DELL. I'm telling you I don't want you to hang around with people like that, Willie!

WILLIE. Hey, look, boy. Don't start telling me how to live, okay?

'DELL. You're my brother and I got a right to tell you how to live!

WILLIE. Lower your voice. You want people to hear?

'DELL. Let them hear! I don't care!

WILLIE. Look, boy. I don't need you for no more hand-outs.

'DELL. What hand-outs? You never heard me make no remarks, did you? I got it I'll give it to you! What do you mean you don't want no more hand-outs?

WILLIE. Look, boy. You want to yell you yell all by yourself. I don't want none of my friends to think I don't know how to behave when I go to a restaurant.

'DELL. You think I go in the ring, I look around, the whole thing stinks and I do it for myself? All right. You don't want to play baseball, you don't have to, but I win the next one you and me are gonna open up a sport store. What do you mean you don't need me any more?

WILLIE. Hey, look! You do what you want and I'll do what I want, all right?

'DELL. No! It's not all right! We first come up here you told me you wanted to play baseball! Remember? And I went around telling everybody I got a brother who's real good, all he needs is a break, and finally you got a chance to try out but you didn't even show up because you were too busy shooting pool! I didn't say anything, Willie, but now I'm telling you, I don't want you hanging around with people like that and I mean it, Willie!

WILLIE. C'mon, boy! Get off it, will you? You got no right to tell me what to do!

'DELL. 'Course I got a right to tell you what to do!

WILLIE. Why? Because you stole two dollars but I got sent up instead? Is that why you got a right to tell me what to do? (*Gets up and starts to walk away.*)

'DELL. Where you going, Willie? I don't want you hanging around with people like that, Willie! You don't need no Mr. Lewis! Here! Take fifty dollars, Willie! Don't go away! Don't you want to go into business with me? I'm your brother, Willie!

(*The light dims on the table and picks up the* BARKER.)

BARKER (*to a reluctant* MARGIE *as he strums a chord on his ukulele*). Come on, Margie! Shake it up a little! Give it what you got! (MARGIE *still doesn't move.*) Hey, c'mon! Let's go! You want to settle down, first you got to shake it up! Come on, Margie, give it what you got! (*And again the* BARKER *strums a chord on his ukulele.*) Makes the old feel young and the young feel foolish! (*But suddenly,* MARGIE *cries:*)

MARGIE. You stink! You stink! You all stink!

(*A woman comes through the curtain, throws a blanket around* MARGIE *and leads her off the platform. And as the* BARKER *looks after her with amazement,* WINDY *enters. . . .)*

WINDY. Hey, c'mon. Let's go! They're waiting for you! You want to watch a cooch show, do it on your own time!

'DELL. I don't want to cut nobody up, Windy! I don't want to cut nobody up in front of a thousand faces I can't stand no more!

WINDY. What do you mean you don't want to cut nobody up? You want to make it look good, don't you?

'DELL. I don't have to do something I don't want to!

WINDY. That's right. You don't have to do nothing you don't wanna. But how about your brother? He gets across the state line, what're you gonna tell him? You could have made some real money only you didn't want to cut nobody up?

'DELL. But supposing he doesn't make it across the state line?

(A GIRL *of nineteen enters, followed by her boy friend,* FRANK.*)*

WINDY. C'mon. Don't give me a hard time. Just tell yourself he'll make it to where you can help him. C'mon. Let's go.

*(*DOROTHY *and* HARRY *make their entrance and* 'DELL *hesitates.)*

(Offstage) You quit now, what are you going to do?

GIRL. Look what it says on his back. " 'Dell"! Isn't that a scream? I don't think he likes us, Frank. I think he's mean.

FRANK. He's all right.

('DELL *looks at* FRANK *and the* GIRL, *then goes off.)*

GIRL. Where we gonna sit, Frank? I want to sit up close.

FRANK. Close as you want. I don't care.

(Enter a PHOTOGRAPHER *and a* REPORTER. FRANK, *the* GIRL, *the* PHOTOGRAPHER, *the* REPORTER, DOROTHY *and* HARRY *all sit down.* FRANK *and the* GIRL *are up front.)*

How's this, close enough?

GIRL. I think it's real exciting, going to a fight, I mean. What's he doing? Is he gonna sit down right in front of us, Frank?

FRANK. It's his corner.

GIRL. You think he can hear us?

FRANK. You talk loud enough, probably.

GIRL. You hear about that nigra they're looking for?

FRANK. No. What nigra?

GIRL. You know. The one they've been looking for since the day before yesterday. My aunt says if they catch him down here they might not even bother giving him a trial.

FRANK. They catch him down here it won't make much difference if they give him a trial or not.

GIRL. You think I'll enjoy myself, Frank?

FRANK. Sure. Everybody does.

GIRL. But don't they sometimes get hurt?

FRANK. Sometimes.

GIRL. You know I can't bear to see someone get hurt, Frank. Frank? What are they doing now?

FRANK. Just touching gloves. They always do before a fight. The bell ought to ring any minute now.

GIRL. Do I look pretty enough tonight, Frank?

FRANK (*preoccupied with the fight which has just begun*). You're beautiful.

GIRL. Sometimes I wonder if a man appreciates what a girl goes through getting dressed up. I bet you'd never guess I spent my whole week's allowance getting a scarf to match this blouse, would you? And the prices they want! They're just out of this world for the simplest little things! Frank. Frank, why aren't you paying any attention to me? What's happening, Frank? Why is everyone shouting? Tell me what's happening! Why is that big nigra just lying there, Frank?

FRANK. He was knocked down.

GIRL. He was?

FRANK. The little nigra caught him with a combination.

GIRL. Is it over, Frank?

FRANK. I don't think so. See? He's getting up. He'll be all right.

GIRL. His eye is bleeding.

FRANK. That's nothing.

GIRL. What are they doing now?

FRANK. The big one's just trying to hang on until his head clears.

GIRL. I think it's cute the way the little nigra keeps pulling up his pants. That 'Dell or whatever his name is ought to be ashamed of himself, just walking around like he didn't know where he was. Frank?

FRANK. What?

GIRL. Tell me something.

FRANK. Tell you what?

GIRL. Tell me why you brought me here.

FRANK. There goes that little one!

GIRL. Where? Where? But why did they stop?

FRANK. The end of the round.

GIRL. He's going to sit down right in front of us again.

FRANK. You shouldn't be so sensitive.

GIRL. He smells, Frank.

FRANK. You work up a sweat and you'll smell, too.

GIRL. Honestly, the things that come out of your head. He's looking at me again, Frank. Make him stop.

FRANK. You're just imagining things.

GIRL. Daddy says you really can't hurt a nigra. He says they aren't built like other people. He says they really don't have feelings like we do. (*quieter, for the benefit of* FRANK *only*) I think it's awfully exciting. I mean being at a carnival. I've always wanted to go to a carnival. Really I have. But you're the first person to ask me. Aren't you glad? It makes you sort of extra special. Did I tell you Bob called me up last week? I told him I was sorry, but I wouldn't be able to see him. Wasn't that sweet of me? If someone you knew called you would you have done the same for me? What are they doing, Frank? They keep circling each other like a couple of dogs.

FRANK. They're feeling each other out.

GIRL. But why don't they hit each other, Frank? That's what they get paid to do, isn't it?

FRANK. Give them a chance, they will.

GIRL. What is it, Frank? What are they doing now? Why is everyone standing up? Tell me what's happening, Frank!

FRANK. The big one has the little one up against the ropes.

GIRL (*standing*). But why doesn't the little one try to get away? Why doesn't he hit him back?

FRANK. I don't think he can. I think the little one's hurt his hand.

GIRL. Don't be silly! He's just not trying, that's all. Come on, hit him back! Just don't stand there! Do something!

FRANK. He would if he could.

GIRL. It's not fair, Frank! The big one keeps hitting him in the face!

(FRANK *and the* GIRL *sit down as the second round comes to an end.*)

GIRL. After the fight, let's go to my house, all right?

FRANK. Will there be anyone home?

GIRL. No. Nobody will be there.

FRANK. Are you still glad I took you to the carnival?

GIRL. Yes. Very glad. I suppose you heard about the party last week.

FRANK. No. What party?

GIRL. The one my aunt gave me.

FRANK. Anything interesting happen?

GIRL. Nothing except someone told me I was engaged and I said "That's news to me" and she said "Well, it's all over town" and I said "People will talk, won't they?" and she said I could trust her. Don't you think that's funny? Imagine some old biddy trying to get around me like that. I told Daddy and he almost died laughing. He keeps looking at me, Frank. Make him stop looking at me, Frank.

FRANK. There goes the bell!

GIRL. Why doesn't the little one do something?

FRANK. There isn't much he can do.

GIRL. You really think he hurt his hand?

FRANK. Sure. See the way it dangles?

GIRL. He just keeps staring at the big 'Dell or whatever his name is.

FRANK. There goes that left in his face again.

GIRL. The little one's trying to hit him back, Frank.

FRANK. He can't do anything with a broken hand.

GIRL. Do you think the referee will make them stop?

FRANK. No. But he'll make them break the clinch.

GIRL. Look at the little one's face, Frank. It's all blood.

FRANK. I don't think he can see.

GIRL. He doesn't even know where to turn.

FRANK. His pants are slipping again.

GIRL. They're starting to laugh at him, Frank.

FRANK. The big one is holding back. It won't last much longer.

GIRL. The blood keeps running into his eyes, Frank.

FRANK. There goes the big one!

GIRL (*turning away*). I want to go home, Frank. Take me home.

FRANK. It'll be over in a few more minutes.

GIRL. Hold me, Frank.

FRANK. The big one is banging his left in his face again!

GIRL. I don't want to watch any more!

FRANK. Just a few more seconds. It'll be over in just a few more seconds!

GIRL. I want to go home. Take me home, Frank.

FRANK (*getting to his feet*)
C'mon! Let him go!
C'mon! Let him go!
Look at the sweat pour down his legs!
C'mon! Hit him!
That's it! Bang him in the face!

(FRANK *becomes more and more excited as he watches the fight and his face becomes a repository for all the fear and hate the crowd feels as it watches one man being beaten to his knees by another man.*)

C'mon, ref! Make them break it up!
Don't let him hang on!
Hit him! Hit him!
C'mon, ref! Make them break it up!
Pull him off, ref! Pull him off!
That's it! Now you got him!
Push him to the ropes, boy! That's the idea!
That'll do it! Now you got him! That's the idea!
C'mon! Hit him! You got a hand free!
Below the belt! That's it! Below the belt!
Do it again!
Now you got him! In the belly! He can't take it in the belly!
Hit him in the head! Hit him in the head and he'll go down!
That's the idea! Now you got him!
There he goes, boy! That's it! Hit him again!
He's down!
He's down on his knees!
That's it, ref!
Keep counting!
Eight, nine, ten . . . and he's out!

(*And as* FRANK *just stands there, his face flushed with hate and his hands clenched, from somewhere in the distance, a loudspeaker opens up. . . .*)

LOUDSPEAKER (*very calm in contrast to the above*). The winner of the fight in two minutes and fifteen seconds of the third round, Adele Griffin. . . .

(*The crowd disperses with* HARRY *and* DOROTHY *the last to go. Enter* WINDY, 'DELL *and the two representatives of the press, the* PHOTOGRAPHER *and the* REPORTER, *in a deserted corner of the carnival lot.*)

WINDY (*the big shot*). Okay, boys, he's all yours.

('DELL *is cornered. Flashbulbs flash and the air is filled with shouts*

*of "That was some show you put on!" "Okay, smile. That's it." "A little
to the left. There. That's better." "When was the last time you saw
your brother?")*

'DELL. Tell them I don't want no picture of me in the paper, Windy!

WINDY. Hey, what are you crazy? A little publicity is good for you.

'DELL. I don't want no picture of me in the paper, Windy!

WINDY. Don't let him bother you, boys. He's the bashful kind.

'DELL. You guys think I like it I go in the ring and all I see is a
bunch of faces I can't stand no more?

WINDY *(to the newsmen)*. Got that, boys? My boy's got feelings.
That's what I call real class.

(To 'DELL*)* And another thing, tomorrow I want you to move out of
that dump you're staying in. I don't want you staying in no cheap
dump. People will get the wrong idea.

'DELL. You want me to live it up on what I make fighting carnivals,
is that what you want?

WINDY *(annoyed)*. What do you mean, fighting carnivals? If it was
someone else maybe it would have been just a carnival fight. Don't
be stupid. I know talent when I see it. You're a valuable piece of
property. Remember that. A valuable piece of property. *(To the newsmen)* Ain't that right, boys? *(To* 'DELL*)* You know what people are
saying?

'DELL. Sure. Look at that big nigger give it to the little nigger.

WINDY. They're saying you're the best middleweight there is. That's
what people are saying. What do you think of that?

'DELL. I think you're a liar!

WINDY *(to the newsmen)*. He thinks I'm a liar. That's what I call
real modesty.

REPORTER. May we ask him some questions? You know, the human
side of the story?

WINDY *(magnanimously)*. Sure. Go ahead and ask him some questions. Ask him anything you want. We got nothing to hide, do we,
Adele?

'DELL. What kind of questions you want to ask?

REPORTER. When was the last time you saw your brother?

'DELL. Why? What do you care when was the last time I saw him?

REPORTER. Do you think he did what they say he did?

'DELL. No!

REPORTER. You plan on helping your brother if they catch him?

'DELL. That's right.

REPORTER. You think he'll get a fair trial if they catch him down here?

'DELL. No.

REPORTER. You used to be a leading contender for the title, isn't that right?

WINDY. What do you mean, used to be? He still is!

REPORTER. May we quote you on that?

WINDY. Sure you can quote me. You can put it in headlines if you want, I don't care. We're just down here for kicks.

REPORTER. We have some more questions.

WINDY. Shoot.

REPORTER. Does he have any immediate plans?

WINDY. Like what?

REPORTER. Does he have any big fights coming up?

WINDY. We had some important people down here looking at him tonight. But it's hard to tell what the future's gonna bring. We'll probably head North again in another week or so.

REPORTER (*scribbling down the reply*). I see. Just a few more questions. (*To* 'DELL) About the fight tonight. Did he hurt you in the first round?

'DELL. He hurt me bad.

REPORTER. Could you explain what happened?

'DELL. I dropped my guard and he caught me with a straight right to the jaw.

REPORTER. But you came back strong in the second round.

'DELL. That's right.

REPORTER. Could you explain what happened?

'DELL. I got mad.

REPORTER. Is that all?

'DELL. He broke his hand.

WINDY. That's a lie! My boy is good. That's what happened.

REPORTER (*to* WINDY). If you don't mind, I'd like to have him answer his own questions.

WINDY. I don't mind. But you don't have to believe everything he says, do you?

REPORTER (*to* 'DELL). You mean after the first round he couldn't even defend himself?

'DELL. That's right. He could hang on. That's all.

WINDY. You want to believe him, go right ahead. But my boy is terrific and nothing you put in your paper will make the people think different.

REPORTER (*to* 'DELL). Didn't it bother you?

'DELL. You mean would it have been better if he was a white man, is that what you mean?

REPORTER. Yes. I suppose that's what I mean.

'DELL. No. It wouldn't have made no difference.

REPORTER. But if he couldn't even defend himself, why didn't you just knock him out?

'DELL. Because my manager, he kept telling me to cut him up before I put him away.

WINDY. That's a lie!

REPORTER. Didn't it bother you?

'DELL. What do you think? Don't you think I got feelings?

WINDY (*to no one in particular*). The guy was a bum! Don't believe a word he says!

REPORTER. Then you cut him up for the crowd?

'DELL. That's right. I cut him up for the crowd.

REPORTER. But didn't he try to stop you?

'DELL. Sure. Every time he got me in a clinch he tried to stop me.

REPORTER. Did he ever say anything to you?

'DELL. He kept saying, "C'mon, boy. Take it easy. Gussie's black, too."

REPORTER. But you didn't let up, did you?

'DELL. No.

REPORTER. And how did you manage to finally break away?

'DELL. I kept hooking him in the belly.

REPORTER. Could you show us how you did it?

('DELL *looks to* WINDY *for advice.*)

WINDY. Go on. Show him how you did it.

('DELL *backs away and pantomimes some of the action of the fight. And as he does so, the gaunt figure of the* DEPUTY *crosses slowly before him on the forepart of the stage, then leans up against a wall to watch.*)

'DELL. Like that. I kept hooking him in the belly.

REPORTER. And he still wouldn't let go?

'DELL. No. The more I hit him the harder he hung on.

REPORTER. And your manager kept yelling it was for your brother so you kept on hitting him?

'DELL. That's right.

REPORTER. And he still wouldn't let go?

'DELL. No.

REPORTER. So what did you do then?

WINDY. Go on. Show him how you did it.

'DELL. I hit him harder.

DEPUTY. You say you did it for your brother, that why you took the two dollars?

REPORTER. And you say you did it for your brother?

'DELL (*confused*). That's right. I did it for my brother!

DEPUTY. They put you in jail, they put you in a cage and they only feed you once a day. . . .

WINDY. Go on! Show him what you did! That's it! Harder! Harder!

(*As* WINDY *encourages him,* 'DELL *becomes completely confused and he continues to stare at the* DEPUTY *as the punches he throws, though directed at nothing, become more and more earnest.*)

DEPUTY. You wouldn't lie to me, would you, boy?

WINDY. Hit him again! See! He's crying! He's crying like a baby!

DEPUTY. Everybody knows Willie's gonna come to no good. . . .

'DELL. That's a lie!

WINDY. But he won't let go! Hit him again! That's it! For your brother, 'Dell! Hit him again! That's it!

DEPUTY. Always talking big and telling folks he's going North where they got opportunity.

WINDY. Hit him below the belt! That'll teach him! Harder! Harder! For your brother, 'Dell! Just tell yourself your brother will make it to where you can help him!

DEPUTY. Mrs. Corbett got a witness, boy. . . .

WINDY. That's it! Rub his back against the ropes! Now you got him! Hit him, 'Dell!

DEPUTY. Somebody got to go to jail, boy, it better be your brother. . . .

WINDY. Now you got him! In the belly! He can't take it in the belly!

'DELL. Make him stop crying, Windy! Make him stop crying!

WINDY. C'mon, you got him in the ropes! Give it to him! That's it! In the belly! He can't take it any longer!

'DELL. Make him stop crying, Windy! Make him stop crying!

(*But* WINDY *can't make him stop crying and suddenly* 'DELL *stops his punching, grabs* WINDY *and throws him to the ground. Silence. Then* 'DELL *slowly pulls himself erect, turns slowly around to face his tormentors and after a pause. . . .*)

Willie! Willie! All I wanted to do was buy you a pair of shoes, Willie!

CURTAIN

ACT THREE

SCENE ONE

SCENE: 'DELL'*s room early the next afternoon. The shade is up and from across the hall comes the muffled sound of a jazz band intermixed with an occasional burst of shrill female laughter.*

AT RISE: 'DELL, *midway between sleep and awareness, sits on the edge of his bed. Suddenly, the sound of the jazz band becomes louder as the door across the hall is momentarily opened and* HARRY *comes out to knock on* 'DELL'*s door.*

HARRY. How would you like to join us for a drink? Dorothy and I are having a little party.

'DELL. I don't want to go to no party.

HARRY. You shouldn't be so anti-social. A little group therapy might be just the thing. Are you worried about . . . what's your brother's name? Willie?

'DELL. I worry about someone it's none of your business, is it?

HARRY. I worry about things, but I never let it keep me from having a good time. It's just a matter of self-discipline.

'DELL. You got nothing to do but bother people?

HARRY. We just thought you might like a little company.

'DELL. I want some company, I'll send you a postcard, all right?

(HARRY *is joined by* DOROTHY.)

HARRY. I don't think he wants our company.

DOROTHY. What is he, independent?

HARRY. He does have a wonderful face.

DOROTHY. Maybe he'll come if I ask him. Some people just like to be coaxed more than others. (*To* 'DELL) We'd love to have you over.

'DELL. What for? You want to look at faces, go on down to the zoo.

DOROTHY (*to* HARRY). You certainly have a talent for picking them. Remember the time I threw a party and you showed up with a mad German who thought he was Christ?

HARRY. Well, wasn't he?

DOROTHY (*to* 'DELL). If you're upset about something the best thing to do is to get out and visit with people.

'DELL. I want your advice I'll ask for it, all right?

DOROTHY. Wouldn't you like to have me sketch your face?

'DELL. I'll think about it, all right?

HARRY. How about coming over and listening to the radio? They broadcast bulletins every hour on the hour.

'DELL. I don't want to listen to no news!

(*There is a moment's pause.* DOROTHY *shrugs her shoulders and the two of them exit. Enter* WINDY.)

WINDY. What's the matter, kid? Anybody bother you?

'DELL. Some people gotta stick their noses in where it don't belong.

WINDY (*sensing* 'DELL's *mood*). About last night. I want you to know I didn't mean no harm.

'DELL. That's okay.

WINDY. You know how it is. I just thought a little publicity wouldn't do no harm, that's all.

'DELL. Yeah. I know how it is.

WINDY. That was a nice fight you put on last night. Everybody says you put on a good show.

'DELL. It was all right, I guess.

WINDY. You feel all right?

'DELL. Sure. I feel all right.

WINDY. You have any breakfast yet?

'DELL. No.

WINDY. You want I should go get you some breakfast?

'DELL. No. I don't want nothing to eat.

WINDY. It's a beautiful day out.

'DELL. Maybe I'll take a walk later.

WINDY. Sure. That's a great idea. Maybe you can work up an appetite.

'DELL. I been thinking.

WINDY. You have? What about?

'DELL. I don't want no more fights.

WINDY. Why? What's the matter?

'DELL. I don't know. I just don't want no more fights.

WINDY. But you're on the way up. You can't quit now.

'DELL. I don't like the faces I see when I go to a fight.

WINDY. What faces? What are you talking about? C'mon, I'll go get you some breakfast. You'll feel better.

'DELL. Why'd you tell me to cut him up, Windy?

WINDY. Hey, c'mon. Get off it, will you? You wanted to make it look good, didn't you? Two guys get in the ring somebody's liable to get hurt, that's right, isn't it?

'DELL. You didn't have to tell me to cut him up, did you?

WINDY. Hey, what is this? Boy Scout Week or something? What do you mean I told you to cut him up? You can use the money, can't you? You won, didn't you? When was the last time you won a fight? It's been so long since you won a fight I almost forgot who was taking the count and started to yell for what's his name to get off the deck. That's what I call gratitude. You get your confidence back for the first time in two years and all you want to do is blame me because maybe you cut someone up a little.

'DELL. You didn't have to keep telling me it was for my brother, did you? What am I? An animal? I got no feelings, is that what you think? You stick me in the ring with some guy who don't know a jab from a cross, he's black and there's a thousand faces looking up at me like I was a freak, all right, but you got no right to keep saying, "Cut him up, boy, cut him up. Just tell yourself your brother will make it to where you can help him." You think it's right for one man to tell another man to cut somebody up because if he don't maybe something bad is gonna happen?

WINDY. Hey, look. I tell you what to do, you don't like it you don't have to do it. Sure, it's my brains but it's your hands, all right? I remember when you first come to see me. You were just a kid and you said what you wanted more than anything else was to fight. I took you on and I taught you everything you know because I figured maybe you had something, remember? So don't get wise with me, kid. All right? If it wasn't for me, you'd never have got started. You'd have been washed up before you ever even begun. Sure. Last night I told you it was for your brother. And you get a fight next week and I'll tell you the same thing. Why shouldn't I? What did your brother ever do for me? Louse you up so bad you never knew if you was coming or going and died after the only real chance at the big time you ever had! Maybe you like it down here, but it's a long way between me and where I come from. (*Disgusted*) You don't want no more fights. Who you trying to kid? You quit now, how you gonna make a living? Go back on the ice truck?

'DELL. I can do something.

WINDY. Like what? Short order cook in a fry house?

'DELL. Don't worry. I'll figure out something.

WINDY. Sure. But supposing I tell you I already got you booked for next week?

'DELL. You got me booked?

WINDY. Sure. That's right.

'DELL. Where?

WINDY. What do you care where? It's a fight, isn't it? Besides, they got a roof over the ring. What more do you want?

'DELL. You want me to do what I done last night?

WINDY. Why? What'd you do last night?

'DELL. Who you got me signed up with, Windy?

WINDY. I don't know. Some guy about a hundred and sixty pounds. I just got confirmation on it about an hour ago.

'DELL. What city?

WINDY. Down in Houston.

'DELL. A colored guy?

WINDY. Hey, look, kid. I don't make the rules. I get you a fight you think I go around asking what color the boy is? Maybe he's green for all I know.

'DELL. You hear anything today?

WINDY. About what?

'DELL. About my brother.

WINDY (*as though it didn't matter*). I heard a little something.

'DELL. Like what?

WINDY. I forget.

'DELL (*suspiciously*). Tell me what you heard, Windy.

WINDY. Nothing. I didn't hear nothing. Here. I'll go get you some breakfast. By the way, you gonna take that fight or aren't you?

'DELL. You heard something, Windy. Tell me what you heard.

WINDY (*caught*). Okay, I heard something.

'DELL. They gonna call out the state militia? Is that what you heard?

WINDY. No. They aren't gonna call out no state militia.

'DELL. Then what'd you hear, Windy? Tell me what you heard?

WINDY. All right. They caught him.

'DELL. They caught him?

WINDY. That's right. They caught him last night.

'DELL. Where'd they catch him, Windy? Tell me where they caught him.

WINDY. I don't know.

'DELL. What do you mean you don't know? Then how do you know they caught him?

WINDY. Because they got him down at the city jail, all right?

'DELL. Down at the city jail?

WINDY. That's right.

'DELL. You're joking, Windy. Tell me you're lying!

WINDY. What joking? What are you talking about? Why should I tell you they got him down at the city jail if I'm only making it up?

'DELL. Did they hurt him, Windy? Tell me if they hurt him!

WINDY. How do I know if they hurt him? All I know is they caught him.

'DELL. I want to go see him, Windy.

WINDY. All right. All right. But first we'll go get him a lawyer.

'DELL. A lawyer won't do him any good. What good's a lawyer gonna do him?

WINDY. All right. All right. We won't argue. We won't get him a lawyer.

'DELL. I want to go see him now, Windy. I don't want to wait till we get him a lawyer.

WINDY. You can't see him now.

'DELL. Why? Why can't I see him now?

WINDY. Because they don't let no visitors in till two, all right?

'DELL. Then I'll go down and see him at two, Windy.

WINDY (*annoyed*). All right. Go down and see him at two. See if I care.

'DELL. Aren't you gonna go with me?

WINDY. What for? What do I want to go see him for? You don't care if you get some bad publicity, it's your business. I can't do nothing about it.

'DELL. I want you to go with me, Windy.

WINDY. Yeah. Okay. I'll go with you. I'll see you down at the city jail at two. Okay? Look. I gotta go. I got things to do.

(WINDY *exits. For a few minutes,* 'DELL *is left by himself. But then the door opens and* HARRY *and* DOROTHY *enter.* HARRY *is in his bathrobe and* DOROTHY *carries a large sketch pad under her arm.*)

'DELL. What do you want? I just told you I don't want no company.

HARRY. I know but we thought you might have changed your mind. I think this calls for a formal introduction. (*To* DOROTHY) This is my across-the-hall neighbor, Mr. Adele Griffin. (*To* 'DELL) This is an old friend of mine, Miss Dorothy.

DOROTHY. How do you do? Would you mind moving over to the window?

'DELL. But I told you I didn't want no company!

HARRY. Once Dorothy makes up her mind that she's going to sketch someone's face there's no stopping her. The best thing to do is to sit still and enjoy it.

'DELL. But supposing I don't want my face sketched?

DOROTHY. Anyone can spare an hour.

HARRY. Besides, we would like to talk about your plans.

'DELL. Plans? What plans?

HARRY. Plans for your future, of course.

'DELL. I got a future, you got nothing to do with it.

HARRY. Are you sure? Aren't you being a little rash?

'DELL. What do you mean I'm being a little rash? I know what I'm being so why don't you go on out and stay out? (*pause*) Well, why don't you go? (*pause*) What are you waiting for?

HARRY. Haven't you heard? Your brother evidently didn't make it across the state line.

'DELL. What about it? What's that got to do with you?

HARRY. We just thought you might like to talk about it with someone who might be able to help.

DOROTHY (*getting her things ready*). You do have time, don't you?

HARRY. Of course he has time. That's something we all have. Today. Tomorrow. Next year if we like.

DOROTHY. It really won't take long.

HARRY. Nothing stops Dorothy. I remember once when she wanted to sketch the face of a Negro who had been sentenced to hang and not even the warden could stop her. She just sat in his cell and didn't finish until just an hour before the poor man was hung.

DOROTHY. I wish you'd move away from the window, Harry. You're blocking the light.

HARRY (*to* 'DELL). Dorothy's always afraid I'll follow her uncle's example. (*To* DOROTHY) The trouble with your uncle is that he didn't have a sense of humor. (*To* 'DELL) Standing by an open window always reminds Dorothy of her Uncle John. He used to stand by the window all the time and nobody thought anything about it till one day, on the fourteenth floor of the Commerce Building, he did what no one thought he would do and jumped.

DOROTHY (*to* 'DELL). If you'll just sit down for a minute. . . .

HARRY. I still don't think he likes us. . . .

DOROTHY. Of course he does. It's just that different people show their emotions in different ways, that's all. (*To* 'DELL) You're really flattered, aren't you?

'DELL (*sitting down*). Flattered? What do you mean, flattered?

DOROTHY. Yes. Flattered. Pleased to think that somebody would want to sketch your face.

HARRY. Dorothy and I were thinking you might like to go on a little vacation, just the three of us.

'DELL. I don't want to go on no vacation.

HARRY. Beautiful country, Italy. Full of nice, quiet little towns.

DOROTHY. Harry knows a beautiful little town in northern Italy, don't you, Harry?

HARRY. A lovely spot. Isolated. Away from everything. No pressure of any kind and a long stretch of white beach. There's a hotel over-looking the bay and no one cares who you are or what you do.

DOROTHY. Much better than places like Rome.

HARRY. Unless you like motor scooters and tourists, of course.

DOROTHY. The nicest thing about it is there won't be any problem about who sleeps where.

'DELL (*quietly—aware of the implication*). Suppose I don't want to go?

HARRY. You would like to have someone testify that your brother wasn't even there when it happened, wouldn't you?

'DELL (*defeated*). I go there, how long do I have to stay?

DOROTHY. As long as you want.

HARRY. After a while, you won't even want to come back. Most of the people who go there never bother returning.

'DELL. About Willie. How you gonna get him a witness?

HARRY. That's very simple. It's just a matter of knowing the right people.

DOROTHY (*cheerfully, as she sketches*). Of course. That's no problem. Not when you come from one of the finest families around just loaded with judges and governors and things.

'DELL (*after a long pause—tonelessly*). What you gonna do with my picture when you finish it?

DOROTHY. Frame it.

'DELL. No. I don't mean that. I mean after you frame it.

DOROTHY. I don't know. Maybe I'll just give it to my husband to hang in the bedroom.

'DELL. You mean across the hall?

DOROTHY. No. I mean my husband's bedroom.

'DELL. You mean you got another husband?

DOROTHY. Don't be silly. Not another. Just one. We don't live together, but he's still my husband.

'DELL. But won't he mind?

DOROTHY. Mind what? I'm afraid I don't understand.

'DELL. Giving my picture to your husband to hang in the bedroom?

DOROTHY. Oh. I see what you mean. No. He won't mind. He's too intelligent for that. Besides, we're still good friends.

'DELL. You are?

DOROTHY. Of course. It's just that we decided it would be better if we didn't live together, that's all.

'DELL. If he was you and you was him, wouldn't you mind?

DOROTHY. Of course not.

'DELL. You wouldn't?

DOROTHY. My husband and I are both perfectly adjusted. We just aren't bound by what most people think is right and wrong.

'DELL. How do you mean?

DOROTHY. Ask Harry. He'll tell you.

'DELL. Why? Does he know your husband?

DOROTHY. They're very good friends. They even went to the same school together.

'DELL. They did?

DOROTHY. It's really very simple once you think about it. Did you ever think about it?

'DELL. Think about what?

DOROTHY. We all have needs you know.

'DELL. Needs? How do you mean, needs?

DOROTHY. Yes. Needs. Why? Haven't you ever heard of the word before?

'DELL. No. Not like that.

DOROTHY. Everyone has needs.

'DELL. I got needs?

DOROTHY. Certainly. Everything that functions has needs.

'DELL. Explain how I got needs.

DOROTHY. It's very simple. Everyone is made up of billions and billions of little cells. Each cell is like a little animal and together they make up a big animal. And just as the little animals that make up the big one have to eat, excrete and multiply, so does the big one. To be healthy is simply to live in accordance with one's needs even if they're different from someone else's needs. Now do you understand? It's really quite simple.

'DELL (*angrily*). That why you got a boy friend, because you got a need?

DOROTHY. There's nothing to get upset over. Harry has needs and I have needs. It's all very reciprocal.

'DELL. I don't think I got as many needs as you got.

DOROTHY. Of course you do.

'DELL. Don't tell me what I got. I know what I got.

DOROTHY. We won't argue about it, but you do. You just repress them more than I do perhaps, but that's about all.

'DELL. You really think everybody is made up of billions and billions of little animals?

DOROTHY. Cells. That's right. Billions and billions of little cells. But you shouldn't take it so personally. That's all anyone is.

'DELL. Then how come you want to sketch my picture?

DOROTHY. What does that have to do with it?

'DELL. But all it is is a lot of little cells. You just said so.

DOROTHY. I told you. I'm sketching your face because it's so beautifully sad.

'DELL. But how could a bunch of little cells be sad?

DOROTHY. I don't have time to explain. Now a little to the right, please.

'DELL. No. First tell me how a bunch of little cells could be sad.

DOROTHY. I told you I don't have the time. Now a little to the right, please.

'DELL. But I want you to tell me.

HARRY. It does make things easier. Thinking of people as lumps of cells, that is.

DOROTHY (*becoming impatient*). Will you please move your head a little to the right? I'm doing your ear.

'DELL. But I want to know.

DOROTHY. Some other time, perhaps. But not now.

'DELL (*getting to his feet and turning to* HARRY). Make her tell me. You make her tell me.

DOROTHY. Don't be a fool. Now sit down and let me finish.

'DELL. But I want someone to tell me! I want someone to tell me how a billion little cells could be sad!

DOROTHY. No one's going to tell you anything unless you stop acting like a maniac. Now sit down and let me finish your portrait.

'DELL (*to* HARRY). But I want to know! Someone has to tell me!

HARRY. You'll get used to it after a while. After a while you won't even notice the candy wrappers on the sidewalks or the hair in men's nostrils.

DOROTHY. Will you please sit down while I finish?

'DELL. I don't want to sit down! I want someone to tell me!

DOROTHY (*picking up her things*). If that's the way you're going to behave, I might as well go now.

'DELL. You think when someone hits me in the face, it don't hurt? Is that what you think?

DOROTHY. No one said anything about hitting you in the face.

'DELL. I go in the ring and someone keeps jabbing a left in my face, you think I don't feel it? You think I like getting hit in the face? Is that what you think? You think it's fun you go in the ring with everyone looking at you like they expect you to kill someone? You think that's fun? That I don't feel anything? And when the bell rings, you move out and maybe just stare at the other guy or feel him out a little because you're scared and don't want to start nothing, but the crowd eggs him on and all of a sudden he snaps a left in your face, don't you think I feel it? (*A moment of silence as* 'DELL *stares at the two visitors*) Well, just don't look at me! Say something!

DOROTHY (*containing her indignation*). No one said anything about hitting you in the face.

HARRY (*to* DOROTHY). I think we'd better go. (*To* 'DELL) You really shouldn't take things so seriously. We'll drop back later when you feel better.

'DELL. Tell me what she said isn't true! Do you hear? Tell me what she said isn't true!

HARRY. Do you want me to tell you something I don't believe?

DOROTHY. I guess some people just can't stand the truth. (*To* 'DELL) We're terribly sorry if we've upset you.

(*The visitors leave and* 'DELL *stares after them for a moment. Then suddenly, he slams his fist against the door with all his might and the pain brings a gradual look of surprise to his face. He raises his fist and looks at it curiously as though he'd never seen it before and then sits down on the edge of the bed where he buries his head in his arms and begins to sob.*)

CURTAIN

SCENE TWO

SCENE: 'DELL *and* WINDY *stand humbly before a desk behind which a* POLICE CAPTAIN *stands with his back turned. His hands are clasped behind his back and he stares out the window in front of him as though contemplating a decision of major importance. Finally, he speaks. . . .*)

CAPTAIN. You ask why should he want to see the prisoner if he is not in fact his brother? I don't know. But even if he were his brother why should he want to see him? That's more to the point. If it were me, I'd be ashamed to even look at him. (*Pause. Then he turns.*) I don't know what to say. I suppose it's only a rule, after all. (*To* 'DELL) What did you say your name is?

'DELL. Adele Griffin.

CAPTAIN. You realize if I let you see the prisoner it will only be for fifteen minutes?

'DELL. Yes, sir. I just want to see him for a little while.

CAPTAIN. And what is it you want to talk to him about?

'DELL. I don't know. I just want to see him, I guess. That's all.

CAPTAIN. All right. You win. But fifteen minutes. That's all. (*Sitting down at the desk*) I need a little information first.

'DELL. Yes, sir.

CAPTAIN (*filling out an official blank*). Your age?

'DELL. You mean how old I am?

CAPTAIN. Yes, how old are you?

'DELL. Twenty-seven.

CAPTAIN. And your present address?

'DELL. One-fifteen Shawney Avenue.

CAPTAIN. How long you been there?

'DELL. Two weeks.

CAPTAIN. Are you a resident of this state?

'DELL. No, sir.

CAPTAIN. Where were you born?

'DELL. I was born here.

CAPTAIN. You were born here but you don't live here any more, is that it?

'DELL. That's right.

CAPTAIN. What's the matter? Don't you like it down here?

'DELL. Yes, sir. It's all right.

CAPTAIN. Ever been arrested for anything?
'DELL. No, sir.

CAPTAIN. Occupation?

'DELL. You mean what I do?

CAPTAIN. That's right. I want to know what you do for a living.

'DELL. I'm a prizefighter.

CAPTAIN (*with an attempt at humor*). Make any money?

'DELL. No, sir. Not much.

CAPTAIN. Your mother living?

'DELL. No, sir.

CAPTAIN. And your father?

'DELL. He's dead, too.

CAPTAIN. Married?

'DELL. No, sir. I'm not married.

CAPTAIN. Nearest of kin?

'DELL. My brother. He's the nearest.

CAPTAIN. Race?

'DELL. Negro.

CAPTAIN. All right. Sign here.

'DELL (*taking the proffered pen*). Here?

CAPTAIN. Yes. That's right.

'DELL. Is there something else I gotta do?

CAPTAIN (*taking his pen back*). No. That's all. Sergeant?

(*The* POLICE CAPTAIN *calls again and a gorilla-like* SERGEANT *appears. His pants legs are too short so that the white of his socks shows above his shoes and his jacket is pulled taut across his back. His arms hang loose and when he walks, he rolls a bit from side to side. The* CAPTAIN *rises.*)

Take this man to cell seventeen, Sergeant.

SERGEANT. Yes, sir.

(*The* SERGEANT *turns to leave.* 'DELL *looks back toward* WINDY *for a moment, but* WINDY *motions him to follow the* SERGEANT *and he does. The* SERGEANT *opens a huge steel door which leads into a long, narrow corridor lit by the light coming from the cells on either side and a single, naked bulb hanging from the ceiling at the far end. The shadow of steel bars lines the corridor and as the* SERGEANT *and* 'DELL *enter, various hands are brought up in gestures of mock salute and nose-thumbing defiance. Immediately upon* 'DELL'S *and the* SERGEANT'S *entrance, the men begin to talk and shout, spitting out their hate and resentment and occasionally sounding off with a Bronx cheer.*)

VOICES.

Hey! Look who's here! The keeper of the keys!

Sure and you know why he works in a jail, boys? Because down inside he still gets lonesome for his cage, that's why he works in a jail!

How come you're still on, sergeant? Ain't it feeding time yet?

Hey! He's bringing us company!

Call that company?

Hey! Black boy! Smile when we talk to you!

Hey, Sergeant! One jigg at a time is enough!

Yeah, Sergeant! We thought this was a high-class jail!

Ain't we got no rights?

'Course we got rights! This is America, ain't it?

Nigger lover!

We'll get up a petition, that's what we'll do!
Nigger lover!

SERGEANT (*goaded beyond his endurance*). All right, you guys! Cut it out! You hear me? You guys better cut it out! I come in here I don't want no more cheap remarks! You understand? No more cheap remarks! I hear any more cheap remarks and you'll all be sorry!

(*The men quiet down and their hands begin to slip from the bars. The* SERGEANT *and* 'DELL *continue on their way to cell seventeen. Feeling a sudden rapport with* 'DELL—)

Bunch of wise guys. That's what they are.

'DELL. Yes, sir.

SERGEANT. You treat 'em good and all they wanna do is insult you.

'DELL. Yes, sir.

SERGEANT. What are you, a friend of his?

'DELL. He's my brother.

SERGEANT (*unlocking the door to the cell*). Yeah? You wouldn't kid me, would you? You wanna know something?

'DELL. What?

SERGEANT. I don't think he done what they say.

'DELL. You don't?

SERGEANT. Naw. I seen a lot of 'em brought in here. He don't seem the type.

('DELL *enters the cell. The* SERGEANT *shuts the door behind him.* 'DELL *blinks his eyes as he tries to get used to the dark of the cell. His brother lies sprawled on a cot in the corner, his face to the wall.* 'DELL *stands motionless for a while, then goes to his brother and taps him gently on the shoulder. As he does so, from out of nowhere comes the sad, lonely music of the calliope once more.*)

'DELL. Willie! Willie! It's me, your brother 'Dell! (WILLIE *rolls over and rubs his eyes.*) Hey! C'mon! Get up! It's me, Willie! 'Dell!

WILLIE (*sitting up and rubbing his eyes*). Hey, boy, what you doing here?

'DELL. I come to see you, Willie!

WILLIE (*yawning*). Yeah? What for?

'DELL. Aren't you glad to see me, Willie?

WILLIE. Sure. Sure I'm glad to see you. How you been?

'DELL. Okay. I been all right. How about you? You tired?

WILLIE. A little. I didn't get much sleep last night.

'DELL. You know what the Sergeant just told me?

WILLIE. No. What did the Sergeant just tell you?

'DELL. The Sergeant just told me even he don't believe you did what they said you did.

WILLIE. No?

'DELL. I'm gonna get you a lawyer, Willie. A good lawyer will get you out of here in no time at all.

WILLIE. Sure. (*Yawning again*) Sounds like a good idea. So how you been? I haven't seen you in a long time. The last time I saw you we had a little argument.

'DELL. I been all right, I guess.

WILLIE. Getting any fights?

'DELL. Some. But what were you doing down here, Willie?

WILLIE. Had a little business I had to tend to for a friend of mine. You know how it is. How about you? What you doing in this part of the country?

'DELL. I been on the road for the last couple of years.

WILLIE. Yeah? It's a tough racket. You ought to give it up and try something else.

'DELL. You think so, Willie?

WILLIE. Sure. There's no sense in getting your brains beat out for nothing, is there?

'DELL. I been thinking, Willie.

WILLIE. Yeah? What about?

'DELL. I know some people who could get you a witness to testify you weren't even there when it happened. That would fix it, wouldn't it, Willie?

WILLIE. You must know some pretty important people. Sounds like a real good idea.

'DELL. You think so, Willie? You want me to I'll tell 'em.

WILLIE. But it wouldn't do no good.

'DELL. It wouldn't?

WILLIE. 'Course not. Not when I already signed a confession, how could it?

'DELL. You signed a confession?

WILLIE. Sure. They catch you down here, you know how it is. I didn't see no sense not to.

'DELL. That's true.

WILLIE. Hey, c'mon, boy. Don't take it so hard.

'DELL. You hungry, Willie? You're hungry maybe I can go out and get you something to eat.

WILLIE. Hungry? Why should I be hungry?

'DELL. I thought maybe they didn't feed you.

WILLIE. They feed me all right.

'DELL. They hurt you, Willie? They do anything to you?

WILLIE. No. They didn't hurt me. Why should they hurt me?

'DELL. I thought maybe they hurt you when they caught you.

WILLIE. I got no complaints. They been real good to me.

'DELL. They have?

WILLIE. Sure.

'DELL. I heard they were gonna use bloodhounds.

WILLIE (*yawning again*). Yeah? I guess I foxed them. I gave up before they had a chance to use them.

'DELL. You gave up?

WILLIE. Sure. I didn't see no sense not to.

'DELL. You got tired of being chased?

WILLIE. No. I didn't get tired of being chased.

'DELL. But they were close to you, weren't they?

WILLIE. I don't know. Maybe they were close, and maybe they weren't. I got no idea.

'DELL. But weren't you scared out in the woods?

WILLIE. In the woods?

'DELL. Weren't you in the woods?

WILLIE. No. I wasn't in no woods.

'DELL. But you had to go through the woods if you wanted to get across the state line.

WILLIE. I wasn't in no woods. I was in Peerville the whole time.

'DELL. Peerville? That's only five miles from Hamilton.

WILLIE. Yeah? I thought it was six miles.

'DELL. You figured they wouldn't look so close, is that what you figured?

WILLIE. No. I figured they would but they didn't.

'DELL. You figured they would but they didn't?

WILLIE. Sure. I wanted to give up.

'DELL. But they won't give you a fair trial this side of the state line, Willie. Don't you know that?

WILLIE. Sure. I know. But it won't make any difference if it's a fair trial or not.

'DELL. Why? Because you're beat hollow inside and don't care?

WILLIE. No. Because I done what they say I done.

'DELL. You did what they say you did?

WILLIE. Sure. That's right. I did what they say I did.

'DELL. Say you didn't do it, Willie. Say she lied.

WILLIE. What do you mean "Say you didn't do it. Say she lied"? What difference does it make? I know what I did, don't I?

'DELL. Say you didn't do it, you hear me, Willie?

WILLIE (*amused*). Hey, what is this, what are you so worried about? Someone's gonna be hanged, it's not gonna be you, is it?

'DELL. Say you didn't do it, Willie, and I'll get you a witness and everything will be all right.

WILLIE. Hey, c'mon, get off it, will you, boy? What do you mean tell you I didn't do it? You still think I'm a real good guy, all I want to do is run a sport store only I never had a chance? Is that what you want to hear? Look, boy, I done something wrong, I did it because I wanted to, you understand? You say that once more, Old Willie's gonna bust right out and laugh.

'DELL. Don't laugh, Willie. You got no right to laugh at me.

WILLIE. Sure I got a right to laugh at you. I got a right to laugh at you because you're a fool, that's what you are. You still can't see what is and what isn't, can you? But I don't want no more whining, you hear me? I don't want to hear no more "Willie, you practice your ball today, Willie? You gotta practice your ball if you want to be a big-time ball player" or "Willie? I hear you been hanging around the wrong kind of people. It's no good if you hang around the wrong kind of people" or "I know, Willie. I know you didn't do nothing wrong, you was only looking." You think Old Willie cares what they do to him? I go to hell I don't want no two-bit liars blowing their noses over my grave and saying "My, ain't it a shame? The poor boy just never had a chance." They put a rope around my neck, you know what Old Willie's gonna do? He's gonna bust right out and laugh. He's gonna bust right out and laugh and when the preacher says, "Boy, this is no time to laugh" Old Willie's gonna say, "Listen, preacher-man, you ever walk down the street and watch the big man beat on the little man and the law come down and arrest the little man and let the big man go free?" You still think I got what it takes to be a big-time ball player or to run a sport store, Adele?

'DELL. Don't laugh at me, Willie.

WILLIE (*more seriously*). 'Course I'm gonna laugh at you. If I gotta go to hell, boy, first I'm gonna laugh. And you know why I'm gonna laugh at you? Because you're a liar. You lie so much you can't even see straight. What kind of world you come from, boy? You work hard, you do right, you go to heaven? That the kind of world you come from?

'DELL. Stop it, Willie. Stop it, you hear me?

WILLIE. Sure. Of course you don't want to listen. But you're gonna listen so you'll see what kind of a world you come from. You come from the same kind of world I come from, only you can't stand it so you gotta make it pretty somehow even if you have to lie. You gotta keep telling yourself there's something clean in the world or you won't be able to get out of bed in the morning. That's right, isn't it, boy? That's why you wanted me to play baseball, because if everything you knew was dirty, at least your brother, he'd be clean. But how about me, boy? What was I supposed to keep clean? You? And if it wasn't baseball, it was sport stores. And if it hadn't been that it would have been something else just so long as you could keep me clean, so if you cut someone up in the ring and you liked doing it, you could always say you done it for me.

'DELL. That's not true, Willie!

WILLIE. Sure it's true. But I got news for you. I never was any good and once I got to Chicago I never even wanted to play baseball, all right?

'DELL. You're lying, Willie!

WILLIE. No. I'm not lying. I took you, boy. I took you good. You just listen to me and you'll see what kind of world you live in. You'll see what kind of brother you got. You think I wanted to play baseball, don't you? But I didn't want to play no baseball. All I wanted to do was live it up till they caught up with me, all right? I used you, boy, and I'm glad. But you still want to think it's just that I never had a chance and that everything I ever did wrong was really your fault, don't you? But you listen, boy, and you'll see just how dumb you are, because nothing I ever done was your fault. You hear me? It was my fault. All of it. Sure. You want to keep me clean, but I won't let you. Nothing I ever done was your fault, I only let you think so, so I could use you. Not even Mrs. Corbett. You hear me, Adele? Not even Mrs. Corbett, because sure, you took two dollars to buy me a pair of shoes when she had her back turned and, yeah, I went to jail for it, but I got news for you. If you hadn't taken the two dollars, I was going to, you hear me? Because that's what I was there for to begin with. . . .

'DELL. You're lying! (*Hits* WILLIE) Tell me you're lying!

('DELL *hits his brother again and* WILLIE *sprawls to the floor and then with horror and as* WILLIE *pulls himself off to a corner,* 'DELL *raises his hands to the level of his eyes, slowly sinks to the floor himself and still staring at his hands, begins to moan and rock back and forth.*)

WILLIE (*after a long pause, broken and with pain*). A witness, 'Dell? What's a man gonna say? He could have been somebody? He could have done something? (*pause*) Only deep down inside he really didn't want nothing . . . nothing. (*pause*) A man see something he can't be . . . he don't want it. Nothing. (*Then quietly and with great gentleness*) 'Dell? You hear me, 'Dell? . . . Can I still be your brother?

CURTAIN

Scene Three

SCENE: 'DELL'*s room late the same afternoon.*

AT RISE: 'DELL *sits with his back to* HARRY *and* DOROTHY. *The shade is up and the wan light of the late afternoon sun filters through the window.*

HARRY. We'd like to apologize for the way we behaved this afternoon. But sometimes people say things and what's said is misunderstood.

DOROTHY. It isn't that we don't understand how you feel. But if someone wants to be your friend, we don't see why you should want to turn them down.

HARRY. Even if there's nothing we can do for your brother, we're still human and we would like to have you join us for supper.

DOROTHY. What Harry means is that whatever the reasons may be, none of us is in a position to refuse what's offered us. Nothing may mean anything, but it's still nice to have company.

(*Enter* WINDY.)

WINDY. Hey, what is this? Didn't I tell you people to leave my boy alone? What do I have to do, get out a court order or something?

HARRY. We just dropped over to offer our compliments.

WINDY. Yeah? Well, my boy don't need no compliments. All my boy needs is a little break and everything's gonna be all right. (*To* 'DELL)

Right, kid? What do you say, kid? You all packed? We got to get
going if we want to catch the eight-ten to Houston.

HARRY. Is he leaving?

WINDY. Sure he's leaving. What do you think he's gonna do, stay
cooped up in a two-bit flea bed like this the rest of his life? My boy
got a future. But you want to get somewhere you can't waste no time.
You got to keep moving.

DOROTHY. I don't think he wants to go.

WINDY. What do you mean he don't want to go? What do you know
about it? I got him all booked up for a week from Tuesday, don't I?

HARRY. I don't think he's packed.

WINDY. Hey, c'mon, get off it, will you? What are you, his lawyer or
something? My boy don't want to do something he got a mouth of
his own, don't he? How come you think you know so much about
what my boy wants to do? (*To* 'DELL) C'mon, kid. I don't know who
these bums are, but tell them to get out of here. We got things to do.

DOROTHY. You may be his manager and he might need someone to
tell him what to do, but I still don't think you're being very polite.

WINDY. Yeah? Well, look, lady, I am his manager and he is my boy,
but I don't know who you are and if I ever find out I promise I won't
tell nobody, all right? So if you don't like it here go someplace else,
because all I want you to do is leave my boy alone. I don't want my
boy getting into no trouble, you understand?

'DELL. I'm not going, Windy.

WINDY. What do you mean, you're not going? You got something
better to do a week from Tuesday? Hey, what's going on around here?
These bums giving you fancy ideas?

'DELL (*turning around*). I'm not going, Windy.

WINDY. What are you, sick or something? This is your chance to get
back in the big time. What's the matter, you got a better match somewhere else?

'DELL. I'm not afraid anymore, Windy.

WINDY. Who said anything about being afraid?

'DELL. You can't make me do anything I don't want any more,
Windy.

WINDY. C'mon. Don't give me that. Who do you think you're
kidding? What are you gonna do, become a civilian? Where do you
think you'll get without me telling you what to do? C'mon. Let's face
it. You're a second-rate boxer and you're over the hill. Without me
you got no connections and if you don't play it smart you'll end up a

bigger bum than you already are. What do you think you're gonna do? Get a job? What kind of job do you think you'll get? Without me you'll end up washing dishes and sleeping it off in somebody's mission house. Without me you got nothing. Without me you ain't even got a friend. Who you trying to kid?

'DELL. You can't scare me no more, Windy.

WINDY. I'm not trying to scare you. I'm just telling you the facts. All right? I got a right to talk, don't I?

'DELL. I got nothing. That's true. But I don't need nothing, Windy.

WINDY. What do you mean, you got nothing but you don't need nothing? What kind of stupid remark is that supposed to be?

'DELL. Maybe other people need something. Maybe other people got to believe what isn't so. . . .

WINDY. Never mind other people. All I know is I tell you what to do, what'd I ever get out of it?

'DELL. I don't know, Windy.

WINDY. Of course you don't. Nothing. That's what I got out of it. So I'll tell you something else. I stuck with you for six years, you think I done it because I thought I'd get rich? You think I didn't know you never had what it took? How dumb do you think a guy can get?

'DELL. I'm sorry, Windy.

WINDY. C'mon. Don't give me that. Guys like you don't get sorry. Guys like you don't even know what the word means.

'DELL. All I know is I'm not scared any more, Windy.

WINDY. Scared. Scared of what?

'DELL. All my life it was like I was scared of the dark. Like you're scared because you don't know what's in front of you so you're scared to move because you might bump into something you don't want to bump into . . .

WINDY. What about it?

'DELL. . . . And you look around and it's like everybody else is different and can see where they're going, but you're in the dark and you want to touch someone and ask, "Please, won't you stay with me awhile?" But you're too scared to even ask. It seems like everybody else got something and you walk on down the street and you see a man got a woman and even a boy got a dog and so it's not so bad for them. But you can't buy not having anything and being in the dark all by yourself, so you get yourself a dream and the dream is like a woman, it keeps you warm. And you'd do anything for the dream because it's like when a man has a woman and as long as the woman is with him, everything is all right. So the dream is like a woman and you'd do anything to keep it because it's the only thing you got. But then something happens and the dream is busted, Windy, and for a while it seems like the blackness is gonna get you and there's no place to hide. And when the dream is busted and the blackness comes pouring in, it's like a big brass band has cut loose in your head except nobody is playing anything but noise. And the noise keeps building up louder and louder till you can't stand it no more and you want to close your eyes and scream. But then all of a sudden, the noise stops, Windy, and you open your eyes and it's still dark out. It's just as dark and cold as it was before, but then you know that the blackness isn't going to get you because you wanted to scream but you didn't. So when you open your eyes and look around you begin to see how scared everybody else really is because most people never had the blackness come pouring in and they're still afraid they're gonna scream if it does. That's when you know you're not scared any more.

WINDY. That's why you don't want no more fights?

'DELL. That's right.

WINDY. And you don't care what happens to you?

'DELL. Nothing's gonna happen to me I can't take care of.

WINDY. You got any plans?

'DELL. No. Not yet.

WINDY. What do you want me to do? Forget about Houston?

'DELL. That's right, Windy.

WINDY. But you gotta do something.

'DELL. I'll be all right.

WINDY. How about coming North with me? You come North with me I ought to be able to fix you up with a job.

'DELL. No. Not now, Windy.

WINDY. You sure?

'DELL. I'm sorry, Windy.

WINDY. You make it sound like you thought I was all washed up or something. I got nothing to worry about. Sure. Only last week I was thinking maybe it's time I ought to go in with a friend of mine, he's got a bar back in Chicago. I only got a card from him a couple of weeks ago.

'DELL. If you say so, Windy.

WINDY. Sure. That's the best thing. A bar's always good for a buck.

'DELL. You won't have any trouble finding him?

WINDY. No. I won't have no trouble. I guess I better get going. It's getting late. I got things to do. I'm not worried, kid, you'll be looking me up. (*Exits.*)

HARRY. I've always admired someone who could cut himself off from a bad acquaintance without a moment's hesitation.

DOROTHY. Someone as sensitive as you can find something better to do than fighting.

HARRY. And now that you have nothing . . . not even a brother. . . .

DOROTHY. And you're not afraid and there's nothing to hold you. . . .

HARRY. And you know who you are. . . .

(*For a moment* 'DELL *seems lost in thought as he looks after* WINDY. *But then he turns toward* HARRY *and* DOROTHY.)

'DELL (*threateningly*). Go on, get out of here.

DOROTHY (*surprised*). But why? We haven't done anything.

'DELL (*louder*). Go on, get out of here! You hear me? Get out of here!

HARRY. But don't you want to go with us?

'DELL. Go on! Look at my face! You still want to sketch my face? You still think all I am is a bunch of cells, some kind of animal? Go on, get out of here! A man don't need nobody like you!

(*And as* 'DELL *stands there in the growing fullness of his anger and pain,* DOROTHY *and* HARRY *move back as they slowly become aware of both the power and the anguish of a man whose new-found strength lies in a heightened sense of isolation. And then the curtain slowly falls.*)

A SIMPLE LIFE

ROBERT E. INGHAM

Presented May 13, 1964, at the School of Drama,
Yale University, with the following cast:

CAPTAIN WATKINS, *Company Commander*
George R. DiCenzo, Jr.

MASTER SERGEANT CHARLES JAMES PURCELL
Robert E. Ingham

SERGEANT FIRST CLASS TROY J. TIPPIN   Jon Jory

SERGEANT DOLEMAN   Marvin B. Lichterman

CORPORAL CLAYTON   Hal Johnson

PRIVATE FIRST CLASS MYLES   Arthur Pellman

PRIVATE PASSACAGLIA   R. A. Harrison

PRIVATE JENKINS   Frederick John Haut

PRIVATE BATES   Joseph Curtis

PRIVATE CONNOR   Heath Bannard

PRIVATE BROWN   Robin Davis Wilkins

OTHER TRAINEES   Maurice Breslow, John Calhoun,
Bob Clymire, David Freeman,
Peter Burbage, Grady Larkins,
Robert Struble, Paul Trent,
Gayther Myers

Directed by F. Curtis Canfield
Settings by Dale Amlund
Costumes by Cletus Anderson   Lighting by Douglas Taylor

Company A, Fifth Infantry, a Basic Training Regiment
at Fort Jackson, South Carolina—1954.

ACT ONE. SCENE 1: *A spring night.* SCENE 2: *4:30 the next
morning, "Reveille."*

ACT TWO. SCENE 1: *Night, a week later.* SCENE 2: *The next
morning, just after "Work Call."*

ACT THREE. SCENE 1: *Night, a week later.* SCENE 2: *The next
morning, between "Reveille" and "Work Call."*

ACT ONE

SCENE ONE

SCENE: *Company A, Fifth Infantry. Fort Jackson, South Carolina. Spring, 1954.*
*The Company Street, narrow and sandy, runs from up right to
down left.*
*Upstage of the street, a barracks front extends from center to
down left. In the center of the barracks there is a raised porch, with
a door leading in. Inside the barracks (unseen) this door gives into a
hallway which runs between two small Cadre Rooms and then empties
into the large squadroom occupied by the trainees. The Cadre Room
on the left front of the barracks belongs to* SERGEANT TIPPIN; *the front
of the barracks on this side is a scrim which flies out when scenes are
played in the room.*
*At the right corner of the barracks stands a tall pine tree. Persons
entering from town or Battalion Headquarters come between the tree*

*and the corner of the barracks. A light bulb hangs from the tree, so that
a person stopping beneath it at night will be—depending upon where
he stops—in a strong down light, a head spot, or general area lighting.*

*There are other light bulbs on the porch, the side of the barracks,
etc., so that at night the stage is lit in pools and splotches.*

*Downstage right of the street, the Orderly Room, a small frame
building cut away, juts onto the stage. It contains a desk, some chairs,
filing cabinet, etc. The right wall of the Orderly Room has a door
marked "Company Supply."*

BEFORE THE CURTAIN: *"Tattoo" plays in the near distance.*

AT RISE: *Late evening. On the porch, a portable radio plays melan-
choly "Rock and Roll" music, very low, with that peculiar fade-in fade-
out quality of late night broadcasts.*

TRAINEES *are working on personal equipment, seated on the porch,
the steps and the grounds. Among them are* BATES, *reassembling a
rifle* (*the radio beside him, leaning against a pile of clothing*);
JENKINS, *brasso-ing a buckle; and* PASSACAGLIA, *sewing a button on a
shirt, painfully.*

A TRAINEE *on guard, in O.D.'s with cartridge belt and rifle, ambles
across from right to left, mentally picking his nose.* PASSACAGLIA
watches him, then speaks:

PASSACAGLIA. Awright there young soldier, you're on guard! Les
walk that post with pride.

GUARD (*turning, mocking and bored*). Ho ho ho.

PASSACAGLIA. Well, I'm just looking out for the honor of Company A.

GUARD. The cat's away, the mice make silly idiots outta themselves.
(*He turns and continues off left. Pause.*)

JENKINS. Hey, "Sick Call." (*No response*) Hey!

BATES. You know my name.

JENKINS. Les hear the radio. (*No response*) You gonna play it,
les play it! Turn it up!

BATES. It's not mine!

JENKINS (*reaching for it*). I don't care!

BATES. Leave it alone!

JENKINS. Hey, man. Who you so scared of, huh? Sergeant Tippin's
in town, man. He can't hear.

BATES (*sotto voce, motioning toward the barracks interior*). Shut
up, will ya?

JENKINS. *Him?* Aw, good god! Who's he?

(*A door shuts inside.* BATES *stuffs the radio under the pile of clothing and turns it off as* CORPORAL CLAYTON *comes breezing out. He is dressed in O.D.'s with a brassard lettered "C.Q." on his arm. He wears cartridge belt and helmet liner.*)

CLAYTON. Hey men! Working hard?

JENKINS. H'o Corporal. (CLAYTON *stops and turns. Pause.*)

CLAYTON. Who's got the radio? Whose is it? (*No reply*) Connor? Where's Connor?

BATES. Don't blame him for everything.

CLAYTON. Is it his?

BATES. I . . . dunno.

CLAYTON. Oh come on, Bates. "You don't know." (*pause*) Well . . . get it out of here before Sergeant Tippin gets back.

PASSACAGLIA (*in a sergeant's voice*). "This here's a Basic Training Comp'ny, not a whorehouse."

CLAYTON. Look, I'm just the Company Clerk. I mean—but I've got Charge-of-Quarters tonight. I don't want him holding me responsible. Take it back in the barracks and put it away, O.K.?

BATES. Good god, don't make me sick.

JENKINS. Aw for godsake, boys scared of their shadows. (*He takes the radio in. Pause.*)

RECRUIT. This is a cra—azy outfit, you know that?

CLAYTON. Where's Connor?

PASSACAGLIA. Who cares?

CLAYTON. What're you doing, Passacaglia? Sewing another button on?

PASSACAGLIA. Yeah.

CLAYTON. Who cut this one off? (PASSACAGLIA *gives him a "Who-do-you-think" look.*) Keep 'em buttoned, he wouldn't bother you.

PASSACAGLIA. "Keep 'em buttoned he wouldn't bother ya." Three weeks inna Army, I sewed this button on a hunderd and fifty times.

(CONNOR *has come on down right; now speaks.*)

CONNOR. You're learning a trade.

CLAYTON. Private Connor. Where've you been?

CONNOR. "Communing with Nature," O.K.?

CLAYTON. This platoon's working, soldier.

CONNOR. Don't make me weep.

CLAYTON. Now you mustn't be hard on us, Connor old friend, just because we can't all operate on your plane of high moral principle. After all, not everybody gets an opportunity to flunk out of Yale.

CONNOR (*sullenly*). Why don't you go to hell?

CLAYTON (*continuing, unperturbed*). I know in my own case, the best my folks could do for me was Dartmouth, and it's a terrible handicap.

(CONNOR *walks away.* CLAYTON *follows, trying to mollify.*)

Look, I'm a draftee, too. I know how you feel—

CONNOR. I don't care "how you feel"!

CLAYTON. The rest of these guys—

CONNOR. If you want to eat this Army up, that's on your conscience, not mine!

PASSACAGLIA. "Conscience," for Chrissake! Oooo, it hurts me, right here.

CLAYTON. To hell with the Army! I'm not talking about the Army! I'm talking about the way you behave. (CONNOR *turns away.*) O.K. It's up to you. But you'd better keep away from Sergeant Tippin, take my word. (*pause*) You take my word.

(CLAYTON *exits.* CONNOR *stands alone; he considers the moon, the sky, etc., and says softly to himself:*)

CONNOR. God, if I could just . . . get away.

A RECRUIT (*softly*). Why don't you "get smart," Connor?

ANOTHER RECRUIT (*in the same tone, as a post-script*). Grow up.

(*They go back to work.* BATES *watches* CONNOR, *then detaches himself from the group and sidles over to* CONNOR, *hesitantly.*)

BATES. That's all right, Dick . . . Richard. Connor. Hell with them.

(CONNOR *ignores him. Enter from the Mess Hall, in high dudgeon,* PRIVATE FIRST CLASS MYLES, *in cook's whites. He hurls his hat to the ground and scoops it up without breaking stride and exits, grumbling.*)

MYLES. Scabby son of a wall-eyed—huh!—no good. . . .

PASSACAGLIA (*this happens frequently*). Whassamatter, Myles?

MYLES (*disappearing into barracks*). Aw, Mess Sergeant. . . .

CONNOR. Hey, Batesy? I noticed something this morning.

BATES. Yeah? What's that, uh—Dick?

CONNOR. The brilliant Sergeant Tippin, who never makes a mistake? Overlooks nothing? He doesn't take roll at Work Call. . . .

BATES. Oh yeah? What do you mean, Richard?

CONNOR. That's very interesting.

BATES. Ah—h how do ya mean?

CONNOR. You watch, in the morning. They check at Reveille, very carefully. But after breakfast, when they fall us out for Work Call, the good Sergeant Tippin takes us off to "make soldiers out of us all," he doesn't bother to make sure he's got us all. . . .

BATES. Heyyy, yeah. I see what you mean. What ah—you thinking about? I mean, doing?

CONNOR. I don't know. But it opens up all sorts of avenues. Indeed it does.

(*Pause. Enter from town* SERGEANT DOLEMAN, *dressed for the occasion in every bit of ribbon, braid and cord imaginable. Instead of collar and tie, he wears a scarf of Infantry Blue, which lolls now about his neck like a beer-stained bib. On his right shoulder he wears a combat service patch, of the First Cavalry Division: a glittering great golden shield with a black diagonal bar and the black silhouette of a horse's head. He regards them unsteadily, with the air of one who knows where the bodies are buried, and then launches himself in.*)

DOLEMAN. Heyyy, goof-ups! Hey, eight-balls! What ya doin', huh?

PASSACAGLIA. Sergeant Doleman! Hey, sarge!

DOLEMAN. 'At's right, 'croot! Ser-geant Doleman, pride 'a the Army. Better believe it!

PASSACAGLIA. Where you been, sarge?

DOLEMAN. Town, boy. Hey! Wher's old Tippin? Wher's old hardhearted Hannah? He out harassing the troops again?

PASSACAGLIA. Town, sarge. Right after you.

DOLEMAN. Huh. So how's my little old third p'toon, huh? Been good little old 'croots?

RECRUIT. No chance to be anything else, sarge.

DOLEMAN. 'At's right. Work ya tail off, keep ya outta trouble. Make soldiers outta ya yet. (*He notices* CONNOR, *standing off.*) What's a matter'th you, boy? (CONNOR *doesn't acknowledge*) I said what's a matter'th you! Sound off'n I talk to you! 'Croot!

CONNOR. Nothing. Sergeant.

DOLEMAN. Awright. Don't get smart'th me cause I'm tough. "Tough but fair." Army way. How's "Sick Call" these days, "Light Duty Slip"? (BATES *says nothing.*) I be damn. I thought all that Light Duty Slip said was you couldn't walk, run, march, stand nor heavy lift, Bates. I didn't know it said "No talking," too.

BATES. I'm fine, Sergeant.

DOLEMAN. Huh. 'At's better.

(CLAYTON *comes back in.*)

CLAYTON. H'o sarge.

DOLEMAN. Hey, buddy.

CLAYTON. How's town?

DOLEMAN. Aw buddy, they loved me.

CLAYTON (*he doesn't stop, but throws this over his shoulder as he exits*). Bet they did. You men get ready to hit the sack now. Hard day tomorrow.

(DOLEMAN *was all set to tell him about it. He notices now and comes back to the small knot of trainees who have drifted out.*)

DOLEMAN. Old Doleman come into town, big silence, y'know what I mean? Awe. Reverence. 'N' then there's this little "ooo" way up the street and all of a sudden all you can hear is—flip flip flop. Flip flop. Skirts. Falling. Underwear, dropping. Women, passing out, falling over, up and down the street, in the sidewalks . . . Doooolemannnnn!!! Ugh!

PASSACAGLIA. You a mess, sarge. You know that?

DOLEMAN. Ain't I though? I'm hard to stop.

CONNOR. Why don't you tell us some good old "Combat Stories," sarge. All about Korea and killing and rapin' and all that stuff.

DOLEMAN. Yeah? Hey. Who you think you playin' with, huh?

CONNOR. Sarge!

DOLEMAN. You wanta drop down and do about a hundred and fifty push-ups, huh? I mean, it's a free country, like the man say. I'll let ya.

CONNOR. I was serious! I love combat stories!

DOLEMAN. Yeah, hell. Wasting my time, trying to educate you wise bastards. You smart, ain't you? Really something! Laugh at a soldier, huh? Well, let me tell you. You maybe went to college, but you know who I was? I talked to a President of the United States! You know that? I was on the Honor Guard! Arlington Cemetery! Yeah. Best damn duty in the world. Handpicked! Me, old Doleman, in 'at old silver helmet, them old white gloves, walking 'at Post! Unknown Soldier! Hup, hup. Them little old high school girls, coming off them busses, in the springtime, in them . . . *dresses*—takin' pitchers! Lord, Lord.

PASSACAGLIA. My my my.

RECRUIT. Tell 'em, sarge!

DOLEMAN. Best damn rifle twiddler in this man's army, you better believe! Wher's me a rifle? Who's got a rifle? Hot damn, I feel the mood comin' on! Here gimme 'at rifle, 'croot! I'm so damn good I don't even need a rifle! Look at this! See this? "Queen Anne Salute?" "Order Arms?" Now watch! A soldier, boy!

(*Clumsily drunken, he whirls through the salute, ending on one knee, head bowed in majestic homage, facing upstage, toward the soldiers grouped around the front of the barracks.* MASTER SERGEANT CHARLES JAMES PURCELL *enters and stands, at the corner of the barracks, framed by the tree, in half light. He is tall and thin, about thirty-five years old, and now quite worn and tired. He wears a rumpled G.I. overcoat upon which, when he steps into the light, is sewn the insignia of his rank, and, on the right shoulder, a First Division patch, a "Big Red One" on an olive green shield, on the left an Eighth Army patch. He carries a heavy bag and a small flight bag. He favors his right hand.*)

PURCELL. Well, thanks for the welcome. Major Bowes, I presume?

DOLEMAN. Uh—tech-hut! Uh—good evenin' sir.

(*He salutes.* PURCELL *steps in, so that his Sergeant's stripes are seen, and puts down his bags.*)

PURCELL. Oh no, don't call me sir. I work for a living.

DOLEMAN. Oh. Hey. Didn't know who you were. I thought you—ah—who are you?

PURCELL. Well, my name is Purcell. If that's any help.

DOLEMAN. Mine's Doleman. How d'ya do?

PURCELL. How do you do? Is this "A" Company of the Fifth?

DOLEMAN. That's right.

PURCELL. Do you have a Sergeant Tippin, Troy J. Tippin, here?

DOLEMAN. Yeah, we sure do . . .

PURCELL. Oh. Where can I find him?

DOLEMAN. Ah . . . oh! Town right now, sarge.

PURCELL. I see. Well, I guess I can wait. I've come this far.

DOLEMAN. Ah—you a friend of his?

PURCELL. Yes. I am.

DOLEMAN. Oh. Well, ah—his room's in there, first door to your right . . . if you wanta wait.

PURCELL. Thanks. (*He starts to pick up his bag, straightens.*) Nice . . . night, huh?

(*There is a blare of music as* JENKINS *comes out, "cakewalking," with* CONNOR's *radio. He has just turned it on, too loud; it blares sud-*

denly as it warms up, and he is turning it back down as he appears. He sees PURCELL *and stops, turning it off. Pause*)

PURCELL. Go ahead. I like it.

(JENKINS *stands for a moment suspiciously staring at this strange new Sergeant, then turns and goes back into the barracks.*)

CONNOR. "Welcome to Company A."

(PURCELL *turns, notices* CONNOR, *who is still down right, looking sour. He steps towards* CONNOR *and speaks sympathetically.*)

PURCELL. What's the matter, son? Spring fever?

CONNOR (*sourly*). Yeah.

PURCELL (*acknowledging the moon, etc.*). How long have you been in the Army?

CONNOR. Three hundred and fifty years.

PURCELL. That long? Hunh. A career man, I take it?

CONNOR (*he begins to retort, but is forced to smile*). O.K. Three weeks.

PURCELL. Yeah. I know how you feel. It's a game, y'know? Stop grousing and play it like a game, you'll be all right. (*pause.*) Well. Good night, gentlemen. (*He bends to pick up his bags.* PASSACAGLIA *jumps up.*)

PASSACAGLIA. Help ya, sarge?

PURCELL. Thank you. . . . No, thanks. I think I can handle it. Good night. (*Exit* PURCELL *into the barracks.*)

DOLEMAN. Huh! Sa'gent Tippin, he come to see.

PASSACAGLIA. Is he—will he be in this company, sarge?

DOLEMAN. How the hell should I know, huh . . . ?

(CLAYTON *crosses, goes into Orderly Room, and on into the Supply Room.*)

CLAYTON. Better hit the sack before the sarge gets home.

DOLEMAN. Yeah, I better put his thing in the hay. Well! (*He exits into the barracks. The trainees break up and straggle into the barracks and off up the street.*)

PASSACAGLIA. I wonder who that was?

CONNOR. One thing for sure; if he's a friend of Tippin's, that's all we need to know.

(*They exit. After a moment, the radio is heard; an* ANNOUNCER'S *VOICE says* "Rain in Korea. . . . The Rotation Blues." *The song begins,* "Rain in Korea/Sho' is cold and wet . . ." *The band fades out. During this, the* TRAINEE ON GUARD *slouches on again, up right, glancing idly about for distraction. His glance falls offstage, up by the barracks corner where everyone has entered from town. He sees something that causes him to straighten up and, highly military and fast, march post off down left. Pause. Enter* SERGEANT FIRST CLASS TROY J. TIPPIN, *sober and immaculate. He pauses by the barracks corner and looks at the empty street, reflects and speaks:*)

TIPPIN. Son of a bitch. (*He comes in toward the porch. The radio fades in again blaring, " 'Way from this Army/From Korea too./ Rotation papers—" It takes* TIPPIN *about this long to bound up the steps into the barracks. There is a squawk, a crash, and silence. Pause.* TIPPIN *comes back out again, throws smashed radio into trash can, and stands in the street.*)

Hunh.

(*Out of the barracks comes* PRIVATE BROWN, *timidly, with a pair of boots, polish, etc. in his hands.*)

BROWN. H'o, sarge.

TIPPIN (*quietly*). Why the hell ain't you in bed, young soldier? (*pause*) Whassamatter, cat got yer tongue?

BROWN. I din't have nothing to do with the radio, sarge. (*Pause. He holds out his boots.*) This all right, sarge? I been shinin' on 'em all night, sarge.

TIPPIN (*goes to him, takes one*). Huh. Look at that. Even in this light, I can see spots in it. 'At ain't no way to shine a gotdam boot.

BROWN. Aw sarge, I'm sorry. I tried. . . .

TIPPIN. What's yo' name?

BROWN. Private Brown, sarge. R. A. 21 385 674. Thirty-year man, sarge. R. A. all the way.

TIPPIN. Huh. Why you in this Army, Brown? Why do you serve?

BROWN. Ah—"To defe' my country against aggression and to pertect the principles of human dignity and freedom as set forth in th' U.N. Charter," Sergeant!

TIPPIN. "Uphold." "Uphold the principles." Not "pertect."

BROWN. Oh yeah. I'm sorry, sarge. "Uphold."

TIPPIN. And say the "Sergeant" first—or "sir," whichever one it is. "Sir! To defend my country . . ." You see what I mean? It gives you time to think.

BROWN. Aw yeah. I see.

TIPPIN. Gimme yer polish. . . . Give me yer polish. Only way to get a shine worth a damn is this. You got a match? (BROWN *hands him a pack from his pocket, hastily buttons it back again.*) You smoke?

BROWN. No sarge! I just . . . carr'em, case anybody wants one.

TIPPIN. Awright. Now this is what ya do. Set fire to it. (BROWN *hesitates, then complies.*) Go ahead. Set fire to it. Let it burn. (BROWN *peers into the flame, an oracle.*)

BROWN. Aww yeahhh. . . . I see.

TIPPIN. Use it while it's still wet, rub it in with a little bit of a real soft rag. She'll shine like a piece of glass. You see what I mean? (*He blows it out, hands it back.*)

BROWN. Yeah I see what you mean. Thankya, sarge.

TIPPIN. Now you get the hell to bed. Hard day tomorrow. (*He turns and starts away.*)

BROWN. Yeah, sarge. Right. Uh—night, sarge?

(*No reply. He exits.* TIPPIN *looks at the empty street again, goes onto porch, reaches inside door, turns off light. Looks at street again, goes inside. Lights up in his room, the scrim flies. We see* PURCELL *asleep on his back on* TIPPIN's *bunk.* TIPPIN *enters, sees the duffle bag on the floor, then sees him.*)

TIPPIN. Now what the hell is this? (*Crosses, looks at the face. To himself:*) Well I'm a son of a gun, old Purcell. Ain't that a bitch. Hey Purcell! Yeah, you still a sleepyhead, I see. Hey! "Yankee Soldier! Etty wa! On your feet!"

PURCELL (*opens his eyes*). As I live and breathe, a "Tool of Wall Street Imperialism."

TIPPIN. Get yer tail outta the sack, Purcell!

PURCELL. Don't rush me—

TIPPIN. Ain't seen a man in three years, what'uz he do? Sleeps!

PURCELL. Ain't seen a man in three years, what'uz he do? Wake me up!

TIPPIN. Where ya been?

PURCELL (*sitting up on edge of bed*). Oh man.

TIPPIN. Looking good. Picked up a little weight there, since the last time I saw you.

PURCELL. Picked up a little weight yourself, I see. On your arm?

TIPPIN. Oh, yeah! Yeah. "Sergeant First Class." Ain't that a bitch.

PURCELL. Ain't that a bitch.

TIPPIN. You on leave or what?

PURCELL. Yeah, on leave.

TIPPIN. Well stand up and let me shake yer— (*He reaches for* PURCELL'*s hand, to help him up.*)

PURCELL. Wo! Watch it!

TIPPIN. Whassamatter?

PURCELL. Oh. Didn't mean to yell at you. I picked up a bum hand here since the last time you saw me.

TIPPIN. How come?

PURCELL. Oh, they—strung me up by it, y'know? Got to laughing too hard, left me up there.

TIPPIN. Chinese bastards.

PURCELL. Yeah.

TIPPIN. Hey! This calls for celebration! You up to some celebration?

PURCELL. I'm sorta tired tonight—

(*Without waiting for an answer,* TIPPIN *has gone to his footlocker, opened it, and is rummaging around in it. He tosses things up onto the bed as he names them.*)

TIPPIN. You hungry?

PURCELL. Yeah!

TIPPIN. I figured you like me, ain't got used to being back wher' there's Army chow three times a day. Chinese bastards shrunk my di–gestive equipment, all that rice and chick-peas.

PURCELL. Stay hungry all the time—

TIPPIN. I got just what the doctor ordered, old buddy. Little bit of everything: Baby Ruth, Milky Way, Apple Taffy—you oughta like that: "Old Virginia Brand." You from Shenando' Valley?

PURCELL. No, Tidewater.

TIPPIN. Well, isshere says "Shenando' Valley Apple Taffy," but I guess that's close enough.

PURCELL. Yeah, little bit of home, huh?

TIPPIN. So wha'ya want? I got some crackerjacks.

PURCELL. Anything's fine. (*pause*)

TIPPIN. I'm sort of partial to crackerjacks, myself.

PURCELL. That's fine with me.

TIPPIN. O.K. (*Coming to sit beside* PURCELL *on bunk, tearing open the box.*) It's funny. I went to a fair one time. Macon. They took a whole busload, all of the kids from the . . . And they had crackerjacks. (*Pause. He pours* PURCELL *some.*) Hey, you get the prize.

PURCELL. Well, I forgot they had those things. "Prize in every pack." (*Pause.* TIPPIN *is throwing crackerjacks into his mouth.* PURCELL *takes one up, looks at it.*) Speaking of . . . Georgia. I stopped off on my way through.

TIPPIN. In Georgia? What for?

PURCELL. Oh—see what it looked like.

TIPPIN. I coulda told you that old buddy. One word.

PURCELL. Yeah. (*pause*)

TIPPIN. Cotton candy, too. At the fair. Couldn't keep that in your footlocker, though.

PURCELL. Not with your longjohns, no.

TIPPIN. Have some more?

PURCELL. No, let me work on this for a while. I'm an old man, y'know. Have to take it easy.

TIPPIN. Old, hell.

PURCELL. What'ya mean, "Old, hell"?

TIPPIN. You ain't so old.

PURCELL. Now don't you get cheeky with me, son. I'm old enough to be your—uncle!

TIPPIN. Uncle hell.

PURCELL. You know what's wrong with this modern Army? Bunch a' young whippersnappers get a couple of stripes, got no respect for their elders, that's what's wrong with it. How old are you?

TIPPIN. Twenty-five. Joined the Army when I was seventeen years old. Eight years of service.

PURCELL. Hunh. Well, I joined the Army when I was twenty-one. Fourteen years ago. Man, that's a long time, isn't it? Sneaks up on you. (*About the crackerjacks:*) It's not bad, y'know? This stuff? Sounds horrible: popcorn dipped in—what, molasses? But it grows on you.

TIPPIN. Yeah, I'm sort of fond of it, myself.

PURCELL. So. Are you—how is it, here?

TIPPIN. Basic Training?

PURCELL. Yeah. Do you accomplish anything?

TIPPIN. I bust some asses trying.

PURCELL. But I mean—do you like it?

TIPPIN. Well, it's got to be done.

PURCELL. Yeah.

TIPPIN. A lot to put up with. Specially now—First Sergeant got hisself transferred out about three weeks ago, got to do half of his work too. (*An idea strikes him.*) Hey. (*He looks at* PURCELL *speculatively. There is the sound of a flare popping in the distance, and then gunfire: machine guns firing rapidly, hysterically, and sporadic rifle fire.*)

PURCELL. My God.

TIPPIN. Oh! that ah—night problem. Some outfit in the second eight weeks is ah—tactical problems. Y'know?

PURCELL. Oh. Boy.

TIPPIN. Yeah. (*They listen.*)

PURCELL. Firing those fifties too fast, aren't they?

TIPPIN. Burn the goddam barrels out.

PURCELL. Small arms, too—weak, scattered. Listen.

TIPPIN. Half of them ain't firing at all. Wonder who thought he trained *them*? (*They listen.*) You . . . going back to the Far East Command?

PURCELL. Oh. No.

TIPPIN. You're not?

PURCELL. No, I—I went back.

TIPPIN. How do you mean?

PURCELL. I went back. That was the only time I was ever really comfortable, you know? In Korea, before the War, "The Hermit Kingdom." You should've seen it then.

TIPPIN. I bet it was.

PURCELL. Get up in the morning, they don't have a word for "Hello." They say "May you walk in Peace. . . . Did you sleep in Peace?" And something crazy always comes along . . . So—I got out of prison, they put me in a hospital for a while, in Japan. Force fed me. And then I didn't have anyplace else to go, so I went back to Korea . . . about four months ago. Just in time for Christmas. Same job. I could have closed my eyes and it was 1950 again, the whole thing never happened. But it's not 1950 again. It's 1954. You know what I mean?

TIPPIN. Damn right I do.

PURCELL (*relating to the sound of gunfire off*). I kept waking up at night. . . .

TIPPIN. So—wha'ya go do? Now?

PURCELL. I don't know.

TIPPIN. We was to go fishing, remember? All them places you knew about, in the Blue Ridge?

PURCELL. Yeah.

TIPPIN. Why don't you stay here?

PURCELL. Fort Jackson?

TIPPIN. I mean right here. First Sergeant. We got a vacancy.

PURCELL. Me, First Sergeant?

TIPPIN. I'll talk to the Captain. He can fix it up.

PURCELL. Wait a minute, I don't know, Troy—

TIPPIN. You got the stripes.

PURCELL. I need to think about that—

TIPPIN. Just what the doctor ordered? Huh?

PURCELL. I'm a desk jockey, Troy—

TIPPIN. You was Infantry in the World War. Got the badge right there. "Combat Infantry."

PURCELL. That was 1945. I haven't worked with troops since then.

TIPPIN. What the hell was in that P.O.W. compound if it wasn't troops, hah? Had to work with them, didn't you?

PURCELL. That's exactly what I mean. Troy, I'll be frank with you. I'll tell you something. The day the Chinese took me out of that compound, put me in solitary confinement—some people might think that was a nasty break, but that was the happiest day of my life. I can take care of me, but I had all I could stand of watching eighteen-year-old people— (*He stops and shakes his head.*)

TIPPIN. Right here is where we see that don't never happen again. You with me?

PURCELL. Troy. Have you got an empty bunk I can use?

TIPPIN. A what?

PURCELL. I've been on a train and a bus all day. Have you got a bunk?

TIPPIN. Oh. Sure. Yeah. 'Course we have.

PURCELL. Good.

TIPPIN. Old First Sergeant's room, matter of fact. Second building up. . . . So what about it?

PURCELL. Let me sleep on it? I'll talk to you later, huh?

TIPPIN. Sure. Here I am, batting your ear off. (*pause*) It gets kind of lonesome, y'know?

PURCELL. Yeah. I know.

TIPPIN. Funny. We won't together but—what was it, month or two? But you the only sumbitch I ever did know that. . . . Come on, I show you the room.

PURCELL. O.K.

(*They start to gather up* PURCELL's *bags, etc.*)

TIPPIN. Stop by the Orderly Room, kick the C.Q.'s ass, get some sheets and stuff.

PURCELL. Oh, that's all right.

TIPPIN. Huh?

PURCELL. Let him sleep.

TIPPIN. What the hell you talking about?

PURCELL. Who needs sheets.

TIPPIN. First Sergeant sleep on a mattress so a P.F.C. can get his beauty sleep? Come on!

PURCELL. I don't need sheets!

TIPPIN. He'll go get you some sheets!

PURCELL. What've I got to do, pull rank on you? Listen! I don't want to wake him up! (*pause*) Oh hell, if it's that important to you—

TIPPIN. No, hell NO! Sleep on the floor! See if I care! Here! (*He takes a folded blanket off his bunk, throws it at* PURCELL.) Take this! I don't need it anyway. Take another one, here!

PURCELL. Troy—

TIPPIN (*throwing the pillow at him*). Take this too! What the hell!

PURCELL. Troy! Thanks! That's fine.

TIPPIN. Awright.

PURCELL. Now lead me to it.

TIPPIN (*pauses, looks at* PURCELL, *grins*). Hey.

PURCELL. Hey yourself.

TIPPIN. I don't mean to be telling you what to do. (*pause*) Come on. I'll show you where to go. (*He picks up the duffle bag and starts out.*)

DIMOUT

SCENE TWO

"*Reveille,*" 4:30 *the next morning.*
It is still dark. Whistles blow, the bugle plays, all over the hill the

troops pour out of their barracks, crying like Indians on the warpath.
TIPPIN'*s voice bellows:*

TIPPIN. Awright Able Comp'ny les go, les fell out in the comp'ny street, les go! Hit it!

(*He is swallowed in sound as the lights come up, and the troops pour out. As they come into ranks, there is a sudden silence.*)

You young soldiers sound like a bunch a Wacs coming out of them barracks. You go let ev'y comp'ny on this hill drown you out? Hah?

COMPANY. No, Sergeant!

TIPPIN. Sound off'n I talk to you!

COMPANY. No, Sergeant!!

TIPPIN.
"Cause Troy J. Tippin is my name,
Soldierin's my game.
You play ball'th me,
I play ball'th you.
If y'don't play ball'th me,
I'm go take bat, ball,
Glove and all,
And shove 'em down yer throats."
Zat clear?

COMPANY. Yes, Sergeant!

TIPPIN. Am I right?

COMPANY. Yes, Sergeant!

TIPPIN. Damn right I'm right. Now les fall back in them barracks; this whistle blows, I wanta see one steady stream, knock them doors loose off their hinges as you come, and les hear it, hah? Now, Fall Out!

(*Screaming, they pour back into the barracks. Silence.* PURCELL *enters from right, with coffee pot and cup. Speaks to* DOLEMAN, *up right.*)

PURCELL. Morning.

DOLEMAN. Watch it, sarge!

(*Because* PURCELL *has passed him and is walking towards* TIPPIN, *who is left, looking off.* TIPPIN *blows the whistle, they pour out again, and almost run over* PURCELL *who has to hustle back right, out of the way.*)

PURCELL. Lord! (*Sotto voce to* DOLEMAN, *after silence returns.*) I know how General Custer must have felt.

TIPPIN. Awright, that looked a little better. P'toon leaders check yer p'toons, Reveille Roll Call. At Ease. Morning, Sergeant.

PURCELL. Morning. (*To* CLAYTON, *entering*)

CLAYTON. Morning, sarge.

TIPPIN. Corporal. This here's Sergeant Purcell. New First Sergeant.

PURCELL. Maybe.

CLAYTON. Glad to see you, sarge.

TIPPIN. Maybe you can show Sergeant Purcell the Orderly Room before Reveille, he can set his coffee pot somewheres.

CLAYTON. Sure, sarge.

(*They cross into Orderly Room. During this,* DOLEMAN *has gone down the ranks of his platoon with a slip of paper in his hand, checking Roll.* TIPPIN *is watching off right, and now he steps up and commands:*)

TIPPIN. Company, tench-hut! Dress Right, dress! Readip, Front, Post! (DOLEMAN *hustles to his post at front of platoon.*) Good morning, sir!

(TIPPIN *salutes. Enter the* CAPTAIN, *a youngish looking middle-aged man, resplendent in tailored fatigues with welt seams, loops and a pocket at the shoulder for cigarettes and pencils, but starched flat, shoulder strap with green baize squares and regimental crests, and form-fit torso. He wears Corcoran boots with zippers up the side, and carries a swagger stick of mahogany with a fifty-caliber casing for tip and top.*)

CAPTAIN. Ready, Sergeant?

TIPPIN. Yes sir.

CAPTAIN. Well then? (TIPPIN *salutes again, the full-armed Old Army way, does about face to face* THE COMPANY.)

TIPPIN. Reeport! (*He snaps his head right, to the First Platoon, offstage right, whose Sergeant is heard.*)

FIRST PLATOON SERGEANT (*off*). First P'toon one man barracks orderly!

(TIPPIN *snaps down a salute and raises another, snapping his head one notch left, to the* SECOND PLATOON SERGEANT, *closer off right.*)

SECOND PLATOON SERGEANT (*off*). Second p'toon one man K.P., two men guard, one man barracks orderly!

(*He snaps his head to* DOLEMAN.)

DOLEMAN. Third P'toon four men K.P., five men guard, one man barracks orderly!

(*To Fourth Platoon, off left.*)

FOURTH PLATOON SERGEANT (*off*). Fourth p'toon one man K.P., four men guard, one man barracks orderly!

(TIPPIN *returns this last salute, as before, commands:*)

TIPPIN. Post!

(DOLEMAN *moves by left flanks to the left of his platoon.* TIPPIN *watches, then does about face. Salutes.*)

Sir! Com'ny all present or accounted for!

CAPTAIN. Take your post.

(TIPPIN *goes up right.*)

At ease! Young soldiers! Today we begin your Third Week of Basic Training. Remember our motto. "Able, Always Able." Best company in the best regiment on this Post, you better believe it. Am I right?

COMPANY. Yes sir!

TIPPIN. Sound off!

COMPANY. Yes sir!!!

CAPTAIN. Thank you, Sergeant. Now. A matter of great importance. Each cycle there is a competition, first in each company, then at Battalion, Regimental, and finally, Post Headquarters level, for a "Soldier of the Month," the best, sharpest recruit on the Post. Needless to say, I don't think I need to tell you this—ah, it's a feather in the cap of the Commander whose Company supplies the winning soldier. Yes, indeed. I don't think I need to say, either, the Able Company, thanks to the talents of your Field First Sergeant, Sergeant Tippin, here—has won that honor the last three cycles. I think we ought to give Sergeant Tippin a little cheer for that. Ready? Let's hear it?

(THE COMPANY *cheers.*)

Very good. Now, there are a number of college men in this company, education level's pretty high, I think you've probably figured out for yourselves by now that when this occurs, Able Company wins for me, I am a very happy man. *I expect to be happy again.* And when you make me happy, some of it may run down to you. How about that, huh? Are we gonna win?

COMPANY. Yes sir!

CAPTAIN. I think you mean it. That little extra effort, that's all it takes! To be superlative! And we demand the superlative! Always! Company, 'tench-hut! Field First!

(TIPPIN *hustles to salute him.*)

Take charge, get 'em in the chow line. Oh. That Sergeant, friend of yours you were talking about. He up yet?

TIPPIN. Yes sir.

CAPTAIN. Good. Tell him to stick around. I'll talk to him—oh, between now and Work Call. I need some breakfast.

TIPPIN. Yes sir.

CAPTAIN. My wife didn't feel like getting up this morning.

TIPPIN. Yes sir.

CAPTAIN. Well then . . .

(TIPPIN *salutes again,* CAPTAIN *exits.* TIPPIN *faces* THE COMPANY.)

TIPPIN. You heard what the man said. (*pause*) Private Bates!

BATES. Yes, Sergeant?

TIPPIN. What'd I just say? Front and center! What'd I just say?

(BATES *comes out of the formation.*)

BATES. Uh—"You heard what the man said?" Sergeant?

TIPPIN. Was that funny?

BATES. No, Sergeant.

TIPPIN. Private Connor, front and center!

(CONNOR *comes to beside* BATES.)

Then will you tell me why you was cutting yo' eyes and grinning at this young soldier?

BATES. Ah—not me, Sergeant.

TIPPIN. Not you?

BATES. No, Sergeant.

TIPPIN. By god, this man *is* sick! I didn't believe him, but he is so sick he don't even know when his own eyes is rolling! Man, he's a mess. (THE COMPANY *chuckles.*) At Ease! Awright. I was faced with an unpleasant task this morning, which Private Connor and Private Bates has just simplified. Battalion has ast for a detail to police the parade ground, in addition to all the other things you young men got to do between now and Work Call, and I was really concerned about which one of you deserving young men was go have to do it. But since Private Connor and Private Bates have volunteered their buddies in the Third P'toon, the rest of you can relax. (THIRD PLATOON *groans.*) At ease! Don't look at *me!* So. I believe the order of chow this morning was Third P'toon first, so it'll have to be First P'toon first, then Second, Fo'th, and the Third P'toon eats last. As the man say, one bad egg can spoil the whole barrel. (*snapping to business*) P'toon Sergeants take charge of your p'toons, get 'em in the chow line. (*Salutes, they return it.* DOLEMAN *comes to the front of his platoon, shaking his head.*)

DOLEMAN. Damn Bates. Awright, fall in, Connor. "Sick-Call-No-

Marchee," you get on the rear of the p'toon and tag along, as usual. . . .
Right, face. Forward, march. (*They exit,* BATES *conspicuously out of
step.* DOLEMAN *lets him go by, grins at* TIPPIN *and pantomimes a kick to
the rear.*) Drag-tail bunch of gypsies, make me miss *my* breakfast!

(PURCELL *comes out.*)

PURCELL. That man—has got a problem.

TIPPIN. Yeah.

PURCELL. Well, what happens now?

TIPPIN. I got to check the latrines, then we go eat.

PURCELL. Oh! I ate already. Got hungry in the night, bummed
some eggs when the cooks got up.

TIPPIN. Oh. Well, I see ya anyway. Stick around, Captain wants
to talk to ya.

PURCELL. Indeed, I wonder why?

TIPPIN. Hey, listen. Don't ah—I mean, if you don't like what he
has to say, don't let that change yer mind. I mean, I run this Company.
He won't give you no trouble.

PURCELL. Oh . . . That's nice to know.

TIPPIN. I see ya then.

(*Exit* TIPPIN. PURCELL *comes into Orderly Room, where* CLAYTON
*is working. There is a general hum of activity, troops marching past
offstage, etc.*)

PURCELL. This is a "Regular Beehive of Activity," isn't it?

CLAYTON. Yeah. Sort of frantic until Work Call. Nobody knows
what anybody's doing. Funny, after Work Call it's a ghost town.
I've been tempted—with all that privacy—I've been tempted, along
about noon one of these spring days to go stand in the Company
Street and sing dirty songs, yell "Screw the Army," or something. No
insult intended. Never have, though.

PURCELL. You sound like a draftee.

CLAYTON. You bet your boots. One month to go, and I'm long gone.

PURCELL. I gather you don't care much for Army Life?

CLAYTON. I can take anything for two years.

(*In the near distance a voice is heard counting cadence: a peculiar,
high, humming voice. The sound approaches.*)

PURCELL. That's a nice sound, isn't it?

CLAYTON. Charlie Company. You can tell Sergeant Peters by his
voice. Better close your ears, sarge.

PURCELL. Do what?

(*By this time, the offstage marchers are passing the A Company Street, just offstage.* SERGEANT PETERS *calls for a cadence count, and 120 young men count at the top of their lungs.*)

I see what you mean.

CLAYTON. Happens every morning.

PURCELL. Any particular reason?

CLAYTON. Jealousy. Sergeant Tippin's a better soldier, we make better scores, Soldier of the Month, all that jazz. So Sergeant Peters takes revenge in noise.

(PURCELL *chuckles.*)

You're a friend of Sergeant Tippin's, huh?

PURCELL. Yes, I am. Admirer, or something.

CLAYTON. So am I. Which is funny, from a dyed-in-the-wool draftee, but I've been here twenty-two months, now—almost twenty-three. . . . I've seen a lot of sergeants. I hope you stay around and help him out.

PURCELL. Do you . . . think he needs "help"?

CLAYTON. I dunno. I'm just an innocent bystander.

(*He goes back to work. Enter* CAPTAIN.)

'Ten-sion!

CAPTAIN. As you were, as you were. Morning, Corporal.

CLAYTON. Morning, sir.

CAPTAIN. And you're Sergeant . . . ?

PURCELL. Purcell, sir.

CAPTAIN. Purcell? Irish?

PURCELL. No sir. Virginian. A little bit of everything.

CAPTAIN. Oh, "F.F.V.," uh?

PURCELL. A later boat.

CAPTAIN. Well, from what Sergeant Tippin tells me, you must be the greatest soldier since General Grant—or maybe I'd better make that General Lee?

PURCELL. Sergeant Tippin gets—over-enthusiastic, at times.

CAPTAIN. Oh, not in this case, I don't believe. Have a seat, sit down, Sergeant. I'm just passing by, little time to kill; thought I'd drop by for a little chat with this "Paradox of Virtue," here. Morning Report done up yet, Corporal?

CLAYTON. Working on it, sir.

CAPTAIN. Uh. Good man. All good men in this company. Have to be; sharp outfit. You're just back, then? From the "Far, Far East, Land of Mystery, etcetera"?

PURCELL. Yes sir.

CAPTAIN. I always wanted to see that place—Japan, Korea. Spent the whole damn Korean War right here.

PURCELL. I'd say you were lucky, sir.

CAPTAIN. Well, it doesn't help the old career any, I tell you!

PURCELL. No sir. I guess not.

CAPTAIN. How long you been in the Army, Sergeant?

PURCELL. Fourteen years, sir. Since 1940.

CAPTAIN. Oh! You were in the "Old Army," then. Lot changed since those days, uh? Lot tougher, back in the old days, from what I hear.

PURCELL. Well sir, I think most of the changes've been improvements.

CAPTAIN. Oh you do? Huh! That's very interesting. You had breakfast yet, Corporal?

CLAYTON. No sir.

CAPTAIN. I see you're—uh—wearing a combat patch from the First Division, there; the old "Big Red One." Second World War, uh?

PURCELL. Yes sir.

CAPTAIN. Boy, you must've seen a lot of action with that outfit, then. Rifle Company?

PURCELL. Yes sir.

CAPTAIN. You know the ropes then, huh? Clayton, why don't you—I hate to see a man go hungry—hop on over, get some chow.

CLAYTON. Oh. Yes sir. (*exit*)

CAPTAIN. Well, I think that's extremely interesting, Sergeant. I have to hand it to you. You ah—how long have you and Sergeant Tippin—old friends, huh?

PURCELL. Well, we're friends, yes sir.

CAPTAIN. How do you mean?

PURCELL. I'm not sure you can call it "old." As a matter of fact, we were only together about two months.

CAPTAIN. Two months?

PURCELL. Yes sir.

CAPTAIN. Oh but now, he said you—I thought you were in a Prisoner of War Camp, together?

PURCELL. Yes sir.

CAPTAIN. Well? I mean . . .

PURCELL. The Chinese split us up.

CAPTAIN. Oh jeez—Huh! Well, then, what the hell are you doing here? I mean—from the way he talked, well, I assumed—I mean, I've heard him carry on about guys he *didn't* like over there, eight-balls, but you're the only man I ever heard him. . . . You got a hell of a lot of influence, you made a hell of an impression, let me tell you that, for a casual acquaintance. I mean, Lord God, I figured you must be long-lost buddies from the way he talked! (*During this,* CAPTAIN *pours himself coffee from* PURCELL's *pot. Absently.*)

PURCELL. I think I know how he feels, sir.

CAPTAIN. You do?

PURCELL. Because—it is a feeling, if you see what I mean. Two months or two years, it doesn't really matter, because this is not just some guy I drank beer with, you see? We were in a place called "Death Valley." The G.I.'s called it that, and it was no joke. The name was no joking matter. It's funny. It just occurred to me last night, while we were talking, that I didn't even know how old he was. There are a lot of "things" I don't know about him. We were too busy staying alive, you know? But I know what counts. You find out fast, in a place like that. And it's hard to forget. It's all . . . hard to forget.

CAPTAIN. I . . . think I see what you mean. Oh—ah, have some uh —coffee, Sergeant. Here.

PURCELL. Thank you, sir.

CAPTAIN. Well, he must've been something to see, uh? In a place like that. . . .

PURCELL. The most impressive sight I've ever seen. And the most . . . puzzling, in a way.

CAPTAIN. How do ya mean?

PURCELL. I saw a lot of people . . . not so impressive. With no better reason than he had.

CAPTAIN. But you never actually "soldiered" with him, though? I mean, in a plain old day-to-day army situation, like, say, here?

PURCELL. No sir.

CAPTAIN. Huh. I think that's . . . extremely interesting. (*Pause. Then, nonchalantly, as a new subject:*) Say! Tell me something. You oughta know something about this. Settle an argument. I've got a friend, was in Korea. And he's always talking about this Chinese Army. Greatest—best disciplined—outfit he ever saw. Anything to that?

PURCELL. I was captured before they came in the war, sir. The only Chinese I saw were prison guards and interrogators.

CAPTAIN. Huh. Well, that's what *he* says. Great discipline. Especially interesting to those of us who have to put up with Training Duty.

PURCELL. Yes sir.

CAPTAIN. Course, they can do it easy. Don't have to worry about the "Mothers of America," all that nonsense. Not that I mean to say it's nonsense, but you stay around here a while, you'll begin to think those Chinese suckers've got the secret, huh?

PURCELL. I couldn't say.

CAPTAIN. You had any experience with Basic Training, Sergeant?

PURCELL. Not since I took it, sir.

CAPTAIN. Well, he tells me these Chinks, they just pick a trainee—and in every cycle you can always find one. Boy, do I know that! A real worthless bastard! And they set him, on purpose! Sooner or later he'll do something that's just right, screw it up real good. So then the Captain—or Sergeant, whoever's there—hauls him out in front of the company, screams and rants so you'd think this piddling little mistake he'd made was the biggest damn crime in the world, stomps and yells and then pulls out that old .45 and—bang—shoots that worthless bastard right in the head and walks away. Huh? Whatta ya think of that? That's what you'd call "direct," huh?

PURCELL. It's direct all right.

CAPTAIN. Never have any trouble with discipline after that, huh?

PURCELL. Maybe.

CAPTAIN. Maybe?

PURCELL. I don't think there's much point in fighting Chinamen if you're gonna act like one yourself.

CAPTAIN. Well, of course, neither do I. But what's the alternative?

PURCELL. Treat these boys like people, they'll do all right.

CAPTAIN. Well, yeah. But haven't you ever seen the time when you'd just like to bust some smart bastard in the tail, huh?

PURCELL. That doesn't mean I've got the right to do it.

CAPTAIN. Huh! Well, I think that's all I need to know, Sergeant. You just got yourself a job.

PURCELL. Oh?

CAPTAIN. Be with your buddy, put your ideas to practice. I'll get Clayton to type you up a letter of transfer, you can go to work right now.

PURCELL. I'm tempted, sir.

CAPTAIN. Good! That's settled, then.

PURCELL. Well, no sir.

CAPTAIN. Nonsense. I'll get the orders cut—

PURCELL. Excuse me, sir. I haven't said I want this job.

CAPTAIN. I guarantee you this: A free hand. If that's what's bothering you.

PURCELL. No sir.

CAPTAIN. Just get results and keep it off my back.

PURCELL. I can't give you an answer now.

CAPTAIN. I need you now.

PURCELL. Captain, I'm sorry! But I'm a Specialist, on purpose—

CAPTAIN. You say you respect, admire, Sergeant Tippin?

PURCELL. Yes sir, I do.

CAPTAIN. Then take this job.

PURCELL (*crossing to door*). Captain, I'm sorry. That's all I want—

CAPTAIN. I haven't dismissed you yet!

PURCELL. I'm not under your command, Captain. You can't—

CAPTAIN. I'm offering you a chance to save his life, Sergeant!

PURCELL. To do what?

CAPTAIN. His career, rank, record in the Army, which I think you'll agree with me, is his life?

PURCELL. What do you mean?

CAPTAIN. What would you say if I told you Sergeant Tippin hit a recruit two cycles ago? Damn well might've killed him, if I hadn't been there to stop it?

PURCELL. He knows better than that. . . .

CAPTAIN. You know what the penalty is for striking a recruit? Hell, that's what it is! For him, for me, too. If I'd been clear out of town when it happened! That's the way things are in this rotten world. The innocent suffer. Well, we hushed it up, that time. Tippin got away by the skin of his teeth and nobody knew. But every cycle I look out this door, and I see one, two, three—worthless bastards! Spoiling for it. And the next one may not scare as easy as this one did.

PURCELL. He wouldn't do that! Dammit, he knows better than that!

CAPTAIN. How do you know? You don't even know how old he is!

PURCELL. I know . . . what he feels about the Army.

CAPTAIN. Maybe he's changed. He's gotten worse every cycle since he's been here. Every eight-ball that bucks him, he gets worse. All you've got's a feeling, Sergeant. A memory. . . . But that's enough. It'll keep you here. I've seen your type. (*He picks up his helmet-liner to go.*) I don't like to push you, Sergeant. But you've got to understand my position. I've got a job to do. I didn't ask for it. But I've got to do it. Any way I can. (*He puts his hat on and starts to go.*) It's a simple life, Sergeant. Dismounted Drill and paper work. It'll grow on you. Just keep Sergeant Tippin aimed in the right direction. (*exit*)

DOLEMAN (*voice, offstage*). To the rear, march! To the rear, march! Watch out, "Sick Call," they'll step all over you! (*The Platoon marches on.*) Untangle yer feet. To the rear, march! P'toon, halt. Good god on a stick! (*He wheels away, playing great disgust. A voice from within the ranks,* CONNOR's, *says:*)

CONNOR. Come on Doleman, let's eat.

DOLEMAN. At ease! As you were! Just cause I play with you . . . !

(TIPPIN *has come out of the barracks to hear this.*)

TIPPIN (*coldly*). What's 'a matter, sarge?

DOLEMAN. Oh! Ah . . . wise guys, no sweat, sarge.

TIPPIN. What's 'a matter, can't you handle this p'toon? You listen to me, young soldiers. I ever hear anybody talk to a N.C.O. like that again, there's go' be some asses in a sling. You want chow, huh? Well, I don't think you deserve none; you don't shape up you sho' god won't get any. (*Quickly, to* BROWN) "Why do you serve, young soldier?"

BROWN. Sergeant! "To defend my country against aggression, and to *uphold* the principles 'a human dignity and freedom as set forth in the U.N. Charter!" Sergeant!

TIPPIN. Uh huh! "Why do you serve?" (*To* PASSACAGLIA, *who freezes*) What's your name?

PASSACAGLIA. Uh—

TIPPIN. Name name name! Sho' god you must know that!

PASSACAGLIA. Uh, P–Passacaglia, U.S. 51—

TIPPIN. U.S. Draftee serial numbers make me vomit. Gi'me ten for not knowing yer lessons like you should. (PASSACAGLIA *begins doing push-ups.*) "What will you do?" (JENKINS, *to whom this is addressed, joins* PASSACAGLIA.) What'll you do?

A RECRUIT. Sergeant! "Defend with my life if need be, I—uh—the principles in which I serve—*believe!*"

TIPPIN. Huh. (PASSACAGLIA *jumps up.* TIPPIN *has swung on* CONNOR, *but now swings back to* PASSACAGLIA.) "If captured, what'll you give?" (PASSACAGLIA *goes back to push-ups.* TIPPIN *wheels on* CONNOR, *who is distracted by smirking.*) "What'll you give?" (*Caught off guard,* CONNOR *hesitates, shuts up.*) Give, give, give—you must be able to give me something! What'll it be? "If captured, what'll you give?"

CONNOR. Name! Rank! Serial number! Date! Of! Birth!

TIPPIN. Gimme ten for tone of voice! Hit it, now! Sound off! (CONNOR *does them, counting. He cheats—i.e., not going all the way down.*) Don't cheat on me! Go allaway down! (*He "helps"* CONNOR, *pushing him with a foot, so that* CONNOR *loses balance and sprawls.* TIPPIN *pulls him up.*) On yer feet!

CONNOR (*tearing away from* TIPPIN). Don't put your hands on me, buddy!

TIPPIN (*freezing, then regaining control to a cold calm*). What'd you say yo' name was?

CONNOR. P–Private Connor, Sergeant.

TIPPIN. "Private Connor, Sergeant!" It's go' be shit by the time I'm through with you. (*Suddenly wheeling on* BATES) "What's yo' name?"

(BATES, *also surprised, follows* CONNOR's *lead: silence.*)

My god I never saw so many men with education in my life that didn't know their gotdam name. Well, Troy J. Tippin is my name, 'at's one you go' recall as long as you live. What's yours?

BATES. Private Bates, Sergeant.

TIPPIN. "Why do you serve?" (BATES *shoots a glance at* CONNOR.) Eyes front! He can't help you none! "Why do you serve?"

BATES (*a desperate scream*). I was drafted, god-dammit!!

TIPPIN. Fifty! Now! Hit now!

BATES. I . . . can't, Sergeant.

TIPPIN. You what?

BATES. You . . . know what. . . .

TIPPIN. Tell me again. Nice and loud, so the whole p'toon can hear.

BATES. I got a light-duty slip—"No Exercise."

TIPPIN (*jumping onto the porch step, crowing*). Oh god! You hear it, men? Private Bates is got a light-duty slip! He can crap on the flag of the United States, that raised him up so fat and free, but he can't do no heavy exercise! And that's why Able Company is the sorriest

outfit you ever saw, they laugh at us! **C**ause everywhere we go, standing
tall like men, "Light-Duty-Slip-No-Marchee" is there, scrobbling along
thirty feet to the rear like a hump-back whore after payday week with
her ass in a sling, is Private Bates! I have had lots of experience with
yo' kind of cat! I have been waiting for you. Y'see where these boys
has scuffed up the sand, marching and running with them old heavy
boots? Well, while they stuffing breakfast in their faces with whatever's left between now and Work Call . . . you smooth it out for me,
with this. (*Takes a toothbrush from his pocket*) Zat light enough to
suit you? (*Angrily, to* DOLEMAN, *as he turns on his heel to go*) Take
charge of yo' p'toon!

DOLEMAN (*fuming, pulls* BATES *to the front of the platoon, by his
cap-brim*). Awright, Bates, fall out chere and hit it. (*He gives* THE
PLATOON *the Command to Dress Right, and, pretending to check the
alignment, backs into* BATES *and falls over him, kicking him, etc.*)
Hot damn there, 'croot! Get outta my way! Les go! Readip, front.
Right, face! For—ward, march. (*By so doing,* THE PLATOON *marches
over* BATES, *some trying to miss him, some to step on him; much
horseplay.* PURCELL *has witnessed this from the Orderly Room. Now
he steps into the street, and bellows in his best voice:*)

PURCELL. Detail—*halt!* (*They stop, confused.*)Sergeant, there's a
call for you in the Orderly Room. Put a trainee to take those men out
and tell that young man whatever the hell he's doing there to get off
his can and in the ranks if he wants anything to eat today!!

DOLEMAN. Sure, sarge. Uh, uh, uh—Brown! Take 'em in. (*He
comes to* PURCELL, *shaking his head, chuckling.*) Them boys, I tell
you. Who's calling me, sarge.

PURCELL. I am.

DOLEMAN. Say what?

PURCELL. Where do you think you are, Sergeant?

DOLEMAN. Aw sarge—

PURCELL. This is the United States Army, soldier. You ever hear
of it? It's a country, in North America, with a strange custom—

DOLEMAN. Now what the?

PURCELL. At ease! (DOLEMAN *starts to remonstrate again,* PURCELL
swings back and looks at him. Silence.) Now. You'd better get zippers
on those stripes, because if I ever see anything like this again, I'm
gonna take them away so fast you won't have time to tear 'em off.

DOLEMAN. Now wait a minute, here. Just who the hell are you?

PURCELL. Company First Sergeant. As of now. Dismissed.

(DOLEMAN *scurries off. The voice of* TIPPIN *is heard, and he comes on.*)

TIPPIN. Awright, you lop-tailed long-eared drag-assed pack of she-sheep, les' go! (*He blows whistle.* TROOPS *scurry in, yelling. Silence.*) Work Call, Able Company! Cause Troy J. Tippin is my name, soldierin's my game! Zat clear?

COMPANY. Yes Sergeant!!!

TIPPIN. Am I right??

COMPANY. Yes Sergeant!

TIPPIN. Damn right I'm right. Ri—ight, face! For-ward, march! Hut hut hut. . . . "You . . . had a good home but you left!"

COMPANY. "You're right!"

TIPPIN. You had a good home but you left!

COMPANY. You're right!

TIPPIN. "Raise yo' head and hold it high!" (*The* COMPANY *repeats.* CURTAIN *begins to fall.*) "Able Comp'ny's passing by!" (*The* COMPANY *repeats.*) "Raise yo' head up to the blue!" (COMPANY *repeats.*) "Able Comp'ny's passing through!" Sound off!

(*As they march off,* PURCELL *follows into the center of the street and watches.* CURTAIN *is closed by now.* TIPPIN's *voice fades.*)

COMPANY. One two!

TIPPIN. Once more!

COMPANY. Three four!

TIPPIN. Break 'em on down.

COMPANY. One two three four, one two . . . three-four!

ACT TWO

SCENE ONE

Night, about a week later.

RECRUITS, *studying and working.*

PASSACAGLIA. An M–1 rifle is worth . . . eighty-five dollars. M–1 rifle worth. . . .

BROWN. Nine.

PASSACAGLIA. Huh?

BROWN. Eighty-*nine* dollars. M–1 rifle.

PASSACAGLIA. Oh. Huh. Yeah. Eighty-nine. Entrenching tool. . . .

JENKINS. Man. Some sort of a way to spend Sunday, ain't it?

PASSACAGLIA. Don't knock it. We had the afternoon off. First one since we been here. "A dollar seventy-fi' cents."

BROWN. Man, it's hot.

PASSACAGLIA. Gettin' hotter.

JENKINS. Summer comin'.

PASSACAGLIA. In April?

JENKINS. South Ca'lina, man.

BATES (*quietly, to* CONNOR).Where'd you go this afternoon, Dick?

CONNOR. I took a walk.

(TIPPIN *comes out with a pair of boots in hand; he wears "C.Q." brassard. Stops and watches, as if trying to think of some way to strike up conversation.*)

TIPPIN. Working.

PASSACAGLIA *and* BROWN. Yeah sarge.

TIPPIN. 'At's good. (*He watches some more. To* JENKINS, *who is cleaning his rifle*) How much is 'at weapon worth, young soldier?

JENKINS. Ah—eighty-fi' dollars, sarge—*nine,* nine. Eighty-nine dollars.

TIPPIN. That's right.

(*Still he lingers. He watches* CONNOR *shine his boots. Reaches down, picks one up, holds it to the light. Sniffs and puts it back. Fidgets. Then he gives up and walks on into the Orderly Room. The* RECRUITS *look at each other and shrug.* TIPPIN *puts the boots on the desk, takes a rag and polish from inside a boot, then realizes he doesn't have a match. Pats pockets, looks in desk, starts to rise to go ask the recruits for one.*)

Hey, any you— (*He decides against it.*) Well, hell . . . (*Sits, puts everything away. Fidgets, looks through the Field Manuals on desk.*)

BROWN (*disgusted with his cartridge belt*). Huh. Never get this thing to shine. Hey Connor? Come on. Trade belts with me.

BATES. He told you no.

BROWN. But this one don't look worth a durn. I'm goin' up for "Soldier of the Month" tomorrow, I need a good belt. (*pause*) Well hell. I'll scrub it again. (*He starts to go.*)

CONNOR. Brown?

BROWN. Yeah?

CONNOR. Here. (*He takes his belt from the pile beside him and takes it to* BROWN.)

BROWN. Awww! (*pause*) Hey. Thankya.

CONNOR. Forget it. It made me look like an R. A. anyway. (*He turns on his heel and goes back to his place.* BROWN *goes in barracks.*)

BATES. Dick? Richard? I noticed what you said—about Work Call?

CONNOR. Yeah?

BATES. You're right. Every morning this week. I checked. He didn't take roll a single time. When we come back in, neither. He don't check. We could sneak back in, just before Retreat. Never know we'd gone.

CONNOR. What about you? You're kind of conspicuous, you know?

BATES. Naw. I been going on Sick Call, every day or so, so they'll get used to me bein' gone. If they miss me, old Doleman'll just think I'm gone on Sick Call and he forgot to write it down.

CONNOR. Old Troy J. Tippin—"Go' make soldiers of us all. Whether we want to be or not." And we won't even be there. . . . And he'll never know the difference.

(CONNOR *starts in, stops by a* RECRUIT *who is busy. Imitates* TIPPIN.) "Shape up ther', young soldier." (*The* RECRUIT *looks at him, goes on working.*) "Stand up'n I talk to you. Pretty plain to me you ain't worth a damn, ain't go never be; I'm'o have to do something about that."

(PURCELL *has come in during this.*)

PURCELL. That's exceedingly amusing, Private Connor. Can you imitate me as well? (CONNOR *decides not to honor him with a reply.*) Where you going?

CONNOR. Barracks.

PURCELL. Don't you walk away when I'm talking to you.

CONNOR. I've got to put my boots away.

PURCELL. O.K. Then come on back. (CONNOR *exits.* PURCELL *comes on in. He carries a small red rubber ball, and is exercising his hand.*) You working hard?

VARIOUS. Yeah sarge.

PURCELL. That's good.

RECRUIT. You working pretty hard yourself, uh sarge?

PURCELL. Damn right. "As God is my witness, I'm gonna pitch in the Polo Grounds again." What you doing, Passacaglia? Got your brow all furrowed up.

PASSACAGLIA. Aw sarge. Learning this old "Cost Consciousness."

PURCELL. Oh yes. Our little sop to the taxpayer.

JENKINS. But what's the sense of it, sarge? Learning all this stuff?

PURCELL. I don't know. Maybe it's just that the Secretary of War is a silly old man. How much is it going to cost you to humor him?

JENKINS. Yeah.

PURCELL. Passacaglia!

PASSACAGLIA (*innocent*) Yeah, sarge? (PURCELL *nods at* PASSA-CAGLIA's *pocket, which is unbuttoned.* PASSACAGLIA *catches on, sees it, and jumps up, disgusted.*) Son of a blue-eyed—hell! Not again!

PURCELL. Yep. Again.

PASSACAGLIA. I didn't mean to do it, honest to God. I just forgot.

PURCELL. You just forgot.

PASSACAGLIA. I mean, sarge? I'm a civilian. Everybody is where I come from. It's an underprivileged area. Saturday night, guys hang out on the corner, unbutton three, four pockets at a time. I can't adjust to changing patterns!

(CONNOR *reenters.*)

PURCELL. It's pretty silly, isn't it?

PASSACAGLIA. Aw sarge. No, it's not. I guess.

PURCELL. Yes it is. It's trivial. You just—what? Took out a cigarette, maybe? There was nobody here to remind you about buttons, so you figured "What the hell? Do it later." So you keep on deciding what's important and when you'll do it, and one of these days you'll put something off until later, and it'll be too late. You're a soldier now.

CONNOR. What if you don't want to be? A soldier?

PURCELL. Let's have a show of hands. How many want to be soldiers? (*nobody*) I'd say you belonged to a large club.

BATES. Well, it's not fair!

PURCELL. No. No, it's not.

BATES. Well, all right. I had a job, I had a car . . .

PURCELL. You had it made for twenty years. And you don't want to spend two defending it.

CONNOR. I don't want to defend anything.

PURCELL. Oh yes, you do. You stop being sophisticated for about five minutes and think about it. You don't want to live in China, son. You wouldn't've liked it in Germany a few years back. It's worth defending, take my word.

BATES. What can I defend?

PURCELL. You can type, can't you? O.K. Now I am sorry you boys have to be here. I'm sorry the world's in the shape it's in. I know how you feel. You get your life all going the way you want it, and some blind accident comes rolling through and screws it up for you. But the point is you are here, so what are you gonna do about it?

CONNOR. Just take whatever's handed out, huh?

PURCELL. No. Just stop asking for seconds. You, and Bates both. You ask for it. What is your gripe, really? That sergeant—some of the people I've met here have seen things you've never even thought of. That they're not hatchet murderers amazes me. And then you bitch because they're not genteel. This *is* home to a lot of people, and what you do is walk in here and snicker at their poor old mother's choice of curtains. And one of these days somebody's gonna throw you through a wall, and I don't want to be here when that happens, because it is not worth it. You can't blow up the Mess Hall because the coffee's bad. Now you'd better sit down and do some thinking—I know it's fun to bitch and gripe and be a malcontent, but you stop and think—what you're here for, what you want to fight for—buttons? And you'd better come up with something better than selfishness or stupidity or sophomore ideals. The first winter I was in prison, up on the Yalu River, in North Korea, so many young men died that the Chinese didn't even bother to bury them. It was like a deep-freeze, anyway. They just stacked the bodies up around the camp, a wall of jobs and cars and ideals. I don't want to see that, or anything like that, happen to you. And Sergeant Tippin doesn't want to see that happen, either. So what the hell? Button your pockets and shut your mouth and relax. It's an experience, anyway. An education in itself. Where else will you get a chance to live at close quarters with a bunch of men like this? There's a guy in the Fourth Platoon who rode Citation, did you know that? He was a stable boy at Pimlico, he's ridden all those horses that you read about. You'd never meet anybody like that at Yale. Or a Master Sergeant who carries a little red rubber ball around with him all the time. Huh? You think about it. Now you go to bed. You been working long enough. I'll see you.

(*He exits into the Orderly Room.* CONNOR *watches him go, taking a cigarette out of his pocket as he does. When* PURCELL *is safely indoors,* CONNOR *speaks for the benefit of the Company:*)

CONNOR. "Good night, Doctor Schweitzer, wherever you are."
(*He looks for approval, but gets very little. As he is about to button his pocket, he catches himself, considers, and then, seeing their eyes on him, unbuttons it again and flips the flap up like a flag and saunters*

into the barracks. The lights dim out on the recruits as they start to go in too.

The Orderly Room comes on. PURCELL *is at the filing cabinet, taking out folders.* TIPPIN, *seated, is looking at a manual.*)

TIPPIN. Not going to town?

PURCELL. Naw. Nothin' to do in town.

TIPPIN. Well, it seems to me you'd take advantage of me bein' on C.Q. tonight to practice up yer markmanship.

PURCELL. Me, practice? Who's been winning all the kewpie-dolls? Troy, I tell you something: If you take me to one more shooting gallery, I don't know what I'm gonna do. I've got so many toy whores and hula-hula girls now I can't close my footlocker, and that's just in one week.

TIPPIN. 'Course I picked up a few myself.

PURCELL. What you reading?

TIPPIN. Oh! Ah—Field Manuals.

PURCELL. Something light for a hot night, uh?

TIPPIN. Yeah. I really am hard up for something to do.

PURCELL. Well, it's a good night to do nothing. Sit around and tell lies. (*starting to light a cigarette—*)

TIPPIN. Hey! You smoke them filthy weeds. Gimme a match.

PURCELL. Sure. What for? (*watches disapprovingly as* TIPPIN *burns polish*) Ruin your leather.

TIPPIN. Good shine. I see Charlie Company had two more guys go AWOL.

PURCELL. Yeah?

TIPPIN. Colonel's go'be fit t'be tied.

PURCELL. Well, he oughta be used to it by now. They'll come back.

TIPPIN. Plead leniency for giving themselves up.

PURCELL. Sure. Why not? Seems to me, AWOL's a fact of life, in Basic Training. Some of these guys, it takes that. Let 'em get fifty miles down the road, all of a sudden they'll realize—"My God, I'm a fugitive from justice." They start thinking, finally, and it'll dawn on 'em that it really wasn't worth all that. So they come back, and they'll do all right.

TIPPIN. You got a hell of a sense of humor, you know that?

PURCELL. I'm serious. The fact that he comes back indicates a change of attitude.

TIPPIN. Indicates he's playing it cute. Company see one man get away with it, they'll all do it.

PURCELL. Man, *you* got a sense of humor! Most of these guys wouldn't go AWOL if you told them to.

TIPPIN. You didn't learn a goddam thing, did you?

PURCELL. Don't take it personally—

TIPPIN. Naw! They put you in that Solitary too soon, Purcell. You didn't see it! I saw it; I had to deal with it, cause you was gone.

PURCELL. I couldn't help that, Troy. I didn't go, I was taken.

TIPPIN. I know that, but you left me. To hold that whole damn compound together, any way I could. So don't talk to me.

PURCELL. Talk to you about what?

TIPPIN. I had a boy stand up to me—a P.F.C., to *me!* "You go to hell," he said. That's what he said. "I was drafted! I didn't ast for this, I ain't about to die for no two-bit alphabet, no U.S. nor U.N. nor U. anything else! I'm sick," he said. Yeah, he was sick. He just didn't want to soldier.

PURCELL. What was wrong with him?

TIPPIN. Aw, he just wanted to get in the damn infirmary, there. We was all sick, you know that. And them Chinese bastards wouldn't let you in the infirmary unless you signed one of them propaganda things, U.S. Army was a Wall Street warmonger, all that jazz. And he was willing to do it, cause he was sick!

PURCELL. What—happened?

TIPPIN. What the hell you think happened? I couldn't stop him. Not then, I couldn't.

PURCELL. What—happened?

TIPPIN. You let 'em do it once, Purcell, they'll do it again!

PURCELL. Troy, these guys here are four weeks in the army! Hell, what if somebody drafted you outta here, made you a—a goddam college boy, for Chrissake? Huh?

TIPPIN (*starts to retort, but the idea makes him laugh in spite of himself*). God damn. Can't you just see me? (*pause*) Maybe you're right. (*pause*) I get . . . Maybe we oughta go fishing sometime, huh? Or something? I can't explain it to you, but I—I wake up tired. Ev'y morning, it's just—even what I like to do, I don't like to do it . . . anybody says anything. . . . I've seen some terrible things. . . . And I can't explain it to you or tell you why it is, so maybe you're right.

PURCELL. "Damn right I'm right."

(*Pause. They relax, go back to work.* CLAYTON *comes in, with books.*)

CLAYTON. Evening, sergeants. Am I interrupting anything?

PURCELL. No. Have a seat. You finished that Supply stuff?

CLAYTON. I'll get to it tonight. Got to do my "homework."

TIPPIN. Homework?

CLAYTON. Correspondence course. Getting in shape to go back to college.

PURCELL. When do you leave us?

CLAYTON. Forty-three thousand . . . (*looks at his watch*) two hundred and fourteen minutes. From now. (*They laugh.* PURCELL *is looking through folders.*)

PURCELL. Hey! How do you like this for a name? "Aloysius No-middle-initial Bates."

CLAYTON. You still reading Form 20's, sarge?

PURCELL. Yep. "Homework." This one's nice, too. Connor's "Richard Alexander Connor the Fourth."

CLAYTON. Now that takes the cake.

PURCELL. Oh, I don't know. What about "Charles James Purcell?" I was named after two Kings of England. Both sons-a-bitches.

TIPPIN. Were you really?

PURCELL. I dunno. That's what my old man said.

CLAYTON. What about "Troy J. Tippin," now, if you want a name?

TIPPIN. Yeah. They ain't no Fourths on that one. Nor Kings neither. (*pause*)

PURCELL. You going back to college, huh?

CLAYTON. Yep.

PURCELL. Well, I hope you like it better than I did.

CLAYTON. Did you go to college, sarge?

PURCELL. Yep.

CLAYTON. Didn't care for it, huh?

PURCELL. Oh, the first two years were great—read books, drink beer, chase women. All those new toys. But the time came to get serious, and I didn't know what the hell to do with myself. My old man, he laid down his pen—or his secretary, whatever it was—and leaned back, and said, "Son, I don't want to push you. It's a free country; take your choice. Law, business, or medicine." I tried to join the R.A.F. That was 1940. Lord God, the RAF. . . . But they wouldn't take me. Said I was blind. Oh, I could see all right, but the reaction was too slow, or something, for fighter planes. So . . . I couldn't fly, I joined the Army.

(*Pause. Enter* MYLES *in civilian clothes.*)

MYLES. Gimme my pass, sarge. I'm going to town.

CLAYTON. Who is it this time, Romeo?

MYLES. Anybody, man. I'm so glad to get outta that mess hall, I'll take anything on two feet.

PURCELL. Hey Myles.

MYLES. Yeah sarge?

PURCELL. I see on your Form 20 you went to Bakers' School.

MYLES. Yeah sarge.

PURCELL. Why don't you bake?

MYLES. Well, you know how it is, sarge. Mess Sergeant says it takes too much time, there ain't no need for all that jazz. And he's got the stripes on me.

PURCELL. What've they got to do over there besides put soap in the coffee?

MYLES. Don't ask me, sarge.

PURCELL. Well, I'm gonna take you off shift. You be the baker. O.K.?

MYLES. Yeah! O.K.!

PURCELL. O.K.!

MYLES. Well hey, I'll fix you some. Hey. How about some hot light rolls in the morning? Celebrate? Yeah. I see you, men. (*Exit* MYLES *happily.*)

TIPPIN. Now that's what I like to see is a man that gets things done.

PURCELL. What's the matter with you, man? Been here—what? Six months? And you let a Mess Sergeant get away with that?

TIPPIN. Man, you know why I didn't do anything! He's got three *of these and I got two.* (*Refers to the "rockers" on his stripes.*)

PURCELL. Well, he has just come to the attention of a man with three and a hickey (*a First Sergeant's chevron is a Master Sergeant's— three rockers—with a diamond inside*) so he'd better watch his step.

TIPPIN. All I can say is you oughta got here sooner! Hot light rolls and butter!

CLAYTON. This outfit is shaping up!

TIPPIN (*relaxed, leaning back, merrily shining on his boot*). Hey hey hey! You talking about "old mans" and names and all—my old man, he give me my name. I ever tell you that?

PURCELL. Troy, you mean?

TIPPIN. Yeah. Oh, I mean I just picked up the "J." Alphabet don't belong to nobody. I come in the Army, I didn't want to keep writing "no-middle-initial" on all them forms, so I just picked her up. (*He laughs.*) They say "Spell out middle name," I just put "J-A-Y," "Troy Jay Tippin."

PURCELL. Huh!

TIPPIN. But it'uz nice, you know? At the Home, all them other boys was "Buck," and "Jim Bob," and "R.C." And I was "Troy."

CLAYTON. Did you—not know, your father?

TIPPIN. No, well, that's what my momma said, they said—to call me that.

PURCELL. Well—you didn't know her either, did you?

TIPPIN. Muh Ma? Oh, yeah, sure. I knew m'ma. Oh yeah. She come out to see me. It was one—Sunday morning, as I recall. I was—oh, eight or nine, I recall. Yeah. She ast me was I her Troy, and I said yesm I was. And she just hugged me. So she ast me was I a good little old boy. And I said yesm I was. So she hugged me again. And then she said, I brought you a little something or other, and I said thankya ma'am. And I got hugged again. And then she ast me what I been doin' with myself, and I said I been shooting cats. And she just hugged me and cried, and she couldn't say no more.

CLAYTON. What were you, shooting cats?

TIPPIN. Yeah, cats. Won't nothing else to shoot. See, them city folks, when they'd have a bunch of kittens, why they couldn't drown 'em or anything like that, so they'd tie 'em up in a gunny-sack and drive out by the woods there and drop 'em off on the side of the road. But I mean they was just little old things; you couldn't let 'em smother. So, we'd watch, and go down and turn 'em loose.

But I mean, what could you do with them? We didn't get enough to eat ourselves, we sho' god won't go give it to some cat. So, they run wild in the woods. Ate up all the little birds and things; pretty soon there won't nothing *but* cats. So, a feller come out from town on a Sunday morning with a four-ten shotgun, and we'd shoot 'em.

And you couldn't kill them? I mean, drop 'em with a shot? They wouldn't die? You'd hit one of them little sons-a-bitches he'd squeal and squall and jump ten feet in the air and take off th'ough the brush like a bat outta hell, and you could hear 'em—all night long. Like a baby.

Few days, whole place smelled like a cat. Got so you couldn't even take a goddam walk th'ough the woods, you'd be thinking about something and stumble upon one of them little sumbitches evvy got-dam time you got-dam turned around.

And my old lady? You know what she brought me? The one time she showed her scrawny ass at that Poorhouse Gate? To remember her by? In a box? With a ribbon? A kitten! *A gotdam cat!*

And my old man! He give me, a word! One high class, second-hand piece of alphabet! They coulda called me Shitbird, for all I cared.

(*Pause,* TIPPIN *methodically, savagely, shines his boot. Finally* PURCELL *rises with his coffee pot.*)

PURCELL. Well. Anybody still in the Mess Hall? I think I'll get a refill on this thing. Bring you anything?

TIPPIN. Not hungry.

PURCELL. Well. I'll . . . see you tomorrow, huh? (*He goes out. Stops. Can think of nothing to say or do. Rubs his eyes. Exit.*)

CLAYTON. Sarge . . .? (TIPPIN *is not responding.*) Hard day tomorrow. I'll . . . see ya, sarge.

(*Exit* CLAYTON. TIPPIN *shines.* CONNOR *comes out onto the porch, looking to the Orderly Room. After a long moment, he crosses, knocks, stepping in.*)

CONNOR. Sarge?

TIPPIN. What you want, boy?

CONNOR. Is Sergeant Purcell—

TIPPIN. Come in here.

CONNOR. I just wanted—

TIPPIN. How many times I told you boys to keep the hell away from this Orderly Room unless you got business? Hah? What's 'amatter, cat got yer tongue? Lemme look at you. (CONNOR's *pocket is unbuttoned.*) Iss yours?

CONNOR. Oh hell! I'm sorry, sarge—

TIPPIN. You don't never learn, do you? (*takes knife out, and lays it against* CONNOR's *chest*)

CONNOR. Sarge! I said I'm sorry—

TIPPIN. Sarge! (*triggers the blade*) This button's the property of the United States of America. I don't think you got proper respect for government property, leaving it hang out here in all this wind and weather, so I'm just go' have to take it away from you. (*cuts it off*) Now get outta here, shitbird!

(*Exit* CONNOR. BATES *meets him in the street.*)

CONNOR. Tomorrow?

CURTAIN

SCENE TWO

The next morning, just after Work Call.

BEFORE CURTAIN: *The Company is heard marching off singing cadence as in* ACT ONE SCENE TWO.

AT RISE: CLAYTON *is alone in the Orderly Room working on the Morning Report.*

PURCELL *enters, grumpily, from the direction of Battalion Headquarters with papers in his hand. He comes into the O.R. and checks his coffee.*

PURCELL. Those jerks at Battalion, they always get their emergencies just before the coffee's cool enough to drink, and keep you until it's frozen. (*He tastes it.*) Yep. Well. Cooks put too much G.I. soap in it again, anyway.

CLAYTON. What was it this time?

PURCELL. At Battalion? Nothing, as usual. "Just want to remind you men that today is Battalion Competition for Soldier of the Month."

CLAYTON. I would never have remembered.

PURCELL. Exactly. "You First Sergeants are responsible for the appearance of the men you send up here." Which is another revolutionary piece of information. So, we got a little check-list, all carefully mimeographed, in case we didn't have sense enough to inspect the candidates on our own.

CLAYTON. Well, the Army doesn't have a monopoly on fools in high places.

PURCELL. It just seems that way. Company get off O.K.?

CLAYTON. Singing merrily to work.

PURCELL. Well, I'm surprised somebody didn't trip and fall on the Captain, or set fire to the Mess Hall, or something. This is not going to be my day.

CLAYTON (*after a short pause*). Sarge?

PURCELL. Yeah?

CLAYTON. Have you—how long have you known Sergeant Tippin?

PURCELL. You thinking about last night?

CLAYTON. Yeah. He never—talked, like that, before.

PURCELL. No, I never heard him quite like that myself. I have a way of bringing out the best in him.

CLAYTON. Well, it wasn't you. It just came. (*pause*) Boy, will I be glad to get out of here. Four more weeks.

PURCELL. Why do you say that?

CLAYTON. Well just look at you! Boy, I'm glad I'm the Company Clerk, I don't have to—man, if I close my eyes and work at it, I'm not even here!

PURCELL. You're probably smart; "If you don't see it, it doesn't hurt you," as the man says. (*He gets up, restlessly, goes into street.*) Man, this *is* a ghost town after Work Call, isn't it? (*He says:*) "O sole mio."

(MYLES *crosses into the barracks, greeting* PURCELL *as he goes.*)

MYLES. H'o, sarge!

PURCELL. "Let's straighten up, there!" (MYLES *laughs and goes into barracks.* PURCELL *comes back to the Orderly Room door.*) Oh, things could be worse. . . . Y'know, I had a teacher once— Shakespeare course. Old man, drinking himself blind. He used to read us the plays—whole plays, in that whiskey bass voice of his, rolling it out. Women, too—in falsetto; if you can picture a whiskey-bass-falsetto. Tears streaming out of his eyes, down across those broken veins and purple. . . . "Romeo, Romeo, wherefore art thou Romeo?" And we would sit in the back of the class and snicker at this silly old man who could weep for something in a book—"Poor Juliet." (*pause*) *They* would snicker. I was lucky that way, anyhow. I didn't snicker when people . . . wept. (*He comes in, puts the clipboard down.* BROWN *comes out of the barracks, treading on eggs to avoid kicking dust on his shiny boots. He is resplendent in Class A uniform for "Soldier of the Month." He sets himself in place, wipes his toes off with a rag, and calls:*)

BROWN. Ready to go, sarge. Look all right?

PURCELL. Yeah, as a matter of fact, you do. See this, Clayton?

CLAYTON. My, my, my.

PURCELL. Nervous?

BROWN. Naw sarge.

PURCELL. Short of breath from smoking too much, huh?

BROWN. I don't smoke, sarge— Oh. Yeah. I guess I am, a little.

PURCELL. Be something wrong with you if you weren't. Now don't let 'em scare you, ya hear me? They like to; officers like to play games with ya. But you just remember, even if they could kill you, they can't eat you, so they aren't so goddam much.

BROWN. Yes sarge.

PURCELL. Got everything marked, now?

BROWN. Yeah sarge.

PURCELL. O.K. Now, I'm the Major. Harump. Now you'll be at Parade Rest, y'see, as I come down the line.

(*He does the Inspection bit.* BROWN *snaps to Attention and Inspection Arms as* PURCELL *comes to face him.* PURCELL *doesn't take the rifle at first, pretending to be engrossed in checking the uniform, then turns away as a sort of head fake and turns back, grabbing for the rifle.* BROWN *is not fooled and lets go at the right moment.*)
Very good. (*He turns away, checking the rifle, and mumbles:*)
What's your name, son?

BROWN (*so busy waiting for the question that he misses it*). Uh—

PURCELL. Watch it. They'll do that. Let's try it again. "What's your name, son?"

BROWN. Sir! Private Brown, Johnnie Dee Junior, R. A. 21 385 674."

PURCELL. What Company?

BROWN. Able Company, sir.

PURCELL. Come on, put a little pride in that. It's Mickey Mouse.

BROWN. Able Company, sir!!

PURCELL. Who's your Post Commander?

BROWN. Sir! Major-General Lucius B. Attenbury!

PURCELL. Battalion Commander?

BROWN. Sir! Lieutenant Colonel Henry B. Taliaferro.

PURCELL. You pronounce it "Tolliver." Better get that right. He's the one who's gonna be doing this.

BROWN. "Tolliver." Yes sarge.

PURCELL (*he plays a little more, than jams the rifle suddenly back at* BROWN, *asking the question as he does*). "Why do you serve?"

BROWN (*expertly fielding the rifle, closing its chamber and returning it to Order Arms as he answers the question*). "Sir! To defend my country against aggression and to uphold the principles of human dignity and freedom as set forth in the U.N. Charter!"

PURCELL. O.K. That's very good. Now just remember, it's a game.

Have a ball, hang loose, take no naps and look serious as hell, you've got it made. 'Tench-hut!

BROWN (*not to be outfoxed*). I'm already at attention, sarge.

PURCELL. Too wise for me, huh? Then why are you talking? You don't talk at attention except to answer direct questions, am I right?

BROWN. Yes sarge.

PURCELL. So don't get cheeky with your elders. About—Face! Right Shoulder—arms! Don't grin, you're at attention! Forward, march! Look at that! Pride of Company A, on the way. Good luck. My, my, my. Makes me feel young again.

CLAYTON. It is a game, isn't it?

PURCELL. Yep. With easy rules. But . . . games are fun, for children. . . . You wake up one morning, you're thirty-five years old. . . .

(CHARLIE COMPANY *approaches,* SERGEANT PETERS *singing cadence.*)

PETERS (*off*). "Ain't no need in going home."

CHARLIE COMPANY. "Honey, honey."

PETERS. "Ain't no need in going home."

CHARLIE COMPANY. "Ba–abe."

PETERS. "Ain't no need in going home,
Jodie's got yo' gal and gone."

CHARLIE COMPANY. Honey, ba–ab–y, mine."

PURCELL. Y'know? I used to love that sound. (CHARLIE COMPANY, *passing by, unleashes a full-voiced cadence count and passes on.*) Maybe we ought to post a sign in the road, when Sergeant Tippin's already gone with the troops. Save poor old Sergeant Peters all that energy.

CLAYTON. You want to check this?

PURCELL. Taking it up now?

CLAYTON. No, I've . . . got to finish that supply stuff. I wasn't in the mood last night, y'know?

PURCELL. Yeah. I know what you mean. You ever see that part of Georgia, where Tippin comes from?

CLAYTON. No.

PURCELL. Neither had I. I'd like to take Connor down there once. When this cycle's over, what happens? Do we get a new batch of shiny-faced 'croots. Or is there a break between?

CLAYTON. We get a week, week'n a half.

PURCELL. Any chance Sergeant Tippin and I might get a few days leave out of that?

CLAYTON. There's some paper work, but talk to the Captain. He ought to let you have a long week-end, anyway.

PURCELL. I'd like to get him away from here, y'know?

CLAYTON. Yeah.

PURCELL. I remember, my old man, whenever things got really lousy, he used to take me up in the Blue Ridge. Sometimes it worked. What do you know about that kid Tippin hit two cycles ago?

CLAYTON. Nothing. On purpose. I'd better start on this stuff.

(*He goes into Supply Room.* MYLES *comes out of barracks.*)

MYLES. Off shift, sarge. Goin' to town.

PURCELL. Not going to stay around and enjoy your creation?

MYLES. I had my fun with it.

PURCELL. Hey, Myles? Thanks, you know what I mean? It's good for the Company to know somebody gives enough of a damn to do something besides open C Ration cans.

MYLES. Sure. Hey, uh—next time you sweep the Orderly Room, you come across any old Corporal stripes layin' around, you ain't got no use for . . .?

PURCELL. Well, I'll keep you in mind, soldier. You don't happen to have any ideas about coffee, do you?

MYLES. Well, now I just happen—

PURCELL. Say no more, say no more. Don't say another word. You'll be a Lieutenant-Colonel by morning.

MYLES. That'll do, that'll do. I see ya. (*Exit* MYLES *to town.*)

PURCELL. Who says this Company isn't shaping up? (*still in the street*) Hey, Clayton.

CLAYTON. Yeah, sarge?

PURCELL (*coming in*). This is O.K., except I think you've got one "one" too many.

CLAYTON. Huh?

PURCELL. "Present for Duty 1,126"? Big company.

CLAYTON. Oh yeah. "126." I guess I was a little preoccupied.

PURCELL. You go on back to your Supply stuff. I'll type it over.

(CLAYTON *during this has come into the Supply Room door, just sticking his head in. Now he disappears again.*)

CLAYTON. Thanks.

PURCELL. It's good practice. (*He sits at the typewriter, putting paper and carbons in.*) If I ever go back to civilian life, I've got a rich future, as a stenographer.

CLAYTON. Are you thinking about it?

PURCELL. What, as a stenographer? (*singing as he types*)
"Oh . . . her name was Lil
And she was a beauty—"
(*He misses the note, tries again.*)
Uh–"beauty!" Hum. (*types on, in good spirits*)

(TIPPIN *is heard, loud and fast, counting double-time cadence.* CON- NOR *and* BATES *stumble on, followed by* TIPPIN. PURCELL *goes out into the street.* CLAYTON *comes to the Supply Room door, listens a while, then goes back into Supply Room.*)

TIPPIN. Les go les go les go! Lift them knees, you givin' out? Hot damn there, Bates! Detail, halt! First Sergeant? I got a little Christmas gif' for you!

PURCELL. What is this?

TIPPIN. Yo' catbirds come home to roost! Hooked outta Work Call, too smart for Troy J. Tippin! Yeah!

PURCELL. Did what?

TIPPIN. AWOL is what they did, took advantage of the fact that we didn't take Roll at Work Call.

PURCELL. Oh, wait a minute—

TIPPIN. But I found 'em; I had my eye on them! And now my fine- feathered friend—

BATES. You ran me!

TIPPIN. I did?

BATES. You ran me! I got a light-duty slip and you ran me!

TIPPIN. Haw haw haw ain't that a shame!

PURCELL. What were you thinking—

BATES. I got my rights!

TIPPIN. You ain't got nothing you don't fight for it!

CONNOR. There's no war!

TIPPIN. How do you know?

PURCELL. Look, will you—

BATES. Oh for Christ's sake!

PURCELL. Bates!

TIPPIN. You too good to serve yo' company, huh?

PURCELL. Troy, don't—

BATES. What do I serve, the Company joke?

CONNOR. Two years of my life!

PURCELL. Connor!

TIPPIN. Your life!

PURCELL. Will you all shut up?

TIPPIN. You don't like the game so you go throw the ball away, zat it?

(*Silence.*)

PURCELL. Thank you. Now will somebody tell me what this is all about?

TIPPIN. Two wise bastards wiping their ass on the flag of their country, that's what it is.

CONNOR. Hah!

TIPPIN. Will you shut yo' face or do I have to push it in?

CONNOR. Go ahead! Hit me!

PURCELL. Troy! You shut your face, young man. Look, Troy. Please, look. O.K. Go over to the Mess Hall and get some coffee. Talk about it later.

TIPPIN. I don't drink coffee, old buddy. Remember?

PURCELL. Well for Christ's sweet sake take it up some time! Too much clean living's bad for you. Go sit down somewhere.

TIPPIN. Why?

PURCELL. Because if you don't, we'll all stand here and wave our hands and rant and shout and rave, and I'll never know what the hell is happening.

TIPPIN (*after a pause*). You go come and have one with me, when you get through talking to these boys?

PURCELL. Yeah, O.K.

TIPPIN. Awright. I be waiting for you, in the Mess Hall. (*He exits.*)

PURCELL. Now. I want to get this straight. First: you know what you did, don't you? I mean, this is not just hooky, a little trouble with the Truant Officer? This is—technically—Absent Without Leave, Article 86 in the Court Martial Manual—Uniform Code of Military Justice. (*silence*) Do you know this or don't you? (*silence*) Look, what's happening here?

CONNOR. Just—the last straw, you might say.

PURCELL. What do you mean?

CONNOR. You wouldn't understand.

PURCELL. I know I'm handicapped, but give me a chance.

BATES. You had a chance.

PURCELL. With what? What is this?

CONNOR. With Tippin!

PURCELL. What—did he do something?

CONNOR. He just—cut off a button.

PURCELL. I'm sorry, I lost you there.

CONNOR. You're damned right you did, Sergeant!

PURCELL. Look, son! You want to spend the rest of your Basic Training career digging holes and filling them up?

CONNOR. Anything you like.

PURCELL. Oh, I see. This is a gesture! A "Blow for Freedom," right?

CONNOR. If you like.

PURCELL. I might have known. You're not on the side of the angels, son. Not yet. Not by a long shot. You know what you are? A sniper! A free-lance sharp-shooter who sits in the brush and takes pot-shots at everything that comes down the pike. And if you hit—anything!—you're a great social critic. That makes a simple life, all right. And the lowest form I know. O.K. Go in the barracks and put on your gear—all of it, rifles, steel pots, the whole thing. Since you were well enough, Private Bates, to walk to your hideaway, the pair of you can hike out to the Rifle Range, join the Company, get your day's training in, and I'll have a little job of work for you tonight. Now, Fall Out!

(*Exit* PURCELL. *They exit into barracks.* TIPPIN *comes around barracks, watching* PURCELL'S *progress into Mess Hall. He comes to Orderly Room, looks in. Seeing no one, and since* CLAYTON *should be gone by now, he is satisfied that he is alone.* BATES *and* CONNOR *clatter out, putting on gear. Stop.*)

TIPPIN. I decided not to have that cup of coffee after all. Sergeant Purcell won't mind; he'll think right highly of me, tending to my duty in spite of all this. I told the cooks to tell him I caught a ride on the Mess Truck, out to the Range. (*pause*) Well. Ain't this a remarkable turn of events? You think maybe you can risk it, and stay? Huh? (*They edge down steps and he circles.*) Which way is it gonna be, young soldiers? Huh? That way is the Range, troops all working hard, pissed off, wonder what you been doin', breezin' in so late; and I wonder what tonight will bring? Or you want to do it the easy way? That way? About a hundred yards past where I found you this morning the Post ends. There's a Main Highway, north and south. You could be half-way to Mexico, hitchhiking, by the time old Purcell finds out. That would be a joke, wouldn't it? I'm just trying to be helpful, like Old Daddy Purcell. Help you boys decide.

CONNOR. You'd like that, wouldn't you?

TIPPIN. Naw! What I would really like is for you all boys to stay. I wanted to see you in jail before, but now all I want is a chance to break yo' got-dam necks, little bit by little bit. You ain't got a China-man's Chance. . . . I tell you what. I see you got your bayonets there. Easier still. Settle it right now. Take 'em out. Huh? Take me on, both of you. You look like fighting types. Me unarmed, nothing but my bare hands. Always say I started it . . . *if* you win. Best deal you go' get all day, come on. Kill me now or I'll get you, in my own good time. I have killed one son-of-a-bitch for betrayin' the uniform he wore. Few more won't make much difference. . . . Unless of course you decide to run. It's a free country. Up to you. (*pause*) Well. Suit yo'self. Oh! By the way. There's a little old country store right on that road, right after you get off Post? Makes a specialty out of selling check shirts and overall pants to young men in uniform, no questions ast. In case you innerested. I see y'all, men.

(*Exit* TIPPIN. *Exit* CONNOR *and* BATES *to "civilian street."* CLAYTON *comes numbly into the street. There is a whoop of joy and* BROWN *dances on, throwing his rifle up, etc.*)

BROWN. Whoooo—eee! Yahoo! Look at me! Look! Look! Them boys didn't have a chance, them boys didn't have a Chinaman's Chance, cause I was sharp! I knew it all! They couldn't none of them touch me, they couldn't none of them catch up to me, 'cause I'm a soldier! "Soldier of the Month!" Cause Able Comp'ny is my name, soldierin's my game! Them boys from Baker Company and Charlie Company, stood there drooling like somebody hit 'em over the head! They couldn't touch me with a pole! They didn't have nothing at all on me! Not none of them! Where's old Tippin? He oughta been here! Old Purcell, where's he? They go be proud of this, they go be proud, 'cause I was sharp! Soldier of the Month! Is Sergeant Tippin gone? (*He dashes off.*)

(CLAYTON *stands in the street. He rubs his eyes as if he were very tired.*)

CURTAIN

ACT THREE

SCENE ONE

Night, a week later.
The troops are working, scrubbing the porch, etc., listlessly, sullenly.
A couple of them are painting butt cans, robin's egg blue. A RECRUIT
crosses, also sullen, tired, dirty, with a bucket and mop.

PASSACAGLIA. Finish yet?

RECRUIT. Hell, no. We only been working every night for a week.
Whattya expect, miracles? (*exits*)

JENKINS (*scrubbing the porch. He wrings out his sponge and*
squeezes it viciously, as if it were the offending parties, and slams it
down.) Mother-chasing god-damn Connor and a son-of-a-bitching
Bates! (*glares for a moment, then goes on scrubbing*)

PASSACAGLIA (*stops work and speaks dejectedly, as if to the Ser-*
geant). But man, I mean: *I* didn't go AWOL. Don't take it out on me.

ANOTHER RECRUIT. I'll be glad when they get back here. (*Pause.*
They go back to work. Enter BROWN, clean. He crosses past them into
the barracks.)

RECRUIT. What are *you* doing?

BROWN. Oh. I'm . . . studying. (*pause*) I got to go up for Soldier
of the Month—at Regiment. I got to get ever'thing ready. (*Pause. They*
look at him.) Sarge say I win it here . . . I got it made—in the rest of
the competition. (*He trails off, and looks at them. Fidgets, and goes into*
barracks.) I got to get ready.

PASSACAGLIA. And we been working our humps off for a week.

(CLAYTON *comes out of the Supply Room, dragging two duffel bags*
which he dumps on the floor. He takes his clipboard and, checking the
name on the bag, begins to sort through its contents, checking them off
on the clipboard.)

CLAYTON. "Private . . . Bates, Aloysius no-middle-initial." Boy,
they didn't leave much, did they? You're gonna have to pay for a lot of
"lost equipment. . . ." God damn, sarge!

(*He begins to check it off.* DOLEMAN *ambles on, watches the re-*
cruits work. They glance at him, work on.)

DOLEMAN. Working hard?

RECRUITS. Yeah, sarge.

DOLEMAN. Well, got to have things nice and pretty for your two buddies when they get back. Show you missed them.

RECRUIT. Every night for a week?

DOLEMAN. My heart weeps for you. (*pause*) Well, look busy. Sergeant Tippin be home soon. (*They look disgruntled and continue. He ambles into the Orderly Room.*) Wher's that bad old Sergeant?

CLAYTON. Which one?

DOLEMAN. Ho, ho, ho. Whatch doin', makin' mudpies?

CLAYTON. Clothing list.

DOLEMAN. "Connor and Bates." Hey, they catch 'em yet?

CLAYTON. Gave themselves up. In Florida.

DOLEMAN. "Gave themselves up." Hunh. Court-martials go light on 'em sometimes for that.

CLAYTON. That doesn't really matter, does it? In this case?

DOLEMAN. Hell yes it matters. Florida, huh? Tippin know?

CLAYTON. Yeah. They're coming in tonight. Listen, he said not to tell anybody. I think he wants to make an announcement at Reveille, while thousands cheer.

DOLEMAN. My my. "I'm in the jailhouse now."

CLAYTON. Sarge? Don't you think Sergeant Tippin's overdoing this a little?

DOLEMAN. How ya mean?

CLAYTON. Well, this whole thing. I just don't—understand, this whole damn thing! He just dumped this stuff on the barracks floor. "Help yourself!" Now he's gonna claim it was lost; Connor and Bates'll have to pay for it.

DOLEMAN. They shoulda stayed to pertect it.

CLAYTON. He can't do that, to them! They're gonna be mad as hell!

DOLEMAN. Mad? I reckon they will. Send me to jail, I be mad.

CLAYTON. He can't prosecute these guys! Come on! He's just making a show for the troops.

DOLEMAN. I'd like to know why not.

CLAYTON. Well, he just—can't.

DOLEMAN. That ain't what I hear.

CLAYTON. He can't do it, sarge! That's why he shouldn't be doing this—aggravate it! Not if he's gonna make a deal.

DOLEMAN. Who's gonna deal?

CLAYTON. Like that guy two cycles ago.

DOLEMAN. Yeah, but he hit that guy. He had to make a deal.

CLAYTON (*pause*). He really thinks he can get away with it— make it stick, this time?

DOLEMAN. Why not?

CLAYTON. Jesus, I hadn't figured that.

DOLEMAN. Hell, them short-timer's cramps getting to your head, Clayton. Last month in the Army, startin' to hear voices and see things, uh?

CLAYTON. Yeah, I guess that's what it is, sarge. Short-timer's cramps.

DOLEMAN. Well, you just relax and let the old soldiers take care of this.

(*Enter* TIPPIN *from town with a small paper bag. He hails the troops in passing and comes into the Orderly Room.*)

TIPPIN. Working hard, young soldiers? (*Into the Orderly Room. Sees the pile of clothing.*) Look like a cyclone hit a cathouse. Where's Sergeant Purcell?

CLAYTON. His room, I think.

TIPPIN. Sumbitch won't go to town with me anymore. I think he's ashamed to admit it.

CLAYTON. Admit what, sarge?

TIPPIN. I was right about them boys.

(*Enter the* CAPTAIN *on his way home.* TIPPIN *calls, "Attention!"*)

CAPTAIN. As you were, as you were. Clayton, if my wife calls, I'm on my way home. (*He sees* TIPPIN *in dress uniform.*) You go to town again, Sergeant?

TIPPIN. Yessir.

CAPTAIN. Every night this week?

TIPPIN. Yessir.

CAPTAIN. Well, dammit Sergeant! With the men working?

TIPPIN. I want these boys to see somebody having a good time.

CAPTAIN. Well, all right, all right. Anything new?

CLAYTON. Nossir.

CAPTAIN. Huh. . . . I was just talking to Purcell. . . .

TIPPIN. Captain, everything's just rosy! Now, don't sweat it.

CAPTAIN. Well, I don't see . . .

TIPPIN. Do you or not? Want to be the man—that his company has the example that ends the AWOL problem on this whole damn hill!

DOLEMAN. Colonel's sho' go' be happy about that!

CAPTAIN. I dunno. . . .

DOLEMAN. Sho' was convenient, them breaking all them rules at one time. Disobedience, stealing (all that equipment they took with 'em). . . .

CLAYTON. But sarge, we found that—the stuff they took with 'em.

DOLEMAN. Out in the woods! Where they ditched it! We hadda look for it!

TIPPIN. That's negligence. Same article.

DOLEMAN. All that plus two counts of AWOL. Lord, Lord.

TIPPIN. One count.

DOLEMAN. Huh?

TIPPIN. One count of AWOL.

DOLEMAN. Two.

TIPPIN. One count of AWOL. The other one's Desertion.

CLAYTON. Desertion?

CAPTAIN. Oh come on now Sergeant! Nobody's gonna prove Desertion in peacetime! You wanna make me look like a fool or something?

TIPPIN. Read yer Court-martial Manual sometime, you learn something.

CAPTAIN. Now hold on, Sergeant.

TIPPIN. "I beg yo' pardon, sir." One case. "Desertion may be proved"—and I'm quoting—"if the defendant can be shown to have absented himself *to avoid punishment for a prior offense.*"

CLAYTON. "AWOL from Work Call, and then. . . ."

TIPPIN. "AWOL to avoid punishment for the prior offense."

CLAYTON. Oh . . . I see.

CAPTAIN. Unh. I—didn't realize that. Sergeant Purcell go along with this?

TIPPIN. Captain, you don't know Sergeant Purcell. He'd be passing out coffee and doughnuts to the whole goddam world if they'd let him.

DOLEMAN. If it's a air-tight case, what can he do?

CAPTAIN. Uhhh . . . what about the Colonel now?

TIPPIN. He'll eat it up! Solve his problems, man. . . . He'll eat it up!

CAPTAIN. Yeah, well. . . .

TIPPIN. Talk to him in the morning. Ask him! He'll tell ya!

CAPTAIN. Yeah, yeah—well—

TIPPIN. Or ya want me to?

CAPTAIN. No, no. Now I can handle it. There's no hitch now? You're sure?

TIPPIN. Captain, I am sure.

CAPTAIN. Hunh. Well. . . .

TIPPIN. They ain't got no defense, unless they lie. And the Colonel's used to that!

CAPTAIN. Well, I'll have to . . . think about it.

TIPPIN. You better do it quick, sir. They coming in tonight.

CAPTAIN. Well, I'll uh—I gotta be getting home. I'll think about it, right? (*exit*)

DOLEMAN. That silly bastard can find more things to worry about.

TIPPIN. Standing there with that expression on his face like he was having dinner at the General's house, and he just bit into something tastes like shit, and the General's wife asts him how does he like her new recipe. . . . Get that crap up. I want you to type up a set of charges and specifications on Connor and Bates: "Desertion," "Disobedience of a direct order from a non-commissioned officer in the line of his duty," and "Destruction of government property," "Willful negligence." I want to read it to the troops. Tomorrow.

CLAYTON. O.K., sarge.

TIPPIN. What's 'a matter with you?

DOLEMAN. Short-timer's cramps.

TIPPIN. Hah! (*He turns on his heel and exits to barracks. A RE-CRUIT comes down to the Orderly Room.*)

RECRUIT. Hey, Corporal?

DOLEMAN. What you want, boy?

RECRUIT. Oh! hi, sarge. Sergeant Tippin looks excited. Connor and Bates coming back?

DOLEMAN. You never know, young soldier.

RECRUIT. Huh. I'd like to have about five minutes with one of them right now. . . . I'd like to have about five minutes with most anybody, right now.

DOLEMAN. You may get your chance. Get back to work.

(*The* RECRUIT *goes back.* PURCELL *comes in.*)

PURCELL. You men still working?

RECRUIT. Yeah sarge.

PURCELL. Huh. Well, get the hell to bed. Enough's enough.

RECRUITS. Right, sarge. (*They pack up and begin to go.*)

PURCELL (*entering Orderly Room*). You still working on that stuff?

DOLEMAN. I see yo' two catbirds comin' home to roost, sarge.

PURCELL. Yeah.

DOLEMAN. Captain talking like a prosecuting man.

PURCELL. Captain changes every time the wind blows.

DOLEMAN. You go oppose it, if the Captain wants to?

PURCELL. Get in line, Doleman. I haven't answered the last 2,338 people who asked me that.

DOLEMAN. I don't blame you none for bein' touchy. They took advantage of your kindness thataway. (PURCELL *doesn't respond.*) Old Tippin's right, though; only way to run an army is take names and kick asses.

PURCELL. Thanks for the tip.

DOLEMAN. Lord, Lord. I can just see old Connor now, that college-boy nose in the air, a jailbird! That old white "P" for prisoner on his back, one of them little sticks in his hand with a nail on the end, picking up trash. M.P. with a pump-shotgun, picking his nose, mooch-ing along to the rear. A prisoner! Can't you just see him? Lord, Lord. Won't get no second chances in the Post Stockade, that's one thing for sure. (PURCELL *does not respond.*) Them little old kids in the Of-ficers' Quarters—little old officers' brats—line up on the road: "Jail Bird. Jail Bird." Troops march by and sing: "Jail Bird." Gettin' along to summer now, good and hot. That's always nice. They save the garbage run for the real hard cases—the ones that give 'em any head. Garbage run in the summer, up in that covered truck. Come along on a Monday morning, troops had fried chicken Sat'day noon—whole post, in them tin cans all weekend long. Handing them cans up to you, got to get them to the back, empty them, throw them back out. Truck get so full you have to kneel in it, crawl, right up under that tarpaulin, air full of dust and corruption, so hot you can't breathe, when you do breathe all you can do is smell. . . . (*pause*) I have a theory you'll smell like that the rest of your life. (*pause*) I ever tell you about the time I slugged that Detachment Commander, Arlington Cemetery? Drunk as a fiddler's bitch. . . . But they can't kill you. (*He sniffs, waits.*

Nothing else occurs to him, nobody responds. He ambles out and up the street.) I'll go see how the Mess Hall's coming. Look alive, there, 'croots! (*exit*)

PURCELL. Can I help you?

CLAYTON. If you want to.

PURCELL. Not much there, huh?

CLAYTON. Nope. (*pause*) Sergeant Tippin dumped it out on the barracks floor and said "Take your pick." (*pause*) So I guess everybody owns a little piece of Connor and Bates.

PURCELL. Damn it. Damn it.

CLAYTON. Sarge? You've got to do something.

PURCELL. I came here to change the world, and I did. Made it worse. "Brighten up the corner where you are."

CLAYTON. You know he's planning to go through with this? Desertion?

PURCELL. I know.

CLAYTON. Do you think he can get away with it?

PURCELL. I don't know.

CLAYTON. Are you going to let him?

PURCELL. Congratulations. You are the one-millionth customer to cross that bridge. Maybe they deserve it, I don't know.

CLAYTON. They gave themselves up. The M.P. Station said so.

PURCELL. "Saw the light," huh?

CLAYTON. Maybe. Maybe if we just transferred them out, they'd be all right.

PURCELL. I know. But he's right, they deserve it. I'd like to kick their tails myself.

CLAYTON. Sarge—

PURCELL. And he says it'll be an example, and I don't know. Basic Training's a crazy world, it's insane. I'd just like to pick up and run —do not walk—to the nearest exit.

CLAYTON. I know what you mean.

PURCELL. And just for simple revenge: the Army's the only thing Tippin's got, and they walked all over it, with no excuse, no justification whatsoever. Just for a joke. If anybody was ever entitled to simple revenge, I think Troy J. Tippin is. (*pause*)

CLAYTON. Sarge? I hate to be the first in my neighborhood to do this—but there's something you need to know.

PURCELL. What's that, Clayton?

CLAYTON. I think they had some justification.

PURCELL (*quietly*). Uh oh. . . . Did Sergeant Tippin do this little something I don't know about?

CLAYTON. I'm afraid he did.

PURCELL. What was it?

CLAYTON. I was in the Supply Room, the day they went AWOL. When you left Connor and Bates, and went to the Mess Hall, Sergeant Tippin came back, and "talked" to them. Believe me, they didn't go AWOL on their own.

PURCELL. He told me he went to the Range. . . . What did he do?

CLAYTON. God, what didn't he do? He—said he was gonna break their necks if they stayed. He offered them a chance to fight him, with bayonets—and you know how much chance they'd have, at *that*. I tell you, I would've run.

PURCELL. I expect I would've, too.

CLAYTON. He even told them where they could get civilian clothes, for godssake.

PURCELL. Well, that makes it a cat of a different color, doesn't it? (*pause*) Well. Since you've been so helpful with the information, maybe you can tell me now, what I should do about it?

CLAYTON. It beats the hell out of me.

PURCELL. So if the Captain pleases the Colonel, and Sergeant Tippin gets his example: if we try to court-martial Connor and Bates . . . they're gonna tell what they know, in self-defense. And if they do, you're gonna have to back them up. Which means there will be a stink; the Captain will have heart failure. . . .

CLAYTON. And recover just in time to nail Sergeant Tippin to the wall. . . . What if I didn't back them up?

PURCELL. I don't think you could do that, could you?

CLAYTON. No. . . . And there'd be a stink, anyway.

PURCELL. What the hell was he thinking about?

CLAYTON. Maybe we could make a deal, like I said. Talk to Connor and Bates.

PURCELL. Ship them out and forget it, huh?

CLAYTON. Sure. Nobody'd ever know.

PURCELL. Tippin wouldn't buy it.

CLAYTON. He's got to. He's in danger.

PURCELL. He doesn't know he's in danger. He never will. Because he is "clothed in the whole armor of righteousness." Have you talked to him about these guys? Lately?

CLAYTON. Yeah. He'd take on Congress, the President, and God. All rolled up in one big ball.

PURCELL. So how do you stop him? And if you don't? Can't you just see Sergeant Tippin in the Post Stockade? Or defending himself in a court-martial for "Conduct unbecoming to a soldier?" I might as well walk over there and shoot him in the head, right now.

CLAYTON. "Troy J. Tippin is my name, soldierin's my game." That's all he's got.

PURCELL. He doesn't even have the name.

CLAYTON. What do you mean?

PURCELL. "Troy," that he's so proud of? Where do you think he got that name, in modern Georgia? Instead of "Jim Bob," or "J.C."? "That's what my papa said to call me—so they said." That's what he thinks. And what kind of papa do you think that was? An insane classical scholar, perhaps? Roaming the countryside, impregnating the sharecroppers' daughters in—what is it—strophe and antistrophe? Sure. Well I spent a week and a half, floundering my way through North Georgia, to find out who or why or what, or "whence came" . . . Troy J. Tippin. But nobody knew what his father was; his mother was "omnivorous," they say. When she turned him in at the County Farm —five minutes after he was born, I imagine—they asked her what name she'd given him. And she laughed, they say. As if she'd never thought of such a thing. And then she said, "What the hell? Call him Troy. His old man would get a bang out of that."

And that's all anyone would tell me. But on the way, I stopped in a filling station rest room, and there it was on a coin slot just above my eyes. Troy is a city in Asia Minor, famous in song and story. Troy is also a brand name—a cheap prophylactic, not always guaranteed to work, sold in all the better roadhouses, dives, and filling station rest rooms in North Georgia. "For the Prevention of Disease only." "Prevent disease, invite disaster." Quite fitting, isn't it?

(*Pause. Then* PURCELL *takes coffee pot and cup, walks out of Orderly Room, across the street, up the steps and into the barracks. Lights up in* TIPPIN'S *room. A knock at the door.* TIPPIN *sits on his footlocker, cleaning his boots.*)

TIPPIN. Come in.

PURCELL. Home early tonight, Sergeant.

TIPPIN. Town's deader'n hell.

PURCELL. Well, that's . . . "The Fortunes of War." (*pause*) I want to talk to you about something.

TIPPIN. Match?

PURCELL. What?

TIPPIN. Match.

PURCELL. Why don't you start smoking? (*Gives him the match. He lights the polish.*)

TIPPIN. This here little something wouldn't have no application to a certain Private Connor and a Private Bates, now would it?

PURCELL. It might.

TIPPIN. You can save your breath to cool your coffee, First Sergeant.

PURCELL. They're coming in tonight, y'know—early morning.

TIPPIN. I'd like to go to Florida. All them oranges.

PURCELL. Don't you feel anything about racking these boys?

TIPPIN. Good riddance, yeah! Comp'ny a hell of a sight better since they been gone.

PURCELL. God damn, Troy! You can't make Training Aids out of people! Or can you? O.K. Look. We can still ship them out, and say it was for an unprejudiced trial.

TIPPIN. Do what?

PURCELL. Wait a week, I'll type you up a phoney set of orders, you can read it to the company while thousands cheer. "We just got word on Connor and Bates. They got a year in jail and D.D.'s, the pair of them." Go ahead, make it two years, exaggerate, for Christ's sweet sake. You won't go to hell for that!

TIPPIN. You got a hell of a sense of humor old buddy, you know that?

PURCELL. I'm not joking, dammit!

TIPPIN. I don't lie about things like that!

TIPPIN. No!

PURCELL. No???

PURCELL. Troy, I'm telling you this for your own good.

TIPPIN. You let me worry about that.

PURCELL (*after a pause*). Troy? I know what you did.

TIPPIN. About what?

PURCELL. Clayton was in the Supply Room, the day they went AWOL. He heard you.

TIPPIN (*after a pause*). So what you go' do about it?

PURCELL. Ship them out and close the case.

TIPPIN. Let them get away with it?

PURCELL. Let you get away with it! You could get a year in jail—

TIPPIN. Purcell, don't talk to me like that!

TIPPIN. You supposed to be my friend!

PURCELL. If I weren't your friend I'd be over there typing up charges on *you,* right now.

PURCELL. Then how the hell do you want me to talk to you, when you do things like this?

TIPPIN. Naw, don't give me that!

PURCELL. Then what the hell do you want me to give you, Troy?

TIPPIN. You know how to figure things out! I don't know. Talk to Clayton. He won't tell if you talk to him.

PURCELL. They'll tell! Connor and Bates! They're coming back to-night! We haven't got time to play around, Troy.

TIPPIN. I'm not scared of them.

PURCELL. I'm scared of the *Captain!*

TIPPIN. Oh for godssake! That gutless wonder? I'll take my chances with him.

PURCELL. Well I won't. I'm scared of him and, take my word, you'd better be.

TIPPIN (*after a pause*). Who the hell are they? Cause all this trouble. A couple of eight-balls? What do you care about them?

PURCELL. You can't do this to anybody; for the Army or anything else. It's a two-way road, Troy. You *are* my friend, and if you keep on, the Captain's going to ruin you. And two, you're wrong. It *has* become a matter of principle, and even if you could get away with it, I'd have to stop you. Because you're wrong.

TIPPIN. You really believe that, don't you?

PURCELL. Take my word.

TIPPIN. You know something, old buddy? Sometimes I think I been talking to a complete damn stranger this whole time? I never saw you before in my life?

PURCELL. I know how you feel, old buddy. I know how you feel. (*pause*) I don't want to fight with you. (*Pause. He takes one of* TIPPIN's *boots and a rag.*) Pass the polish.

TIPPIN. New can in the footlocker; ain't been set fire to yet.

PURCELL. What the hell, it's your boot.

TIPPIN. Oh, hey. Almost forgot. I brought you something.

PURCELL. From town?

TIPPIN. Yeah, that little old shootin' gallery down by the Capitol. Just got 'em in. S'posed to be a geisha girl.

PURCELL. Oh. Thanks.

TIPPIN (*taking it from footlocker, giving it to him*). Don't look like much, but I figured you'd get a laugh out of it if it was Jap-looking.

PURCELL. You win it?

TIPPIN. Yeah. Fourteen of 'em. Give 'em all away.

PURCELL (*looking on the base*). Hey. "Made in West Germany."

TIPPIN. It's what?

PURCELL. Says right here.

TIPPIN. Ain't that a bitch. So it does. "West Germany." Can't trust nobody, can ya?

PURCELL. Well, it looks good. (*pause*) Basic Training's hard duty. You told me, but I didn't believe you. Everything gets so tense.

TIPPIN. We always arguin' with each other, but don't—don't worry about that. Sometimes I think if we didn't have nothing to argue about, we wouldn't have no way to pass the time.

PURCELL. Maybe you're right.

TIPPIN. Purcell, it's just that I—I wake up in the night sometimes, and it's like a river of waters, rolling down. . . . All by myself, I'm— all boxed in and tied up and I can't—esplain it to you, can't get out of it.

PURCELL. Out of what, Troy?

TIPPIN. Let's don't talk about it. . . . But I'm right, Purcell! I know I'm right! If it ain't right, everything I done. . . . That boy in Korea, in 'at P.O.W. Camp—that was a little thing. All he wanted was to get in the hospital; but to get in the hospital, he signed his name—as a soldier—to a piece of paper that said some awful things. . . .

PURCELL. Yeah, but who believed that stuff? Nobody in his right mind.

TIPPIN. That ain't the point. It's the principle of the thing. He signed.

PURCELL. What were you going to let him do? Die? It wasn't that important.

TIPPIN. He was as much my enemy, enemy of the cause I served, as if he was wearing a padded suit and a star on his hat.

PURCELL. What . . . did you do? Troy?

TIPPIN. I had to show the rest of those boys . . . (*He clenches his hand, opens it like a judo blow, and lets it drop.*)

PURCELL. Oh man. . . . (*pause*) Well, I won't argue with you any more. . . . Let's just do it the Army way. This is a direct order, Sergeant: Private Connor and Private Bates'll be coming in tonight. They will be transferred out of this company to complete their Basic Training in another Regiment as soon as I can get them packed and get orders cut. They will be punished under Article 15, extra duty two hours a night for thirty days and no passes or privileges. That's all. You will in no way interfere with this, you will not speak to or otherwise concern yourself with Private Connor and Private Bates. Agree or not, this is an order. I've got three and you've got two. (TIP-PIN *shines his boot.*) O.K.?

TIPPIN. Zat all you got to say?

PURCELL. That's all I've got to say.

(*There is a knocking at the door and* BROWN *tears in, with two O.D. uniforms which have been streaked with robin's egg blue paint.*)

BROWN. Sarge? Can I come in? Look what they done, sarge.

TIPPIN. Who did this?

BROWN. Just painted all over 'em. Just got paint all over my O.D. uniforms.

TIPPIN. Who did this?

PURCELL. What's that? (*There is a piece of paper pinned to one.*) "Why don't you work?"

BROWN. Huh?

PURCELL. That's what it says—"Why don't you work?"

BROWN. Sarge! How'm I to go up for Soldier of the Month to-morrow? These the only O.D. uniforms I got.

TIPPIN. I'll find out who did this. . . .

PURCELL. What were you doing tonight?

BROWN. Huh?

PURCELL. What was your detail tonight? Troy?

TIPPIN. He was working for me.

PURCELL. Doing what?

TIPPIN. Learning his chain of command. I don't know.

PURCELL. He learned that. You had these boys working all night, while Brown paraded doing nothing?

TIPPIN. He earned it.

BROWN. Sarge, what am I—

PURCELL. "The good prosper," huh? What the hell is he, another Training Aid? Another week and they'll be ready to break *his* neck. Is that "for the good of the Army" too?

TIPPIN. What the hell are you talking about?

PURCELL. This is your system, right here. This is what you get. Now will you see I'm right?

TIPPIN. I think you gone outta your damn mind, Sergeant.

PURCELL. Brown. I'll see if I can find a uniform to fit you in the morning. But as far as I'm concerned, you brought it on yourself. Both of you. I'll see you in the morning. (*exit*)

TIPPIN. Don't worry, boy. I'll fix it.

CURTAIN

SCENE TWO

The next morning, after Reveille.
CONNOR *and* BATES, *in civilian clothes, are eating in the Orderly Room, guarded by* CLAYTON *with a rifle.*

TIPPIN *comes out of the barracks, and into the Orderly Room. He sits, dead-faced.*

CONNOR *tries to speak to him, hesitantly.*

CONNOR. Sergeant?

(CLAYTON *catches* CONNOR's *eye, and signals "No."* PURCELL *comes in, sees* TIPPIN. *Pause.*)

PURCELL. Captain not back yet.

CLAYTON. No.

PURCELL. Damn. What's this Colonel like?

CLAYTON. Narrow-minded bastard.

PURCELL. You finished eating?

CONNOR. Yes, Sergeant.

PURCELL. Go put some fatigues on. Hustle it up. Captain'll want to talk to you when he gets here.

CONNOR (*starts to go, stops*). Sarge? I'm sorry.

PURCELL. Yeah, I know. (CONNOR, BATES *and* CLAYTON *exit.*

TIPPIN *rises after them, and trails to the door, watching them.*) You had breakfast yet?

TIPPIN. What?

PURCELL. Get some chow.

TIPPIN. Not hungry.

PURCELL. What the hell are you trying to do to yourself, Troy?

TIPPIN. I'm just . . . trying to think, Purcell.

PURCELL. About what?

TIPPIN. What difference does it make?

PURCELL. Go to town, or something.

TIPPIN. I got a duty to perform.

PURCELL. Get outta here!

TIPPIN. I wanna hear what the Colonel's got to say!

PURCELL. Who cares what he says now? He doesn't know!

TIPPIN. You go tell him?

PURCELL. Not if I can help it, no. That's why I want you out of here when the Captain comes.

TIPPIN. So you can lie to him?

PURCELL. Troy, don't—look, don't talk like that. You know better than that.

TIPPIN. I know what they did! What this Company did to Brown last night! Keep on doing!

PURCELL. I gave you an order, get out of here. So I can try to save your skin!

TIPPIN. I got a duty here. I don't care how many stripes you got. (*pause*) And you can't make me.

RECRUIT (*offstage*). 'Tench-hut! Morning, sir.

CAPTAIN (*off*). Young soldiers! (*The* CAPTAIN *breezes into the Orderly Room.*) Sergeant Tippin! Sergeant. Well, I've just been talking to the Colonel. Where are the Rover Boys?

PURCELL. In the barracks.

CAPTAIN. You got a guard on them?

PURCELL. Yes sir.

CAPTAIN. Good. The Colonel wants to make a little noise with Private Connor and Private Bates. Where's uh—Clayton?

PURCELL. He's guarding them.

CAPTAIN. Well, get him over here. Get somebody else to do that.

We've got things to do. Colonel wants a full report this morning, including the court-martial papers: Desertion, Disobedience, the whole works.

TIPPIN. Uh huh! That's what I figured!

PURCELL. Sergeant Tippin, go get me some coffee.

TIPPIN. No thankya.

PURCELL. Don't take this little game too far, old buddy.

CAPTAIN. Now wait a minute. What's the matter with you, Purcell?

PURCELL. Sir, I'd like to speak to you alone, if I may.

CAPTAIN. I don't think there's anything Sergeant Tippin can't hear.

PURCELL. It's not his hearing that bothers me, sir.

CAPTAIN. I know what you're gonna say, Sergeant. Save your breath. The Colonel's decided, the matter's closed.

PURCELL. Sir, I request the Captain's permission to speak to the Colonel.

CAPTAIN. What? Permission refused.

PURCELL. Sir—

CAPTAIN. Absolutely not.

TIPPIN. Maybe you oughta go get some coffee, old buddy. Let the men handle this!

PURCELL. Troy, for Christ's sake, you're killing yourself! O.K. Let's put it this way: I'm sorry you went off half-cocked and got the Colonel all excited, sir. Because you're gonna have to figure out some way to calm him down. You can't prosecute Connor and Bates for going AWOL because they didn't go. They were sent.

CAPTAIN. Sent? What do you mean?

PURCELL. This "paradox of virtue" here.

CAPTAIN. Did what?

PURCELL. Clayton can give you the details. He was a witness. Sergeant Tippin threatened to kill them if they stayed in the Company. He made them desert.

CAPTAIN. I might have known it, I might've known it. You did this?

TIPPIN. They're—lying!

CAPTAIN. You threatened them?

TIPPIN. They were wrong!

CAPTAIN. Who gives a damn about that? You threatened them, that's what I want to know! You know what you could get for this?

TIPPIN. You left me to run this company—

CAPTAIN. That's all I want to hear from you!

TIPPIN. You go' hear a lot before I'm through—

CAPTAIN. You stand to attention if you can't—

TIPPIN. Don't you 'tention me!

CAPTAIN. As you were!

TIPPIN. No sir! As I am!

CAPTAIN. That's all, soldier! You are dead, as far as the Army—

TIPPIN. *I am not dead!* You can't talk to me. . . . (*He lunges towards the* CAPTAIN, *assaulting a chair that is between them, and this action stops him.*)

CAPTAIN. Why don't you hit me, soldier? Really make it nice. This ought to be worth a dishonorable discharge and a few years in Leavenworth. And I'll be willing to disappoint the Colonel about Connor and Bates to get you there. I've been waiting for you.

You, Sergeant. Put this man under guard. I can trust you for that, I hope? And I'll deal with you all when I get off the hook with the Colonel. (*He stops in the door to look at* TIPPIN.) You call yourself a soldier. You're a disgrace to the uniform you wear. (*exit*)

TIPPIN. Purcell?

PURCELL. I can't do anything for you, Troy.

TIPPIN. Well, I'm'o do something. (*He jumps up and goes for the door.*) Where are they?

PURCELL (*moving to stop him*). Don't go out there!

TIPPIN. Oh yes! (*Pushing him out of the way, he goes into street, as* CONNOR *and* BATES *come clattering out of the barracks, as in* ACT TWO, SCENE TWO.) Well, there you are. All buttoned up.

PURCELL. For the last time, listen to me.

TIPPIN. I did that. (*To* CONNOR *and* BATES.) I understand there's go be some vacancies 'fore long. Ought to get your old buddy Purcell to put you in for 'em. Connor here'd make a good Field First, take my place, wouldn't you? New Army.

(*No response. Other recruits come in.* CLAYTON, *with the rifle, edges towards* PURCELL.)

Run it all then, yo' way. Pretty nice, uh?

(*He steps away, then wheels and hits* BATES *in the belly, knocking him down.*)

PURCELL. That's great, sarge! What else do you need to do, to make it perfect? Set fire to the Mess Hall?

TIPPIN (*turns, looks at him dully*). I don't know.

PURCELL. Go to your room.

TIPPIN. I can't hear ya.

PURCELL. O.K. I'll talk your language. (*He steps up to* CLAYTON, *takes the rifle, clicks off the safety and levels it on* TIPPIN.) Do what I say.

TIPPIN. Don't do me no favors.

PURCELL. It's up to you. (*pause*)

TIPPIN. You one hell of a killer, old buddy! Look at this! Work the bolt, if you go' get tough, start shootin'. You ain't even got a round in the chamber yet.

PURCELL. I can take care of it if I have to.

TIPPIN. Yeah. Oh, yeahhh. You the man I been wantin' all along. Take me on. (*He takes out his knife.*)

PURCELL. I don't intend to fight with you, Sergeant.

TIPPIN. Nawww. Look at this! New Army! Am I right? (*no response*) Damn right I'm right. Cause Troy J. Tippin is my name. . . . You oppose me, kill me. Come on. (*He triggers the knife.*) I give this Army everything I got to give. (*a step*) You can't, I can. Old Army.

(*He lunges for* PURCELL, *who drops to one knee, works bolt, fires.* TIPPIN *spins from the impact and falls. Long pause.* PURCELL *goes to look at him. Holds the rifle out behind him, without looking.* CLAYTON *comes and takes it.* PURCELL *exits as the troops open a path for him.*

During this, in the distance, the voice of SERGEANT PETERS, *of* CHARLIE COMPANY, *approaches, counting cadence.*)

SERGEANT PETERS (*off*). Gimme yer left, gimme yer left, gimme yer left, right, left. Hut hut hut haw. (*He begins a cadence song:*) "Ain't no need in goin' home."

CHARLIE COMPANY. "Honey, honey."

SERGEANT PETERS. "Ain't no need in coming home."

CHARLIE COMPANY. "Ba—abe."

SERGEANT PETERS. "Ain't no need in going home.
          Jody's got yo' gal and gone."

CHARLIE COMPANY. "Honey, ba—aby, mine."

SERGEANT PETERS. "If I die in a combat zone."

CHARLIE COMPANY. "Honey, honey."

SERGEANT PETERS. "If I die in a combat zone."

CHARLIE COMPANY. "Ba—abe."

SERGEANT PETERS. "If I die in a combat zone,
      Box me up and ship me home."
(THE CURTAIN BEGINS TO DROP.)

CHARLIE COMPANY. "Honey, ba—aby, mine."

(*They are right beside Able Company now, and the noise is extreme, as* PETERS *calls for a cadence count.*)

SERGEANT PETERS. Count, cadence, count!

CHARLIE COMPANY (*at the top of their lungs*). "One! Two! Three! Four! One! Two! Three! Four!"

(*The sound diminishes as they go away.* CURTAIN *should be closed by now.*)

SERGEANT PETERS. Count, cadence, count.

CHARLIE COMPANY. "One two three four. One two three four."

SERGEANT PETERS (*his voice dying away in the distance*). Hut hut hut haw. Hut hut hut haw.

CURTAIN

HONEYMOON IN HAITI

WILLIAM KLEB

Presented January 20, 1965, at the School of Drama,
Yale University, with the following cast:

THE PRINCE   Ralph Bates
THE WAITER   Alan Skog
THE PRINCESS   Minnie Gaster

Directed by Frank McMullan
Settings by James F. Göhl
Costumes by James B. Harris   Lighting by Margaret Turrill

SCENE: *The veranda of one of a row of cabanas overlooking a
Haitian village and commanding a spectacular view of the Caribbean
Sea.*

*During the twenties and thirties this small, French-speaking town
had been a fashionable—if slightly recherché—winter resort, offering
among its several attractions a particularly languid and hypnotic
climate as well as a native population that had been found on numerous
occasions to be unusually congenial. As a result of the town's sudden
popularity, a luxurious Hotel (La Victoire) with an accompanying
Casino had been erected, fronting on a lingering boardwalk and at
the base of the cliff upon which was perched this row of picturesque*

153

cabanas: favorite quarters of those desiring to withdraw from the more obtrusive social atmosphere of the Hotel below.

These days, however, due in part to an increasingly anxious political situation (internal unrest coupled with the ever-present threat of external intervention) and to an even greater degree due to the cruel whimsy of those who dictate fashion, the Hotel Victoire is no longer considered the "dernier cri."

In fact, for some years now, the town's population, so dependent upon the appetencies of its former guests, has gradually dwindled, leaving only what might be called a "skeleton crew" at the Hotel to accommodate those few nostalgic visitors who do occasionally return in January or February to indulge their memories in one or another of the favorite island specialities.

AT CURTAIN: *It is mid-July, around seven in the evening, hot, bright and breathless. The jungle behind the cabana is thick and dark and green. The edge of the veranda is downstage, the audience being what the characters will refer to as "the view." On the veranda, which is set precariously on several suspicious-looking wooden posts, are a wicker table and two wicker chairs: as everything else, nicely weathered. At the back is a door leading into a bedroom and hung with a bamboo curtain; a window, also curtained, looks onto the veranda and the view beyond.*

To approach the cabana one must ascend a rather risky wooden footpath and cross a small, narrow bridge.

The place has not been entirely abandoned to the jungle though for there is a large vase of freshly cut flowers on the table and a faded cushion or two in the chairs.

As the CURTAIN GOES UP *the stage is empty.*

THE PRINCE'*s voice is the first to be heard and he appears almost immediately thereafter, striding gingerly along the path and crossing the bridge.*

THE PRINCE. (*Coming into view: a man past middle age, above average height, carefully dressed in a tropical suit and an interesting tie and wearing sunglasses. He still has a full head of hair—dark—and might once have been good looking.*) Ah yes, here we are. Here we are, Lucille! Just as I remember it! Just a few steps farther my dear. Yes, yes. Come along. Come along.

(*A* WAITER *is the next to appear: huge, muscular, Negro, wearing a white jacket and carrying a tray upon which rests a bottle of champagne and two glasses.*)

Oh, it looks just the same. (*Calling back down the path to someone as yet out of sight.*) In a minute you'll be able to see the view Lucille! It's divine! Come along, my dear.

(THE PRINCESS LUCILLE *appears, grasping what there is of a rail in both hands and teetering along on a pair of three-inch heels. She too is past middle age, colorfully dressed in a flowered frock and matching hat and also wearing sunglasses.*)
Careful, it's narrow there. Oops. That's right my dear. Step there. Now there. Now careful.

(THE PRINCESS *steps onto the bridge. There is the sound of cracking wood. A horrified look comes across her face. She freezes.*)
Oh. (*To* THE WAITER:) Here, here, let me have that. (*He takes the tray.*) Don't move my dear. I'm sending the waiter. Just hold on, hold on. . . . (THE WAITER *reaches* THE PRINCESS *and helps her along.*) O.K. O.K. Now . . . now careful . . . careful, careful, careful. Now step, that's it. (THE PRINCESS *has made it.* THE PRINCE *turns and walks grandly onto the veranda.*) Here we are. Ah, at last. Come along my dear.

(THE WAITER *helps* THE PRINCESS *onto the veranda. She collapses into a wicker chair and kicks off her shoes.* THE PRINCE *hands the tray back to* THE WAITER *who takes it and remains standing motionless.*)
Look! The view! What a view. I'd forgotten. There's simply no view like that in the Western Hemisphere! It's divine. (*noticing* THE PRINCESS) My dear, are you all right?

THE PRINCESS (*at last regaining her breath*). I could've been killed! *I could have been killed!* Just what in hell do you mean bringing me up here, Harold?

THE PRINCE (*unaffected by this, he tests the table for dust*). Well my dear, I'm terribly sorry, I had no idea it would be so run down.

THE PRINCESS. Run down? It shoulda been condemned twenty years ago. Would you look at the roof? It's caving in. I want to go straight back down to the Hotel, Harold! I am not staying overnight in this place. It's uncivilized!

THE PRINCE. Now my dear, my dear, you mustn't get excited. You know your heart.

THE PRINCESS. What do you mean my heart? There's nothing wrong with my heart except that you just made me climb the side of a cliff that would scare the piss out of a mountain goat!

THE PRINCE. Really Lucille, your language.

THE PRINCESS. My language hell. Honey, this place is uncivilized. It's falling down. I was almost killed on that ridiculous bridge and you're trying to tell me we're going to spend a week up here? You must be out of your god-damned mind Harold.

THE PRINCE. Oh look, fresh flowers, how nice.

THE PRINCESS. Harold, are you listening to me?

THE PRINCE. And there's a telegram. (*He tears it open.*)

THE PRINCESS. Harold!

THE PRINCE (*completely ignoring her*). Shall I read it? (*She shrugs and takes a compact out of her purse.*) "To their Highnesses the Prince and Princess Hohenhagen." How nice. "Have a terrific honeymoon kids. Stop. Life begins at . . . seventy-five." Well really! (*He tears it up.*)

THE PRINCESS (*laughing*). Oh Harold honey, it's just a joke. It's a joke. Who's it from, the girls?

THE PRINCE (*taking the flowers out of the vase and marching to the rail*). My dear that joke was in abominable taste. Seventy-five indeed. I don't know where you pick up people like Irene Davis and Bunny Gross and the rest of the "girls," Lucille, but my advice is to get rid of them immediately. (*He throws the flowers over the edge.*) Oh, look, there goes the boat. They're vulgar and they have no morals and what's worse they have no sense of humor.

THE PRINCESS (*looking up from her compact*). What boat?

THE PRINCE. They say that Davis woman is just this side of nymphomania.

THE PRINCESS. Harold, what boat?

THE PRINCE. The boat we came on of course. (*He is testing the rail.*)

THE PRINCESS. Well, where in hell's it going?

THE PRINCE. Oh back to Porte au Prince I suppose—I don't know.

THE PRINCESS. You mean it doesn't stay here? You mean, well Harold, how in hell do we get out of here?

THE PRINCE (*turning back to the table*). Oh it comes back my dear. It comes back. Ah, le champagne. Mettez-le la. Bon.

(THE WAITER, *who has been standing at attention directly behind the table, puts down the tray.*)

THE PRINCESS. When?

THE PRINCE. (*Tests the temperature of the wine—not quite right. He returns it to the bucket.*) Oh once a day my dear, or is it twice? Or is it every other day? Oh well, I'm not sure about this time of year. They've raised their rates too I've noticed. Outrageous. Twenty-five dollars one way. Honestly, the things people get away with these days.

THE PRINCESS. Harold—

THE PRINCE. Of course Vivian and I used to come down in February and that may have made a difference. At any rate, it was much cheaper as I remember. Everything was cheaper then. But I just don't know how things work in July. They may raise their prices in the summer but then, on the other hand, one would expect them to be lower wouldn't one? The prices. After all, it is the off season. (*He has produced a handkerchief and is dusting the table and a chair—which he finds rather unsteady.*)

THE PRINCESS (*returning to her make-up*). Harold honey, I am not spending the night up here.

THE PRINCE. But my dear, it's so magnificent, so green, so private. And soon there will be shadows and a lovely breeze and the nights, Lucille! Wait until you see the stars down here. I have never seen so many shooting stars. (*turning back to her, cajoling*) And it's really much nicer than the main building, Lucille. Really. With all those tourist people. Let me tell you my dear, Vivian and I stayed down there once and it was unbearable. I . . . well, I lost over a hundred thousand at chemmy and what with everyone running about it was simply impossible to be alone. (*He reflects.*) Impossible.

THE PRINCESS. For god's sake Harold, act your age.

THE PRINCE. Lucille, there is no need to be unpleasant.

THE PRINCESS. Well honey, I didn't see anyone at that Hotel at all. Not a soul—

THE PRINCE. Just what do you mean by "act your age"?

THE PRINCESS. Nothing Harold, nothing. You are so sensitive.

THE PRINCE (*after a pause*). Sometimes I don't think you're in love with me, Lucille.

THE PRINCESS. Oh really Harold, are we going to go into that again? I married you didn't I? I agreed to come down here to this Porto des whatever it is . . . in the middle of July—

THE PRINCE. Well sometimes I think you despise me.

THE PRINCESS. Harold, just because I object to this *place* you've brought me to doesn't mean I despise you. I just don't see why, since you're so set on this honeymoon business, why we couldn't have gone to Switzerland or Denmark or someplace not quite so close to the equator.

THE PRINCE (*exiting through the bamboo door into the bedroom*). Well I like it here. And I thought you would too.

THE PRINCESS (*calling after him*). Well, I don't. No one comes to Haiti in July, Harold! No one! And besides, I have a million-and-one things to do in New York. We could have taken a nice suite at the St. Regis for a few days or gone out to Irene's place in Southampton while the movers . . . (*She catches herself.*)

THE PRINCE (*off*). What dear?

THE PRINCESS. Nothing Harold, nothing. I just said I have a million-and-one things to do in New York, that's all. (*To herself:*) God, it is simply suffocating up here. (*She notices* THE WAITER *standing by the unopened bottle of champagne.*) Listen sweetheart. Could you open the champagne? (THE WAITER *remains blank.*) You don't speak English do you? Anglais?

THE WAITER. Non Votre Altesse. Je parle seulement le français.

THE PRINCESS. It figures. Ouvrez, O.K.?

THE WAITER. (*Still blank, but taking the bottle from the cooler he slowly, elaborately, almost with ceremony, begins to open it.*) Oui, Votre Altesse.

THE PRINCESS. You have enormous hands honey, you know that?

THE WAITER (*stopping, putting the bottle down and standing to attention*). Pardon Votre Altesse?

THE PRINCESS. Nothing dear, rien. Your hands, they're divine. Eh bien, as they say.

THE WAITER. Pardon Votre Altesse?

(THE PRINCESS *looks at him for a moment, then smiles slightly to herself.*)

THE PRINCESS. Nothing dear. Nothing. Oh what the hell. (*She opens her purse, takes out a bill and gives it to him.*) That's 'cause you have such gorgeous hands. Ton mains. Comprends? Now just ouvrez, O.K.? Your mother's parched.

THE WAITER (*accepting the money and returning to the bottle*). Merci, Votre Altesse.

THE PRINCE (*re-entering, he has resumed his cheerful attitude*). Well my dear, it seems to be quite all right in there. Everything in order. A trifle musty perhaps, but clean. I'll have them send up some more fresh flowers and everything will be cheerful and gay. (*He comes up behind her, leans down and kisses her on the cheek.*) I'm sorry Lucille, we mustn't start out our honeymoon with an argument now must we dear?

THE PRINCESS (*pulling away*). Harold, I am trying very hard to be pleasant but honey I am not staying here overnight. Can we just get that straight? I don't care how green and private it is. It's unsafe. It's falling down.

THE PRINCE. Now, now Lucille. (*He takes the unopened bottle from* THE WAITER.) Here, I'll do that.

THE PRINCESS. And there are probably a million snakes and lizards and things and well, my dear, I'm just not going to subject myself— (*She is working on her lipstick.*)

THE PRINCE (*struggling with the cork while* THE WAITER *watches impassively*). Nonsense Lucille, nonsense—

THE PRINCESS. Nonsense? Look at it. Will you just try to look at it objectively? It may have been divine when you and your first wife were here in 1933, but honey right now it's falling into the Caribbean Sea!

THE PRINCE. Now just relax my dear, relax. You're simply acting like a child. Now we're going to have a nice cool glass of wine to celebrate our first day together as man and wife. Then you'll feel much better. We mustn't let a silly little argument spoil a day like this now must we?

THE PRINCESS. Listen Harold. Why don't you just let the waiter do it hunh? I'm dying for a drink. (*She puts away her cosmetics.*)

THE PRINCE. And soon there will be shadows and a lovely breeze off the sea and then the sun will set just over there and everything will be lovely. . . . (*Over his shoulder, rapidly, to* THE WAITER:) Les baggages.

THE WAITER. Votre Altesse!

THE PRINCESS (*forcing her shoes back on*). You should have been a poet, Harold.

THE PRINCE. Well actually my dear I have published a line or two. Nothing elaborate. When I was younger. . . .

(*At that moment a crackle—like gunfire—is heard in the jungle behind.* THE WAITER, *who is crossing the bridge, freezes.* THE PRINCE *and* PRINCESS *look up, puzzled.*)

THE PRINCESS. What's that?

THE PRINCE. I don't know.

THE PRINCESS. It sounds like firecrackers.

THE PRINCE. Well, perhaps someone's celebrating something.

(*At the same moment they see* THE WAITER *standing motionless on the bridge, listening. They watch him as the sound continues. Then suddenly the cork—alarmingly, unexpectedly—pops out of the bottle and sails into the jungle. The bottle gushes beautifully and everyone is startled, including* THE WAITER, *who hurries away down the path.* THE PRINCE *hastens to cope with the overflowing champagne and* THE PRINCESS *keeps her skirts out of the way.*)

THE PRINCE. Oh. Ah. Ha. Here we are. The glasses, quick.

THE PRINCESS. Be careful Harold. Be careful.

THE PRINCE. Here we are. Here we are. My goodness wasn't that unexpected?

THE PRINCESS (*back to her shoes*). Where'd he go in such a hurry?

THE PRINCE (*pouring*). I'm having some hors d'oeuvres sent up. I thought they might be pleasant with the wine. Here we are. Here we are. (*He hands her a full glass.*)

THE PRINCESS (*downing it, practically in one gulp*). Thank god.

THE PRINCE. Oh my dear! Really! A toast! A toast!

THE PRINCESS (*holding out her empty glass*). Sorry. (*He refills it.*)

THE PRINCE. To us.

THE PRINCESS. To us.

THE PRINCE. And really Lucille my dear you shouldn't drink quite so fast you know. In this heat. You'll get a headache.

THE PRINCESS (*avoiding an affectionate hug, she rises from her chair and walks cautiously to the railing*). I already have a headache. (*She touches it suspiciously and looks over the edge.*) Harold, it's suffocating up here. It must be a hundred and thirty. I really would like to get back down on solid ground, O.K.?

THE PRINCE (*pursuing her, lovingly*). Lucille. . . .

THE PRINCESS (*moving away*). Now this is no reflection on my love for you or anything Harold but this place makes me uncomfortable. There isn't anything below us.

THE PRINCE. Nonsense my dear. Soon there will be shadows and a lovely breeze—

THE PRINCESS (*irritated*). Why do you keep saying that?!

THE PRINCE. Just look at the view, Lucille. You can see everything from up here. And relax, I think the climb did you good. You're looking twenty years younger . . . (*She gives him a withering look.*) You know Vivian always used to say that the sea reminded her of a big blue diamond. I think that was it. A blue diamond. And that the hills were the perfect setting . . . green velvet. Just like a gigantic display at Van Cleef and Arpels—

THE PRINCESS. You're such a romantic, Harold.

THE PRINCE (*pausing sensitively*). Well yes, I suppose in a way

I am. Oh, I know it sounds silly, but well, the world's so . . . I don't
know, so cynical these days. I was just saying to Emmett Frazer the
other day—we had lunch at the Cloche d'Or, awful—I was just saying
to Emmett Frazer, the other day, no one thinks about anything but
money anymore. Money and sex. (*She has left his side.*) It's so de-
pressing. Lucille?

THE PRINCESS (*fanning herself with her handkerchief*). God.

THE PRINCE. Well, it's the American way, my dear, isn't it? American materialism. I thank god we don't have to worry about things like
that. Don't you? Don't you Lucille? (*He puts his hand on the railing
and a portion of it breaks away, falling into space.*)

THE PRINCESS (*turning abruptly*). Harold will you please—?
(*noticing that he is looking over the edge*) What's the matter?

THE PRINCE (*looking up*). Oh, oh nothing, nothing. You're empty
again my dear, aren't you? Here let me. (*He takes her glass and goes
to the table.*) When Vivian and I were here in '33 on our honeymoon
we would just sit for hours and hours . . . just where you're standing
now . . . poor Vivian . . .

(THE PRINCESS, *very bored, turns away and walks to the opposite
end of the veranda. When her back is turned,* THE PRINCE *carefully,
surreptitiously withdraws a small bottle from his coat pocket and starts
to open it as he talks, his back to* THE PRINCESS.)

She belonged to another age really. Another era. I proposed to her
on the very night she was elected an honorary member of the I.W.W.
Her father was worried. She had so many bizarre interests—

THE PRINCESS (*suddenly turning and cutting him off. He freezes
for an instant and then quickly puts the bottle back into his pocket.*)
Oh will you cut it out, Harold?! Where's my drink?

THE PRINCE (*regaining his poise*). Oh, ah, yes, here you are my
dear . . . (*He hands it to her.*)

THE PRINCESS. Can I have a cigarette?

THE PRINCE. Certainly my dear. (*He produces a pack of cigarettes,
offers her one and lights it.*)

THE PRINCESS. (*Inhaling deeply, she takes her glass and walks
back to the rail. She seems to have gained new strength.*) I'm sorry
Harold, honey, what were you saying? (*She is resigned.*)

THE PRINCE. Oh, well, I, I was just saying . . . oh yes, about
poor Vivian. Well, she was a communist, but in the end we convinced
her that the depression couldn't last forever, no matter how much fun
it was. And after all Lucille. . . . (*he comes up to her and slips his*

arm around her waist) there have been Princesses Hohenhagen for over four hundred years you know.

THE PRINCESS. Harold—

THE PRINCE. (*His grip tightening on her waist. He could be about to kiss her—or hurl her over the edge.*) Since 1536 to be exact.

THE PRINCESS. Harold, I . . . let go. (*She breaks away with some difficulty.*) Please! Now Harold I . . . I've made a decision. (THE PRINCE, *in his turn, stares out at the sea and though we cannot see his eyes, exasperation can be noticed in the firm set of his lips.*) I . . . I want to go back to New York.

THE PRINCE. (*Irritated, he goes back to the table and pours himself a drink.*) Nonsense my dear, nonsense.

THE PRINCESS. No Harold, no really—

THE PRINCE. Did you know that Vivian's great-grandmother had been a gypsy? A Roumanian gypsy?

THE PRINCESS. Harold—!

THE PRINCE. (*They look at each other. A moment passes.*) Lucille my dear, please. . . .

THE PRINCESS (*walking to the back of the veranda with a sigh*). Oh what the hell. (*She looks critically at the cabana.*)

THE PRINCE (*lighting a cigarette*). Don't . . . don't you think that's romantic? I mean about Vivian's great-grandmother being a Roumanian gypsy. (*He downs his second glass and pours another . . . which he also drinks rather hastily.*) And Vivian was rather dark. But she had a good heart. Her father came to America in nineteen hundred and made a fortune in canned soups. (*He has finished his third glass and pours another.*)

THE PRINCESS (*looking out at the undergrowth*). Harold, honey, would you mind if we didn't talk about your first wife, O.K.?

THE PRINCE. Why, why yes, of course. I'm sorry dear.

THE PRINCESS (*turning back to the table, where she puts out her cigarette*). It reminds me of my first husband. (*She lights another.*) Good old Walter. *We* went to Biarritz on our honeymoon. He rented a villa for the entire season.

(*Again the crackle of gunfire is heard in the jungle behind. They both look up, pause and then go on—dismissing it as a celebration.*)

THE PRINCE. Biarritz? Well, personally I never cared much for Biarritz. It always seemed to be raining. The last time I was there I lost over a hundred thousand at chemmy.

THE PRINCESS. Walter used to say I was the most beautiful woman in the world.

THE PRINCE. Oh you still are, my dear, quite attractive.

THE PRINCESS. Good god, a forty-two-room villa for an entire season. We did nothing but play bridge and make love. Walter wasn't much good at either, but he was mad about me.

THE PRINCE (*conversational*). And he left you everything when he died?

THE PRINCESS. Every penny. (*She refills her glass.*) Poor Walter. He . . . well he died in a plane crash. Did I ever tell you that story? He, well his plane crashed into a mountain in Switzerland. They had a terrible time getting the body down. He was all frozen. . . .

THE PRINCE (*turning back to her, again cheerful*). Well, all that's in the past isn't it my dear? Walter's crash. Vivian's heart. Vivian died of a heart attack. No one ever dreamed she had a weak heart. We had a very simple service for her in the little church you passed on the way from the boat. Oh look, isn't that the boat coming back now?

THE PRINCESS (*turning*). Here? She died here?

THE PRINCE. Yes, didn't anyone tell you? But let's not talk about her. I think I see the boat. See? Over there. . . .

THE PRINCESS. The boat, where?

THE PRINCE. There. Over there. Come here. You can see it from here. (*He motions for her to join him at the edge.*) There, do you see it?

THE PRINCESS. No. Where?

THE PRINCE (*moving behind her*). Isn't . . . that . . . it?

THE PRINCESS (*quickly, moving away with disgust*). No. No, I don't see anything. (*She slaps a mosquito.*) And these damn mosquitoes are driving me out of my mind.

THE PRINCE. Oh, ah, well, I was sure I saw it. Just a point of light I guess, playing across the waves. Across the endless sea, as Vivian used to say. . . .

THE PRINCESS (*turning to face him*). Harold, honey, your first wife died right here? Here?

THE PRINCE (*returns to the table to refill his glass*). Yes, didn't anyone tell you? The summer of '43 I think it was. Naturally I was heart-broken. I haven't been back since.

THE PRINCESS. But Harold, why, why would you want to come back now? For another honeymoon of all things. It must be filled with awful memories.

THE PRINCE. Oh no, no, no, on the contrary, the happiest days of my life have been spent here. The Hotel Victoire was divine then, really the dernier cri. They had everything. Of course one had to book months in advance. Months and months. But they did have everything. (*He comes up to her, his voice becoming smooth and romantic.*) Ah Lucille, my dear, you have made me so happy.

(*There is a long pause as their sunglasses meet.*)

THE PRINCESS (*finally speaking*). Harold, honey, there is something I want to say. Now I want you to just be quiet for a minute and let me finish. I'm very fond of you Harold . . . but . . . well . . . I want a divorce.

THE PRINCE (*after a pause*). I beg your pardon.

THE PRINCESS (*walking past him, back to the table, where she lights another cigarette*). A divorce Harold. A divorce. I've decided I don't want to go on with this ridiculous charade any longer.

THE PRINCE (*after a pause he finally turns to her*). But Lucille I . . . I thought you loved me. (*He takes a few steps toward her. She is still at the table, her back to him.*) And after all, we've only been married . . . (*he looks at his watch*) eight hours.

THE PRINCESS. Well, I don't love you Harold. I never have. I'm taking advantage of you. I needed someone *like* you Harold, and you were the only one around. But I guess I made a mistake.

THE PRINCE. What do you mean?

THE PRINCESS (*still with her back to him*). That's all I have to say. I'm sorry Harold, I feel rotten about this but I just don't think we can make it work. I don't think I can LIVE with you.

(THE PRINCE *is standing directly behind her. She is trying to be sympathetic yet firm: she knows how much he loves her and would like to spare him any unnecessary pain. After a moment* THE PRINCE—*very deliberately*—*lifts his glass and pours it down the back of her dress. General confusion.*)

THE PRINCESS. Oh! Harold! Oh for Christ's sake! Look what you've done! Really! I'm soaked!

THE PRINCE (*simultaneously pulling out his handkerchief*). I'm terribly sorry my dear. Terribly sorry. So stupid of me. I'm awfully sorry. (*leading her to the door of the bedroom*) There are fresh towels in there. I'm terribly sorry, why don't you try to . . . oh dear, I'm terribly sorry.

THE PRINCESS. Really Harold, how can you be so god-damned clumsy?! Christ!

THE PRINCE (*all but pushing her into the cabana*). Just through there. . . .

THE PRINCESS. No! I am not going in there! It's unsafe!

THE PRINCE. Nonsense, nonsense.

THE PRINCESS. No Harold, no, I'm—

THE PRINCE. It's quite all right. There are towels by the bed—

THE PRINCESS (*disappearing through the bamboo curtain*). Harold . . . Harold. . . .

THE PRINCE. Now, now my dear, just by the bed. Do you see them? By the bed. (*He walks quickly back to the table where she has set her glass of wine.*)

THE PRINCESS (*off*). This place is filthy!

THE PRINCE. Nonsense, my dear, it's just your imagination. (*He produces the bottle once again, keeping his back to the cabana.*) Did you find the towels? They should be right there by the bed. On the chair. Did you find them?

THE PRINCESS. What?

THE PRINCE. The towels.

THE PRINCESS. Yes. They're filthy too.

THE PRINCE. Nonsense my dear, nonsense.

(*Just as he pours the contents of the bottle into* THE PRINCESS'S *glass* THE WAITER *enters along the path with two huge suitcases. He is unnoticed by* THE PRINCE, *who picks up the two glasses of wine and advances to meet* THE PRINCESS, *who is just emerging from the cabana, towel in hand, trying to dry her dress.*)

THE PRINCE (*beaming*). Ah my dear, everything all right? I'm so sorry. Can you forgive me? (THE PRINCESS *is mumbling curses under her breath.*) Here, here my dear, a fresh glass.

THE PRINCESS. Harold did you take a good look at that place? It's horrible. It has a mosquito net and a double bed . . .! (*Just as she is accepting her glass she notices* THE WAITER *coming onto the veranda with the bags.*) Harold. (THE PRINCE *turns, following her gaze.*) What's he doing with my bags? Didn't you tell him we weren't staying up here?

THE PRINCE (*rather nervous*). Oh, well, my dear, cheers! I, well . . . I thought you might change your mind. Cheers.

THE PRINCESS (*setting her glass down on the table*). No. No, definitely not. In fact I don't want to spend another minute in this ridiculous banana port. I'm sorry Harold, I want you to call that boat right now and get it out here. Wherever it is. I want to go back to New York tonight.

THE PRINCE. Well my dear really—

THE PRINCESS (*gathering her purse*). Tonight!

THE PRINCE. Well, I'm afraid that's impossible; it'll be dark soon and—

THE PRINCESS. Listen, there's a phone in the bedroom. Use it. Tell them you'll pay anything they ask but get us out of here. I'm sorry, Harold honey, hot weather brings out the worst in me. I find it very difficult to be pleasant with sweat running down my back!

THE PRINCE. Lucille now stop it—!

THE PRINCESS. And these god-damned mosquitoes—!

THE PRINCE. Stop it—!

THE PRINCESS. Harold, I've had just about enough out of you—!

THE PRINCE. Lucille!

(*Suddenly there is another volley of gunfire in the jungle: much closer and much more violent. It is obviously gunfire because splinters fly and the vase on the table is broken.*

For a moment everyone is frozen. Then both THE PRINCE *and* PRINCESS *race for the cabana in confusion.* THE WAITER *crouches behind the suitcases, produces a revolver and begins firing back down the path. Another burst from the unseen attackers and all is quiet. The silence endures.* THE PRINCE *and* PRINCESS *are out of sight. After a few moments* THE WAITER—*who has been wounded in the arm— moves cautiously away from the protection of the suitcases and down the path.*

More silence: the stage is empty.)

THE PRINCESS (*a voice*). What the hell's going on Harold? Harold? For god's sake get up. Jesus. (*a pause*) Give me your handkerchief. (*another pause*) Harold! For Christ's sake pull yourself together and give me your handkerchief! (*After a moment* THE PRINCESS's *hand emerges, waving* THE PRINCE's *white handkerchief.*)

THE PRINCE (*a whisper*). What . . . what's happening?

THE PRINCESS. I don't know.

THE PRINCE. Do you see anyone?

THE PRINCESS. No, now shut up will you and give me the phone. I'm going to call the American Embassy and find out what in hell's going on up here. (*a pause*) Harold! Get up and give me that phone! (*From one side of the door a phone is pushed across on the floor to a hand on the other side.*) Oh for Christ's sake. Hello? Hello? Hello? . . . Hello?

THE PRINCE. (*His voice remains a whisper in contrast to hers, which gradually regains its normal tone.*) Lucille?

THE PRINCESS. It . . . it seems to be dead.

THE PRINCE. Dead? Oh my god. Oh my god. (*a pause*) Lucille, what are we going to do? Lucille?

THE PRINCESS. Shut up.

(*Her hand appears again and waves the handkerchief. After a minute of this,* THE PRINCESS's *head emerges. Then, summoning her courage, she comes onto the veranda, staying very close to the building and looking around cautiously. Every now and then she waves the handkerchief.*)

THE PRINCE. Lucille! Don't go out! They might attack!

THE PRINCESS (*low*). Shut up.

(*The sound of gunfire again in the jungle but this time in the distance.* THE PRINCESS *prepares to rush back inside the cabana but her curiosity gets the better and she decides to try to find out from which direction it is coming.*)

THE PRINCE (*still invisible, his voice an urgent whisper*). Lucille!

THE PRINCESS (*edging away from the door*). I think, I think it's coming from down by the Hotel.

THE PRINCE. What?

THE PRINCESS. I said it's coming from down by the Hotel!

(*She is watching and listening closely.* THE PRINCE's *head emerges for the first time: about knee level.*)

THE PRINCE. Lucille, what's happening?

THE PRINCESS. I don't know. It's stopped. I don't think they were shooting at us. I think they hit the waiter. I think they were trying to get the waiter.

(*There is a pause while they wait for more shots, but none occur.* THE PRINCESS *finally gets up enough courage to go to the table for a cigarette, always on the alert.*)

THE PRINCE. Lucille! Stay back! What . . . what are we going to do?

THE PRINCESS (*lighting a cigarette*). Shut up. (*There is a pause. She takes several deep drags which restore her confidence. She is thinking.*)

THE PRINCE. Lucille?

THE PRINCESS (*turning and seeing his ridiculous posture*). Oh, pull yourself together Harold. It's stopped. Now the way I see it is we've gotten ourselves into some sort of a revolution or something . . . you know how these South American countries are. Don't they all have communists running around in the hills and things? Well, what we've got to do is figure out a way to get the hell out of here. Now the shooting seems to be coming from down by the Hotel . . . Harold, are you paying attention to me?

(THE WAITER *has re-entered. His arm is bandaged and blood is seeping through. He has a sub-machine gun slung over his shoulder and carries another bottle of champagne and a tray of hors d'oeuvres.*)

Harold. . . .

(THE PRINCE *is staring past her at* THE WAITER. *She realizes that something other than herself has his attention and turns to see what it is. Her amazement is profound. To herself:*)

Good god.

(THE WAITER *walks onto the veranda and sets down the second bottle of champagne and the hors d'oeuvres on the table. He straightens up. There is a moment's silence, then he begins to speak:*)

THE WAITER. Vos Altesses. La direction de l'Hôtel Victoire demande pardon à Vos Altesses pour ce regrettable incident . . . que Vos Altesses se rassurent, cela ne reproduira pas; ils sont tous morts. (*His voice begins to change. His fists clench and after a pause he goes on.*) C'étaient des saboteurs . . . des saboteurs venus de l'autre côté de la frontière. . . . (*He is attempting to control himself but his voice has become low and passionate, trembling with hate.*) Des communistes. Des communistes qui, qui essayaient de faire sauter notre hôtel. (THE PRINCE *and* PRINCESS *are watching him, speechless.*) Et ils voulaient aussi faire sauter le casino. Notre casino! La semaine dernière, ces salauds-là ont attaqué la centrale et . . . et ils ont tué mon frère. (*a pause*) Mais on les a bien eus: on les a tous abattus, les salauds, tous. . . . Et c'est ce qui attend tous ceux qui essairiont de faire sauter notre hôtel: on les crévera tous! Tous!

(*His speech, kept low and intense, has however risen to a crescendo of hate. Suddenly he stops. There is a moment, and then he quickly opens the second bottle of champagne.*)

THE PRINCESS. (*As the cork goes off she is brought back to herself. In one swift movement she walks to the table, sweeps up her things and starts swiftly—if a little unsteadily—to the steps leading down.*) Come on Harold! We're getting out of here! I'm not staying another minute in this place! COME ON Harold! We'll just have to take the chance. But I'm not staying another minute—! (*She is just about to cross the bridge.*)

THE WAITER (*brusque, a command*). Madame!

(THE PRINCESS *freezes.*)

Votre Altesse . . il y aurait peut-être quelque danger à descendre tout de suite. Peut-être vaudrait il mieux attendre la nuit . . .

THE PRINCESS (*after a moment, her back to the veranda*). What's he saying Harold? Harold?

THE PRINCE (*still in the cabana but on his feet now*). He, ah . . . he ah says that it might be safer if we waited until after dark . . . to go down . . . to the Hotel. . . .

THE PRINCESS (*another pause*). Why?

THE PRINCE. He . . . well there still may be saboteurs around, communists from across the border and—

THE WAITER. Vous serez plus en sécurité ici.

THE PRINCE. Ah, he says we'll be safer here Lucille. (THE PRINCESS *doesn't move.*) I, I'm sorry, I, I want to leave as much as you do Lucille but well . . . it'll be dark soon and if he thinks that it's safer . . . I mean after all . . . if it's safer. . . .

(*There is a long pause. Finally* THE PRINCESS *turns abruptly, climbs quickly back onto the veranda, goes to the table, throws down her purse, downs her glass of champagne, refills it, eats an hors d'oeuvre and walks to the railing.*)

THE PRINCE (*still inside, not quite sure which glass she has drunk and afraid to say anything at all*). Lucille?

(*No response.* THE PRINCESS *merely stares in fury at "the view."*)

THE WAITER (*producing a revolver from under his white jacket*). La direction suggère que vous preniez ceci . . . simple précaution. . . .

THE PRINCE. Oh no, no that's not . . . (THE PRINCESS *turns back to them very slowly.*) It's ah . . . I'm . . . ah sure it's not necessary. Pas nécessaire.

(THE WAITER *makes a bow as if to take it back.*)

THE PRINCESS. No. Keep it.

THE PRINCE. Oh. Well, all right, if you think we should but . . . Thank you, thank you, that's all . . . that will be all. (*He emerges a few steps from the cabana, fumbling in his pockets for some change to tip.*) Ah . . . ah . . . I, I don't seem to have . . . I seem to be out of change . . . do, do you have . . . anything my dear?

(THE PRINCESS *marches quickly, furiously, to the table and dumps the contents of her purse on it. She grabs up all her money and gives it to* THE WAITER.)

THE WAITER (*not in the least amazed by the large sum he is receiving*). Merci Votre Altesse.

THE PRINCE. Lucille! My dear! (*Though he is shocked he keeps his voice down and is constantly, nervously, keeping his eye out for the "saboteurs" in the jungle.*)

THE PRINCESS (*pouring yet another glass of wine*). You better have him leave the sub-machine gun too.

THE WAITER. Vos Altesses. (*He backs off the veranda. When he gets to the bridge he turns, crouches and rushes off.*)

THE PRINCE. Lucille! You shouldn't over-tip the waiters. They'll think they can take advantage of you.

THE PRINCESS (*sitting*). Great!

THE PRINCE (*still practically inside the cabana*). No telling what he'll expect next time.

THE PRINCESS. Shut up Harold honey, you make me sick! (*She kicks off her shoes.*)

(*There is a long pause.* THE PRINCE *finally gets up enough courage to sit down next to her. His attention is divided: the poisoned glass and the invisible "saboteurs."*)

THE PRINCE (*his voice low*). Now, now Lucille, I'm very sorry my dear. How was I to know that this would happen? I mean, I—well, . . . I mean after all my dear, I only wanted us to be alone together. Just for a few days. . . .

THE PRINCESS. Shut up Harold.

THE PRINCE. This marriage . . . this marriage is a very important thing to me Lucille . . . (*He pushes the glass towards her.*) I desperately want . . . well, I desperately want things to work out. Lucille I . . . well I love you. I do.

THE PRINCESS (*staring straight ahead*). Harold. You must be out of your mind. I mean didn't you understand what I was saying? A minute ago? Before we were attacked!

THE PRINCE (*keeping his voice down*). Lucille . . . (*he pushes the glass a little closer*) please don't talk so loud.

THE PRINCESS. I want to go back to New York tonight and I want a divorce tomorrow. There are just limits Harold, that's all . . . just limits to what can be endured!

THE PRINCE. But Lucille, I thought you loved me. You said—

THE PRINCESS. I was lying.

THE PRINCE. Lucille. How can you say that? I'm sure you don't mean what you're saying. You said you loved me . . . in New York.

THE PRINCESS (*her anger lessening*). No. No Harold, I don't love you. (*a long silence*) I'm sorry Harold. I'm real fond of you and I know you love me and hell. . . . (*she takes off her sunglasses*) I'm damn sorry I'm hurting you honey but look, I just don't think we could spend too much time together . . . you know what I mean? Time. Living. (*She hiccups.*)

THE PRINCE. I, I don't think you know what you're saying Lucille. I mean, my dear, then, well then, why did you marry me?

THE PRINCESS. Well Harold . . . honey . . . do you really want to know? Really?

THE PRINCE (*pushing the glass under her nose*). Well yes . . . here dear, why don't you finish mine. I think I've had enough.

THE PRINCESS. Harold . . . honey . . . I married you because I'm broke. Flat. I have "run out of gash," as Bunny Gross puts it. The bitch. Do you know what she's trying to do to me . . .?! Well, never mind!

THE PRINCE (*a very, very long pause*). You're what?

THE PRINCESS. I'm sorry, Harold, that's it. Now listen sweetheart, I'm only telling you this so you won't feel so bad about divorcing me, O.K.? What the hell Harold, I'm not worth your love honey. I'm just . . . I'm just a . . . well, never mind. I thought we might make it work, you know. Sort of a marriage of convenience, you know what I mean? But I guess, well, I guess I just hadn't counted on you loving me so much Harold. I know this is a hell of a thing to say but, well the girls and I had a long talk and we decided that I'd just better get married. The bills were piling up. Well you were just about the only eligible bachelor around, I mean really eligible so to speak, and well . . . (*a little self-conscious laugh*) well frankly Harold, well frankly honey, we weren't quite sure about you . . . I mean you know what I mean . . . I mean you know . . . I mean you're so elegant. I mean I'm sure you're just as much of a man as anybody else but . . . ah shit Harold, well jesus, I feel terrible about this. I know how much you love me. (*She pours out another drink, ignoring the full glass before her.*)

THE PRINCE (*after a long pause*). Lucille . . . what do you mean . . . exactly?

THE PRINCESS. I'm broke, honey. Can't you understand English? I'm flat. I even had to sell the apartment to pay my Elizabeth Arden bill—

THE PRINCE. You sold your apartment—?

THE PRINCESS. Hey listen, I'm out of cigarettes, could I have one of yours?

(THE PRINCE *fumbles in his coat—a vague, uncomprehending look on his face.*)

Thanks honey. (*She lights one.*) Now listen, when we get back to the Hotel we'd better call New York and stop the movers. I was having all my furniture moved down to your house in the Village. And we'd better call Cletus too . . . he was going to help me redecorate. I love your house but I can't stand the way it's done. I was going to surprise you. (*She hiccups again.*) Hell. Harold . . . honey . . . listen, I'm sorry. Harold, it won't work and I don't want to make your life hell. It's the only decent thing to do. I mean I won't ask for much alimony: just enough to live on comfortably . . . (*another soul-searching pause*) and, well, you see Harold . . . well I . . . I have a lover. At least I think I do. Anyway. . . . (*her voice grows soft*) he's very young and very handsome and I guess I kinda like him, so you see Harold I could never love you too honey. I already have a lover. Don't you see, Harold? (*She puts her hand understandingly on his.*) Don't you see? Harold?

THE PRINCE (*looking at her*). Yes. So do I.

THE PRINCESS. What dear?

THE PRINCE (*irritated, pulling his hand away and walking to the rail*). I said I have a lover too—a mistress!

THE PRINCESS. Well . . . well Harold I thought . . . I thought you loved me.

THE PRINCE. Love you?! No of course I don't love you. You disgust me. You must put on your lipstick with a palette knife.

THE PRINCESS. ! . . . ! . . . !

THE PRINCE. Lucille, how could you have spent so much money? All that money. It's unnatural!

THE PRINCESS. Harold! Well! Hunh! So I disgust you you little— (*suddenly struck*) well Harold, that's . . . that's great. Harold honey, listen, that's just great. If I disgust you then we don't have to get a divorce do we? I mean you disgust me too. And you have your mistress and I have my lover—(*her tone changes*) Harold, listen, I'm sorry, I didn't mean all those nasty things I said. Listen, everything'll be great, no kidding, once we can get out of this ridiculous place.

THE PRINCE (*his voice high and tense*). Oh, for god's sake shut up Lucille!

THE PRINCESS. Harold, honey . . . (*she is putting her shoes back on*) you're going to love the way I've done the house. Early American downstairs—you know, the real stuff—then French Provincial on the second floor. . . . (*She slaps a mosquito.*) Cletus says we'll need extra supports for the rock garden on the roof but I've always liked natural beams and your house has such possibilities. . . .

THE PRINCE (*who has been pacing nervously, deep in thought, his panic growing*). Shut up Lucille will you?! Shut up, shut up!! I've sold it! I've sold everything! Everything!! Now will you just shut up? I've got to think.

THE PRINCESS. Harold honey, what're you talking about?

THE PRINCE. I sold my house to Geoffrey Jones last week! Now Lucille—

THE PRINCESS. You what?!

THE PRINCE (*his voice shaking*). Lucille, my dear . . . now just a moment ago you said you sold your apartment . . . right? And just a minute before that you said you were broke?!

THE PRINCESS. Well, well yes, that's right! God, these damn mosquitoes are driving me out of my mind! I probably should have told you before we were married, Harold, but well, I didn't want you to think I was . . . (*a little laugh*) marrying you for your money. Now everything's gonna be all right honey, you'll see. How long do you think it'll be before we can get out of here? I really want to get back to New York. It's the only place I really feel at home. You know I get kinda keyed up if I'm away too long.

(THE PRINCE *rushes to the phone, left on the floor by the door. He picks it up and frantically begins playing with the receiver.*)

Harold? What're you doing? It's dead.

(*He remembers.*)

Listen, when we get back down to the Hotel I want to make a phone call. I don't trust that god-damned Bunny Gross!

(THE PRINCE *stands and begins pacing again.*)

She's offered Dickie a job at her place on Long Island, the bitch. Listen, when we get back I'll introduce you to Dickie, Harold. You'll love him. In fact maybe you could help him get set up in a little business. He's sort of a construction worker. I found him in a hole on West Forty-third. He was digging. You should see the size of his hands!

(THE PRINCE, *who has been pacing rapidly, walks quickly to the table, picks up the poisoned glass and starts to take a drink. He realizes what he is about to do and puts it down. He is trying desperately to remain calm.*)

Harold, are you all right? I'm feeling a little dizzy myself. It's this heat. Come on Harold honey, you're not mad at me are you? I thought you loved me, that's all. Here, drink up. (*She offers him the glass but he waves it away and walks to the rail.*) I figure we can finish the second bottle before dark. Hell it's free. (*She slaps at another mosquito and refills her own glass.*) These mosquitoes are driving me out of my mind. Here, light a cigarette. It's an old fisherman's trick. (*She lights two cigarettes.*) Walter taught me. He was a sportsman. Smoke keeps 'em away but you've gotta keep smoking, just keep smoking. . . .

(*She holds one out to him.*)

Here honey. Harold? Aw come on. I was telling Irene just before we left how kinda sweet it was, you bringing me down here for a honeymoon and all. At your age. (*She laughs to herself.*) The same place you and your first wife . . . (*She stops.*) When I kept saying I would just as soon stay in New York. . . . (*She has stopped smoking. A mosquito takes advantage of the pause and gets her. She slaps it.*) Harold? Why, why in hell did you bring me down here? If I disgust you?

(*The sun is beginning to set. The sound of gunfire is heard in the jungle again and completely ignored. It continues intermittently throughout the remainder of the play.*)

Harold . . . why did you bring me here? To this place. Harold?

THE PRINCE. I, I . . . well I thought you . . . I thought you . . . you were worth millions. Simply, simply millions. I, I mean everyone thinks . . . (*his voice becoming higher as his panic grows*) good god, Lucille. How could you have spent all the Sloan money?!

THE PRINCESS (*slurring*). What're you talking about?

THE PRINCE. I, I just don't understand, that's all. Everyone said you were worth millions. (*He pounds on the railing, and another piece goes.*)

THE PRINCESS. Harold!

THE PRINCE. How could you have spent all that money?!

THE PRINCESS. Harold!

THE PRINCE (*almost manic—very decisive*). Well, I've got to get back to New York tonight! My furniture is being moved tomorrow. (*He is at the top of the steps leading down.*) Oh hell! Lucille, Lucille listen, how much do you have now? I, I mean cash. Right now. With you. (*He rushes to the table and begins going through the contents of her purse.* THE PRINCESS *is amazed.*) I've, I've only got twelve dollars left and . . . and where's your money, Lucille? Don't tell me you gave it all to the waiter?! Good god! Did you give him all your cash? You

gave him all your cash! Lucille! Jesus! You must be out of your
mind! Just how, I mean just how, I mean just how in hell are we going
to get back to New York? Do you have any more? Your luggage! Do
you have anything in your luggage? (*He goes to the bags and opens
them and begins frantically strewing things about.*) What did you
bring with you? Did you bring any jewelry? Maybe we could sell your
jewelry. You must have brought some jewelry. I've got my gold cuff
links and my signet ring. Where's your jewelry box? Didn't you
bring it?

THE PRINCESS (*finally pulling herself out of her amazement*).
Harold, what're you . . . ? Stop it! Stop it! (*He is strewing articles
about.*) Get out of my things! (*She throws her empty glass at him.*) Get
out of my things! Harold! (*Now she is down on the floor with him and
they are pulling fiercely at the clothes.*) Harold!! (*Finally, she smashes
him across the side of the head. He stops, dazed, drunk, the force
drained out of him.*) What in hell are you doing? Are you out of your
mind? Harold! Harold!

THE PRINCE. I, I, I, just don't understand. How are we going to
get out of here?

THE PRINCESS. What do you mean, how are we going to get out
of here?

THE PRINCE. I, I, I gave my last five hundred to the coroner. I
thought sure you'd have some cash. Maybe I can get a check—

THE PRINCESS. What? What did you say?

THE PRINCE. But that takes days—

THE PRINCESS. Harold! (*She shakes him.*)

THE PRINCE. Lucille stop it! Lucille I . . . How could you have
spent all your money?! (THE PRINCESS *is staring at him trying to understand what's going on.*) Do you think they'll take a personal check?
Maybe? No. And anyway, it takes days and I, I've got to get back to
New York tonight. . . .

THE PRINCESS (*after a moment*). Didn't you get round-trip tickets?
Harold?

THE PRINCE. What?

THE PRINCESS. Round-trip tickets.

THE PRINCE (*suddenly remembers*). Well yes . . . yes, yes I did I
. . . I forgot.

THE PRINCESS (*after another pause*). How many?

THE PRINCE. Ah. . . . One.

(*There is silence. After a moment* THE PRINCESS *rises and goes back* to her chair. *She sits down and faces* THE PRINCE *who is still on the floor by the suitcases.*)

Ah, ah, but . . . but, well Lucille we can . . . listen, we'll phone at the Hotel . . . we'll, we'll, we'll phone one of your friends and have them send us some money. That's it and then *you* can get a ticket too and . . . Lucille? Well, I don't have anyone I could ask. I owe everyone so much already. And . . . and you have so many friends. One of the girls? You know Kitty or Irene or Bunny? (*nervously starting to put the clothes back into the bag*) It was stupid of me just to get one wasn't it? Oh well ah, we'll need cash for the boat too, so you'd better ask for about five hundred . . . (*notices a dress that he is folding*) Where did you get this? It's lovely. (*He puts it into the bag.*) Maybe you could have them send a thousand. Irene won't mind. Tell her something came up. . . . (THE PRINCE *hesitantly looks up: he is being stared at fiercely.*) I, I . . . I'm sorry Lucille.

THE PRINCESS. Go on, Harold.

THE PRINCE. I . . . well, I. . . . (*it's a struggle*) I'm broke too.

THE PRINCESS. Why did you bring me here, Harold?

THE PRINCE. Oh Lucille really I. . . .

THE PRINCESS. Harold.

THE PRINCE. Well, I brought you here to . . . because I . . . I, well you see, I thought you loved me and I just didn't think I could, well I mean I can't, well, I can't stand you Lucille, physically and, and, I mean I have nothing against you as a person but well . . . I, I knew you'd inherited all the Sloan money and I, I . . . well, I owe so much. I owe everyone. I mean I even had to sell my house last week to avoid a mess. I, I don't have anyplace to go and all my furniture's being moved to your place. Tomorrow in fact. It's all I have left. And, since you sold your apartment—which was irresponsible!—I . . . I, don't have anyplace to go.

THE PRINCESS. And the coroner?

THE PRINCE. Well he, he's waiting down at the Hotel right now. I, I've known him for years. He took care of Vivian. For, for five hundred dollars he'll say anything's a heart attack. Simply anything. But Lucille, my dear. . . .

THE PRINCESS. And the coroner's waiting down there for me? Harold?

(*There is a long pause. The gunfire can still be heard in the jungle— now and then a mortar shell.*)

THE PRINCE. Well Lucille I, I'm sorry . . . I, I'm sorry. But well, let's just forget the whole thing O.K.? Listen, we'll call Irene from the

Hotel, all right? Lucille? (*He is quickly repacking her bag, gathering up the articles.*) Here my dear. I'll just put everything back inside. You're not angry with me, are you my dear? I mean we've got to stick together Lucille. When, when we get back to New York well, well, I mean we've got all that furniture. And we can, we'll sell it Lucille. When we get back to New York. Maybe, maybe we could, listen, maybe we could go into interior decorating. That's it. With all your furniture and my title it would be . . . Lucille? I mean that's quite respectable. Really it is. And with your furniture and my title it would be . . . well, we could sort of say it's a hobby. I mean I rather like that sort of thing . . . anyway. I don't know about you but if we said it was a hobby . . . you know, decorating.

THE PRINCESS. Shut up, Harold.

THE PRINCE. And you have all that marvelous Louis Fifteenth and that wonderful gold piano—

THE PRINCESS. Shut up!

THE PRINCE (*continues repacking*). Well Lucille, it's a possibility. . . .

THE PRINCESS (*watching him pack*). Walter was a sportsman. Did you know that? Harold, do you know where I met Walter?

THE PRINCE (*busy*). No dear, you've never told me that story.

THE PRINCESS. At Longchamps. We shared a table one day at lunch. I had a tuna salad on toast and an ice-tea. I was very beautiful then. He offered me everything. Who offered it to you Harold?

(*Just as she says this line* THE PRINCE *clicks shut the suitcase and looks up. He has been paying no attention.* THE PRINCESS *picks up the pistol and pounds it on the table.*)

Listen! I said who offered it to you?!

THE PRINCE. (*About to get up, he stops when he sees she has the gun.*) What? Lucille, my dear, you're drunk . . . I mean . . . well I'm sorry but there's no need to, to . . . be careful my dear . . . (*She continues to stare at him. He is intimidated and stays down.*) Lucille? Are you all right? My dear, do you think we could get a little loan from one of your friends? I'm almost sure that Orlan Foxe will take us into his shop with your furniture and my title. Do you remember Orlan? Well, he's really after Louis the Fifteenth and the Empire and well he's been after my name for years. . . .

THE PRINCESS. (*She pounds with the gun again.*) Shut up!

THE PRINCE (*pauses and goes on*). Lucille. And . . . and you've got those marvelous Goupil engravings which are worth at least six hundred each— (*She pounds again. He is standing now, moving back, away from her.*) And all your Russian Easter eggs. Lucille be careful with that gun dear. It might go off. . . .

THE PRINCESS. When did you change your name Harold?

THE PRINCE. What?

THE PRINCESS. Your name. When did you change it?

THE PRINCE. Why, why Lucille, I . . . I . . . I don't. . . .

THE PRINCESS. Cut it out. Everyone know's your title's a fake. I just want to know when you changed it that's all.

THE PRINCE. Well really, Lucille!

(*She pounds again, quickly, with the gun. It is a demand. There is a long pause. Their eyes meet.* THE PRINCE *looks away; his voice lowers and softens.*)

Oh. Well, I . . . I changed it . . . years ago. Years and years ago. When I was younger. When I was a child.

THE PRINCESS. I changed mine a long time ago too. From Lucille Barnes to Mrs. G. B. Walter Sloan. I still kind of like the sound of that. (*hard:*) What'd your name used to be? (*There is no response from* THE PRINCE. *Again* THE PRINCESS *pounds with the gun.*)

THE PRINCE. Oh. Ah. Murray . . . Murray Watson.

THE PRINCESS (*derisive*). Murray Watson? I don't like it. It sounds common.

THE PRINCE. I know.

THE PRINCESS. Is that why you changed it?

THE PRINCE (*hesitates*). No.

THE PRINCESS. Then why?

THE PRINCE (*evasive*). Oh, it's . . . a, well oh, it's a long story. . . .

(THE PRINCESS *pauses for a brief instant and then brings down the gun with tremendous force.*)

THE PRINCESS (*with detestation in her voice*). Harold! . . . Murray. I want to hear why you changed your name and I want to hear why you became a different person. The ridiculous person you are now.

(THE PRINCE *doesn't answer, merely remains motionless. The pistol strikes the table three times.*)

THE PRINCE. Oh. Well. All right. (*confidentially*) But, but you mustn't breathe a word. It was just after I got out of the army in oh . . . I don't know, I don't remember the date. I was, well, working in France . . . and getting nowhere but I was very good looking . . . when I was younger and well, it occurred to me, ah, Lucille, that a title might be helpful, so, well, I spent a week in Vienna going through the archives until I found one, a title, that had died out, oh, I don't know, I . . . I, oh about a hundred and seventy-five years ago and well I ah, so well I borrowed it. . . . (*This last line is barely audible. The pistol sounds again.*) I! I don't know why I did it. I just don't know why. It seemed, well, it seemed necessary. I don't remember why. (*a pause*) And everyone knows it's a fake?

THE PRINCESS. Everyone. Why do you think that telegram's so facetious? It's a joke . . . Murray.

THE PRINCE (*accepting this calmly*). Oh. Well, I didn't realize that. No one ever said anything.

THE PRINCESS. Of course not. They never do.

THE PRINCE. But my French and German are perfect, Lucille, and everyone always wanted me on lists at balls and parties and things . . . Vivian's father. . . .

THE PRINCESS. Naturally, Murray. You're a prince.

THE PRINCE. But . . . but I'm not . . . really.

THE PRINCESS. No. (*a pause*) How were you going to murder me, Murray?

THE PRINCE. Oh Lucille really I, I. . . .

(*The pistol slams onto the table again.*)

Oh I don't know. Poison, that glass of champagne has poison in it.

THE PRINCESS (*looks at the glass in amazement*). This . . . ?

THE PRINCE. Yes. Lucille, please. . . .

THE PRINCESS. Did you poison Vivian too?

THE PRINCE. Oh no. No, no . . . no we got along very well together. Vivian and I. (*his old tone returning*) We, we came back here every February for two weeks. Of course everyone came here then. It was really the dernier cri. You had to book months in advance. Months and months. We always got this little cabana. Vivian liked the view. She liked to watch the endless sea—

(THE PRINCESS *pounds the pistol again, twice.*)

Well she did!

(*Then quieter. Sometime during the following speech he absently removes his sunglasses.*)

She liked to look at the sea. I mean I never paid much attention to that sort of thing but we always stayed up here, except for that dreadful time in '43 or was it '44 or was it '45—I'm not too good at dates anymore. . . .

THE PRINCESS. When she died.

THE PRINCE. Yes. She . . . well, she found me . . . making love . . . to someone else. I was usually very careful about that sort of thing but we had to stay down at that awful Hotel and it was impossible, I mean simply impossible, to be alone. It was dreadful!

(THE PRINCESS *uses the pistol again.*)

She committed suicide that night. She jumped off here. They found her body two days later on the beach, five miles away. She had never been particularly attractive. And the scandal was hushed up. A heart attack. That's what the coroner said. (*a long pause*) She had a heart attack and fell off the veranda into the sea.

THE PRINCESS. And in her will, she left you everything?

THE PRINCE. Oh yes, everything.

THE PRINCESS. Yes, Walter left me everything too.

(*There is silence. The trial is over.* THE PRINCE *is looking out at the view.* THE PRINCESS *puts out her cigarette, picks up the gun in both hands and looks at it for a moment, trying to determine how it works. Then she cocks it. The noise causes* THE PRINCE *to look up, then he turns around slowly to find* THE PRINCESS *with the gun leveled at his stomach.*)

THE PRINCE. Lucille . . . my dear, ah, don't . . . point that . . . ah, you ah . . . Are you . . . are you . . . ? (*The words are spoken quietly, civilly, almost to himself.*) Because . . . because I . . . I don't want to die. Yet.

(*There is a slight pause, then* THE PRINCE's *body relaxes, his arms at his sides.* THE PRINCESS *fires point blank.* THE PRINCE *jerks and collapses to the ground. She fires at him three more times and then sits in silence and watches the body for a moment or two. Finally she rises from the chair, in her stocking-feet, walks to the body of* THE PRINCE *and with one foot pushes it over the edge of the veranda and into the sea.*

Just a moment later THE WAITER, *his submachine gun ready, comes charging along the path and across the bridge. He climbs onto the veranda and stops, still crouching, ready for anything, his gun pointing directly at* THE PRINCESS.)

THE PRINCESS (*realizing that he is there but in no particular hurry to notice him. The alcohol has made her movements sluggish and unsteady. She turns back to the table and puts down the gun. When she speaks her tone is matter of fact and unemotional—there is even, after the first few remarks, a trace of humor. She is going through the scattered contents of her purse looking for cigarettes. She speaks, almost in an undertone:*) He's dead, honey, morte. Moi, j'ai . . . oh what the hell. (*She turns and addresses* THE WAITER.) I'm out of cigarettes. You don't understand a word I'm saying do you sweetheart? (*She stands a moment and looks at him.*) Don't point that thing at me. I'm old enough to be your mother. Put it down, O.K.? (*She walks to him and puts her hand on the gun just where his is.*) Now here, give it to me. (*Her grip tightens and she starts to pull.*) Put it down, dear. PUT IT DOWN. (*There is a very brief struggle and she takes the gun from him and puts it in the chair.* THE WAITER *straightens up, resuming his official attitude.*) Ha. Oops. Ha. I'm sorry honey, I've had just a little too much vino. (*She takes the second bottle from the table and walks to him.*) Vino. Here. It's the American way. Right out of the bottle. Come on, come on, I'm old enough to be your mother. (*She holds the bottle to his lips but he won't respond.*) All right. All right honey. Have it your way. (*She takes his hand and kisses it. He pulls it away. She stands and looks at him: there is deep hate in her eyes. Then she turns, goes back to the table and fumbles through the contents of her purse. She finds a little change and counts it out. To herself:*) Well, that'll hardly do. . . . (*Then she gets an idea: she takes off her wedding ring.*) Here. (*She turns back to him.*) This . . . this is all I have left. I mean, I've already given you everything I have . . . sweetheart. (*She goes up to him.*) But look. It's a diamond. A real one. A big blue diamond. (*with self-irony*) Like the sea. Whata ya think about that? Listen. Listen. How much'll it buy? Everything? (*He takes the ring.*) Un-hunh. That's what I figured. Just about everything. The whole god-damned world. (THE WAITER *is entranced with the ring.* THE PRINCESS *slips her arm under his and slowly leads him toward the cabana. As they pass the table,* THE PRINCESS *pauses and with what might be called a gesture picks up the poisoned glass. Then, glass in one hand,* THE WAITER *on her arm, she leads him through the bamboo curtain and off.*

The sun is about to set: the world is gold.)

CURTAIN

THE GOOD LIEUTENANT

ROBERT MURRAY

THE GOOD LIEUTENANT ROBERT MURRAY

LIONEL JACKSON	THREE ITALIANS
MASTER SERGEANT HEATH	LIEUTENANT SAWYER
ORIOLE	A DRILL SERGEANT
COLONEL SAUNDERS	A PLATOON OF TRAINEES
A CAPTAIN	THE GENERAL'S ENTOURAGE
GENERAL DUNCAN	GUARDS
SECOND LIEUTENANT STUART LANSING	

ACT ONE. *The Administration Building and Quad of an American Disciplinary Training Compound, Northern Italy, at the close of World War II.*

ACT TWO. SCENE 1: *The same, a month later. Morning.* SCENE 2: *The same, four days later. Late afternoon, evening.*

ACT THREE. *The same, the following morning.*

ACT ONE

The setting is two arenas, one smaller and overlapping the other. Stage left, the larger arena, represents the open Quadrangle of the Disciplinary Training Compound. A pole stands in the center of this area upon which several spotlights stem, angling in different directions over the ground below. At the foot of this pole there is a cage-like structure, approximately 6' x 6', in which a makeshift shelter has been built, resembling a tent. LIONEL JACKSON, *resting beneath this shelter, is visible only in shadow. The smaller arena, stage right, represents the Administrative Building of the DTC. There are two desks separated by the suggestion of a partition and several chairs. The desk at extreme right represents the* COLONEL'S *office. The desk center is* SERGEANT HEATH'S *and represents the Orderly Room area. This arena is slightly elevated from the area representing the Quad. A flight of three steps connects the two. A cyclorama against which prison fencing, barbed wire and a guard post perched atop a crow's nest are silhouetted, completes the background.*

CURTAIN: *The stage is dark except for the lights atop the pole, center of Quad, which criss-cross solid beams of illumination ending in islands of light on the ground below.*

THREE ITALIANS *carrying shovels and picks cross upstage right to left beyond the fence. They hesitate. One of them begins to whistle.* LIONEL JACKSON, *a tall, bearded man, emerges from the shadows and, standing within the cage, fingers gripping its mesh, listens. The* TRIO OF MEN *continue off left, whistling quietly.*

ORIOLE, *a young Negro dressed in Army fatigues patched with prison identification, moves from upstage left toward Administration Building, stage right. He is escorted by two armed guards who walk right and left behind him.*

JACKSON (*singing*). "Oh they hanged him from a high tree
They hanged him good and long
Now today his soul's free
And buzzards sing his funeral song."

(*The* GUARDS *halt* ORIOLE *and turn threateningly on* JACKSON *whose song tapers off.* JACKSON *retreats into shadow.* ORIOLE *and* GUARDS *continue to Administration Building, stage right arena, where* SERGEANT HEATH, *the Provost Sergeant, a large man, impeccably uniformed, stands facing the door, waiting.*

ORIOLE *enters hesitantly. He stops, facing* HEATH. *The* GUARDS *remain outside on the steps.*)

GUARDS. Here he is.

HEATH. Yeah, here he is. (*To* GUARDS) That's all.

(GUARDS *exit up left across Quad.* ORIOLE *and* HEATH *remain immobile, facing one another.*)

HEATH. Relax. Nothing to be scared about. You've been a good boy. (ORIOLE *remains stiff and wary.*) Come on in, Oriole. I ain't gonna hurt you. I said come in! Sit down!

(ORIOLE *steps into the room, walks cautiously toward chair.* HEATH *intercepts him, takes hold of one of the buttons on* ORIOLE's *jacket and twists. It does not come off.*)

You *are* a good boy. No loose buttons. No demerits. You keep this up, Oriole, and I'll send you out of here free as a bird. Of course good boys have to take on little responsibilities. Sometimes that makes staying a good boy hard. Sit down, Oriole. (ORIOLE *sits.*) You're going to take on a little responsibility this morning. A little favor for me. You don't mind doing a favor for me? (HEATH *waits for reply.* ORIOLE *shakes head, "No."*) Know what I'm going to do? I'm going to let you go. Open the gate and let you go. I'm going to give you a vehicle. Open the gate and let you drive out. What do you think of that? (ORIOLE *remains motionless.*) You'll escape Oriole! But only so far— only so far as the railroad. Your trip will be straight to and straight back from the train station. I want you to stop at the Rail Office where you will find—now, what will you find? A lieutenant! One Lieutenant Lansing. You bring Lieutenant Lansing back here and we'll snap the gate behind you. That's all there is to it. I can trust you to do this favor for me, can't I? Of course, as you ride outside the gates, the fences getting smaller behind you, you might take a wrong turn. Oh, that's understandable. You ain't seen the road for some time now. You might forget and one wrong turn might confuse you into making another and soon you might not be able to find your way back to us. Now if that happens, this (*holds up a manila folder*) would be wasted. Know what this is? (ORIOLE *shakes head, "No."*) This is *you!* Papers signed, papers stamped—all that's left of *you.* And the papers here on top tell me that Oriole is getting to be a good boy and if he continues to be a good boy we won't want him no more. Only bad boys here. We'll send him back to the Twenty-ninth and forget all about him. That's not for sure, of course. You might have a loose button someday or you might be a second late for drill—and you might get lost on your way to the good lieutenant. Even so, there's no guarantee on this. (*indicating folder*) Take your choice. Make a wrong turn on the way to the station and hope you don't get caught or bring the Lieutenant back and hope you don't stub your toe around here.

(HEATH *stands watching* ORIOLE. ORIOLE *twists nervously in chair, then stands, head bowed.*)

ORIOLE. Please. No.

HEATH. You don't want to do me no favor?

ORIOLE. No. I don't mean that.

HEATH (*beginning to roll the manila folder as if to discard it*). As you say. 'Course it'll be remembered that you didn't cooperate—

ORIOLE (*anxiously*). I'll go. I'll go.

HEATH. Good. You'll pick up the jeep at Gate 3. There's a temporary permit in the compartment and a strip map from here to the RTO —and back. The guards will expect you to depart at 0800. It's a twenty-minute drive. Check in with the stationmaster, he'll deliver the lieutenant to you. Bring him back. That's all.

ORIOLE. Why do you make me do this, Sergeant? I don't know my way.

HEATH. Why? Because you're a good boy and good boys must accept responsibility. I've got your pass and all instructions typed out—

(GUARDS' VOICES *are heard calling Post to Post.* HEATH *and* ORIOLE *listen alertly. The voices become louder and begin to fade, culminating in a burst of machine-gun fire.* HEATH *dashes to steps, peering across the Quad.* LIONEL JACKSON *comes forward within his cage.* ORIOLE *remains frozen beside his chair.* A GUARD *dashes across Quad to* HEATH.)

HEATH. What is it?

GUARD. Escapee over at South Gate.

HEATH. Get him?

GUARD. Yes. He wouldn't stop. Cut him down hanging on the fence.

HEATH. Which one was it?

GUARD. Darby.

HEATH. Anything left to look at?

(GUARDS *enter carrying a body on a stretcher.* HEATH *steps down, examines the corpse perfunctorily, lifts dog tag to verify identity.*)

HEATH. Darby. You know where to take it.

(GUARDS *begin to exit up right.*)

I want all them reports on this by 1200 hours. All of them!

(GUARDS *have halted momentarily in assent to* HEATH's *order, then continue off.* HEATH *re-enters office. To* ORIOLE:)

What's the matter with you?

ORIOLE. Darby? Is Darby dead?

HEATH. None of your business.

ORIOLE. Please. I don't want to go. Don't make me go outside the fence. I'll do something else for you. Don't make me go outside.

HEATH. Stop telling me what you'll do! I'm telling you. Listen, you took on the assignment, you do it. You do it and do it good and it'll be a gold star for you. You do good, Oriole, and you'll keep the lead out of your belly. Give me any sass and I'll set your record so far back in the red you'll never get out of here. Now, beat it! Get over to Gate 3 and make it fast!

(ORIOLE *moves obediently toward door. Once again* HEATH *intercepts him, twists button. It remains fastened.*)

HEATH. Now you're on your own. There's a catch to everything, Oriole. Even bein' good.

(HEATH *releases* ORIOLE *who exits across Quad.* JACKSON, *who has remained standing within his cage, watches the exit. After a pause,* JACKSON *begins a strange moaning sound increasing in volume.* HEATH *raises his head, listening, then rushes to door. Spotlights attracted by the sound sweep across the Quad and fasten on* JACKSON *who can be seen clearly for the first time. He is a tall, elderly man. Handsome except for his disarray. His clothes hang slack and torn, his beard unkempt. He wears over-size boots with no laces. He stands, head thrown back, hands clutching the wire mesh of his cage, moaning full volume.*)

HEATH. Quiet! Do you hear me? QUIET!

(JACKSON *cuts his moan off suddenly, leaving* HEATH's *last "Quiet!" resounding foolishly across the silent Quad. Several* GUARDS *enter but are waved away by* HEATH.)

You're a little noisy, ain't you, Jackson?

JACKSON. Sorry if I disturbed you. I was only performing a fitting, if primitive rite.

HEATH. Who asked you?

JACKSON. It was for the dead. I presumed he was dead. (*Resumes moaning.*)

HEATH (*moving to cage*). I said Quiet!

JACKSON. I don't expect you to understand, Sergeant. It is an expression requiring some sensitivity to comprehend. Nonetheless I did choose a relatively primitive—

HEATH. Shut up!

JACKSON. Are you denying the dead their rights?

HEATH. I'm denying you the right to cause a disturbance. Don't push it Jackson. I don't think I could find anybody to moan over you.

JACKSON. If you believed that you would have plugged me long ago. You can't cow me like you can the rest of the menagerie. I don't scare like that nigger. What did you do to him? Steal his buttons?

HEATH. You want dirt in your rations? If that's what you want, Jackson, I can see to it.

JACKSON (*chuckling*). Got your goat again, haven't I? Ah, it's so easy, so easy. You're cock-of-the-walk to the rest of them, but to me, a human being, you're just another ape.

(HEATH *springs to cage where he catches* JACKSON'S *fingers against the wire. He squeezes until* JACKSON *kneels, then releases him.*)

HEATH. You buckle just like all the rest of 'em, Jackson. I don't see no difference.

JACKSON (*suddenly old and feeble*). Someday somebody's going to come and help me out of here. Somebody with intelligence. Somebody who has some decency. Some *human being!*

(*Dawn has been rising throughout the preceding scene. It is now almost full daylight. The morning* DRILL PLATOON *made up of Trainees and commanded by a relentless* DRILL SERGEANT, *escorted by several* ARMED GUARDS *and a Cadence Drum, marches in loudly. The* PLATOON *moves like a solid block of automatons. Their entrance severs the exchange between* HEATH *and* JACKSON. HEATH *returns to Administration Building.* JACKSON *retreats into cage.*

The PLATOON *is put through several moments of rapid-fire drill before the* DRILL SERGEANT *orders "Halt!" and puts the* PLATOON *at "Parade Rest" and then "Attention."*)

COLONEL SAUNDERS, *a middle-aged man of medium height, whose brisk martial manner belies nervousness, enters. The* DRILL SERGEANT *and* GUARDS *salute as he crosses Quad to Administration Building. As he enters the building, the* PLATOON *is marched off up left.*)

HEATH. Good morning, sir.

SAUNDERS. Good morning, Heath. Any word yet on when the General is going to stage his inspection?

HEATH. Nothing yet this morning.

SAUNDERS. God, I wish we'd hear. Let's hope he gives us a week's notice. Apparently he wants this prison looking like a resort. (*referring to* JACKSON'*s cage:*) I wish to hell we could get rid of that damned eyesore out there.

HEATH. Easy, sir. Tear it down. Throw the old man in with the others. That's where he belongs. He's the lousiest crook we've got.

SAUNDERS. And the most important. I'm afraid that would get us further in the red than that cage will. He's still a civilian, Sergeant. And innocent until proven guilty. Until they call for him, he remains our guest.

HEATH. Too bad he don't try to get away.

SAUNDERS. What do you mean?

HEATH. It would be worth it to get rid of him.

SAUNDERS. Erase that thought from your mind, Heath. It would *not* be worth it. You and I would suffer considerably if he were to escape. Know what would happen if Jackson got away? He would be well taken care of by his friends. They'd have a hell of a time using him as a martyr, an artist abused and defiled. It would be too embarrassing, Sergeant, for all of us. It would be particularly embarrassing for you and me. We must treat him differently than the others but he must not ever get away!

HEATH. Well, he's still a nuisance. He's a demoralizing factor and keeping him separate from the others is like putting him on display. If they think he's so innocent why the hell don't they put him up at some hotel?

SAUNDERS. His innocence is but a technicality, Sergeant, a technicality. All it means is that he hasn't had benefit of trial yet.

HEATH. But Colonel, he's been here two months! I really think we should push through a request to get rid of him.

SAUNDERS. Oh no. We're going to sit tight. Our instructions were to accept him and keep him and no complaints. Let's not ruffle any feathers until after this damned inspection. Any more scenes from him?

HEATH. This morning again.

SAUNDERS (*going through papers on desk*). What was it about this time?

HEATH. We had an incident early this morning, sir. I've got reports working on it. Escapee. They knocked him down at South Gate.

SAUNDERS. Another! Jesus, Sergeant, couldn't that have been avoided?

HEATH. How do you mean, sir?

SAUNDERS. I don't know how I mean, Heath. I just mean that we can't afford any more incidents around here. That makes the third one in two months. Two months! If we're running a tough jail, why do they think they can get out? That's what the inspectors are going to ask us, Sergeant. That's what they're going to ask us!

HEATH. But sir, they can't gripe when we prevent the escape. If we had a riot or a breakthrough maybe then—

SAUNDERS. They don't like having to explain why they had to kill one of their own men, that's what they don't like. They prefer to let the enemy do it. Regardless of what gives us the right to fire, once it's done, nobody understands. If it proves awkward, they blame us for not discouraging the escape in the first place. Which one was he?

HEATH. Darby. Rapist. General Courts Martial last October. Thirty-third Infantry, Naples.

SAUNDERS. What do we have to do to impress these bastards that they can't get out? Something's wrong. We're going to have so many investigators down here on our necks that we'll wish we were interned here, not running the place.

HEATH. The guards followed instructions, sir. It would have been worse if he got away.

SAUNDERS. They're not going to complain about the corpse. They're just going to imply that we're slack. Everybody climbing fences when we're supposed to see they can't even get near them.

HEATH. This morning will serve as a lesson for the rest.

SAUNDERS. A damned expensive lesson as far as we're concerned.

HEATH (*pause*). Jackson's being here don't help.

SAUNDERS. How do you mean?

HEATH. His yelling around, getting away with murder. The rest see him, hear him. It sets them on edge. They see him getting away with it and they try something.

SAUNDERS. That's one we'll have to sit out. We can't very well answer complaints with passing the buck on Jackson. It would only put them on our backs all the more. We're stuck with that old bird. You say you've got reports working on this?

HEATH. Yes sir. They'll be complete by noon.

(*A* CAPTAIN, *the Graves Registration Officer, a smug, cynical man, enters the Administration Building from across the Quad.*)

SAUNDERS. Good morning, Captain. What can we do for you?

CAPTAIN. Good morning, Colonel. I've come to bury the dead.

SAUNDERS. You're very punctual.

CAPTAIN. You're keeping me quite busy these days.

SAUNDERS. Comparatively speaking, I suppose. Nothing compared to the Front, however.

CAPTAIN. You'd be surprised how the Front's quieted down. Once a war has ended, business slacks off.

SAUNDERS. Unfortunately our little war here has not ended. We haven't noticed any difference.

CAPTAIN. Nor, apparently, has the General, sir. He seemed upset about another attempt down here. I don't suppose you can really blame the prisoners for trying though.

SAUNDERS. No. But they don't receive much blame here. The administration seems to accept most of that for them. Where is the body, Sergeant? Perhaps the Captain can do his job while I finish here.

HEATH. Over behind the Dispensary, sir.

CAPTAIN. Very well, Colonel. Was it with an M–1?

HEATH. No sir. Browning Automatic. Two of them.

CAPTAIN. Well, that means a quick burial.

SAUNDERS. I'll join you shortly, Captain.

CAPTAIN. No hurry, Colonel.

(*The* CAPTAIN *exits the Administration Building as* GENERAL DUNCAN *accompanied by an* AIDE *and two* ENLISTED MEN *enters across Quad briskly. The* CAPTAIN *holds salute until the* GENERAL *enters the Administration Building then exits casually. The* GENERAL's *entourage waits outside.* HEATH *stands at "Attention."*)

SAUNDERS (*saluting*). Good morning, General.

DUNCAN (*returning salute and continuing into* COLONEL's *office*). I presume, Colonel, that you know why I've come this morning? You have an inspection in the very near future and it is imperative that this Compound meet its requirements. Now, this incident this morning—

SAUNDERS. It was an escape attempt—

DUNCAN. I don't give a damn what it was. This Compound is to afford no escapes either realized or abortive. Any such indiscretion on the part of your prisoners is a reflection on you, Colonel. It means, in short, that the impossibility of escape has not been impressed upon them.

SAUNDERS. But I'm afraid, General, that some of them prefer this kind of suicide to their existence here.

DUNCAN. The possibility that you are "afraid" of any such rationalization strikes me as unbecoming to a man in your position. It is a mistake, Colonel, to assign too much sensitivity to your prisoners. If they had any sensitive inclinations to begin with they would never have managed to get here. Understood?

SAUNDERS. Yes, General.

DUNCAN. Now, this inspection that I'm to conduct will take place when I think you have had sufficient opportunity to recover from this morning's fiasco. I want you to get this place back in order. I do not want, Colonel, any more conspicuous events here. This Compound is to function and its inhabitants are to behave unobtrusively. They already cost more than they are worth. Am I understood?

SAUNDERS. Yes, General.

DUNCAN. Do you have anything to say?

SAUNDERS. Is there any possibility of Lionel Jackson being evacuated?

DUNCAN. I did not come here this morning to discuss individuals; I have no idea what is in store for Lionel Jackson. I suggest that you manage him as well as the others, to the utmost of your capability, Colonel. Just don't ever *lose* Lionel Jackson. Good morning.

SAUNDERS. Good morning, General.

DUNCAN. Another thing, Colonel. Coming from the west I could smell your latrines for a mile up the road. I suggest that you bury them and dig new ones before I return. It will put me in a bad frame of mind for the inspection if I detect the foulness before I arrive.

(COLONEL SAUNDERS *salutes,* GENERAL DUNCAN *exits Administration Building and crosses off Quad with his* ENTOURAGE.)

SAUNDERS (*to* HEATH). I trust there's nothing else worth mentioning?

HEATH. No sir. Except maybe the new lieutenant. He's due in this morning.

SAUNDERS. Oh Jesus. What's his name again?

HEATH. Lansing. Second Lieutenant Stuart Lansing.

SAUNDERS. You've got his file?

HEATH (*handing it to* COLONEL SAUNDERS). Yes sir.

SAUNDERS. Looked at it?

HEATH. Yes sir.

SAUNDERS. What do you think?

HEATH. I'd rather not say, sir, concerning an officer who's going to be second in command around here.

SAUNDERS. In other words you hate him. Well, don't worry too much, Heath. It won't mean that your duties will be interfered with.

HEATH. No sir.

SAUNDERS. What time is he coming in?

HEATH. He's due in at the RTO at 0830. I sent a jeep down.

SAUNDERS. What did you do, get one of the supernumeraries off post at that hour?

HEATH (*hesitating*). I sent one of the trainees from the clemency list.

SAUNDERS. You did *what!* Are you losing your mind, Sergeant?

HEATH. It's accepted practice, sir, to give clemency candidates certain responsible duties.

SAUNDERS. Don't inform me, Sergeant. I know what procedure is. We can't even keep the bastards inside the fence let alone you opening up the gate for them. Jesus, Sergeant! A little discretion! A little discretion!

HEATH. He won't try nothing. He's got too much to lose. He's on top for parole next period.

SAUNDERS. You don't know whether he'll try anything or not, Sergeant. That man this morning didn't consider his life too much to lose in trying something. You don't mow them down at night and then turn around in the morning and push them through the gate!

HEATH. I made arrangements before the other happened.

SAUNDERS. I don't accept that from you, Heath. We don't make any arrangements around here that can't be broken.

HEATH. Yes sir.

SAUNDERS. Which one did you send?

HEATH. Oriole. Colored. Twenty-ninth Infantry.

SAUNDERS. What's he here for?

HEATH. Barracks skirmish. Knifed a buddy.

SAUNDERS. That's fine, Sergeant. You may not be any keener on having some punk Lieutenant around here than I am, but you had better sweat a little until that Lieutenant walks in here without his throat cut.

(*During last speech,* LIEUTENANT LANSING *has entered down left. He is a thin, ascetic-looking young man of twenty-three. Although he is not a prepossessing officer there is an intensity about him. He stands looking over the Quad for a moment.* JACKSON *emerges from rear of cage. The two exchange looks and then* ORIOLE, *carrying the* LIEU-

TENANT's bag, *enters behind him, indicating the Administration Building. The two cross to it while* JACKSON *watches.*)

HEATH (*looking out door*). He's here, sir. No sign of blood.

SAUNDERS. Lucky for you. (*Going into his office, looking at* LIEUTENANT LANSING's *folder*) Send him in. Get those incident reports in this afternoon without fail. All of them! (*Phone rings on* COLONEL SAUNDERS' *desk.*) Colonel Saunders here. That's right, sir. This morning, early. Yes, I presume it was unavoidable. Graves Registration is here now. No, I have not received his report—

(*During the telephone conversation* LIEUTENANT LANSING *and* ORIOLE *enter the Administration Building.* HEATH *feigns preoccupation at desk as* COLONEL's *dialogue fades.*)

LANSING (*after awkward pause*). Sergeant?

HEATH (*looking up as if surprised*). Oh, Lieutenant! You're Lieutenant Lansing, is that right sir?

LANSING. Yes.

HEATH. I'm Heath, Provost Sergeant. The Colonel and I have been expecting you. The Colonel asked to have you come in when you arrived. (*Indicating* COLONEL's *office:*) You can go in, Lieutenant.

LANSING (*to* ORIOLE). Thank you for the lift, Oriole.

HEATH (*to* ORIOLE). That's all. (*Goes to door, blows whistle. A* GUARD *appears.*) Take this one back to work detail.

(ORIOLE *steps down to waiting* GUARD *who calls him to "Attention" and marches him off across Quad at double cadence.*)

LANSING. Does he need a guard on him?

HEATH. He's a prisoner, Lieutenant. Regulation.

LANSING. But he's free to go outside without one?

HEATH. He's up for clemency. He's allowed certain privileges. He's trusted only on unimportant missions.

LANSING (*pause*). The Colonel's in here?

HEATH. Yes sir.

(*The* LIEUTENANT *knocks on* COLONEL's *door.*)

SAUNDERS. Come in.

LANSING (*entering and saluting*). Lieutenant Lansing reporting to the commanding officer.

SAUNDERS (*returns salute, eyes* LANSING *candidly for moment*). Ordinarily you'd be welcomed to a new assignment. Under the circumstances (*gesture, indicating DTC*) the grimness of our locale and our peculiar function preclude any such joviality. I can imagine your disappointment on first seeing our layout. One gets used to it. The bitter with the sweet. Your not being a professional soldier doesn't give you benefit of stoicism. Sit down, Lieutenant. I see here that your last assignment was at Salerno. Why didn't you stay there, Lieutenant?

LANSING. I believe my commanding officer had my transfer prepared.

SAUNDERS. There's no letter of reprimand in your file, Lieutenant. And yet I know that officers are not transferred to such godforsaken spots as this when their presence is not required. No matter. I won't pursue it further.

LANSING. Sir, my former commanding officer objected to my giving rations to civilians.

SAUNDERS. Yes?

LANSING. I gave them only a little. Not enough.

SAUNDERS. So?

LANSING. I was told that an American soldier would go hungry because of my action and I volunteered to be that soldier. I insisted on not eating for several days—to compensate for what I had given away. My commanding officer thought this peculiar.

SAUNDERS. Why did you do it?

LANSING. Why? I don't know, sir. I never thought why. But there they were. Men. Women. Just looking at the food and they were going to die from looking at it. Never asking for it, never reaching for it, never taking their eyes from it. It became theirs just looking at it. They would return, of course, and bring a friend, but they never presumed that I would be generous. They never asked. They just came. I gave it to them. Anyone would have.

SAUNDERS. No. You would think so, wouldn't you, but no. Your generosity is more unusual than you think.

LANSING. My commanding officer told me that my food was not being eaten by these people but sold for money. He said they got rich bargaining with the mothers of hungry children. (*pause*) I am not unhappy about my change. This place is not any blacker than what I saw in Salerno. And there are no hungry children here, are there?

SAUNDERS. No. I have not seen any. But we do have 197 trainees. The cream of the crop. Each has been convicted under General Courts Martial for such misdemeanors as murder, rape, desertion. . . . We have three guard platoons that operate alternately around the clock with supernumeraries. Rules are strict and punishment severe. We keep the trainees busy at drill or manual labor so that they are, we hope, too exhausted to try anything. Occasionally we have an escape.

But the fences are high and the guards don't hesitate to ask questions. That, in a nutshell, is the "predicament."

LANSING. Why do you say "predicament"?

SAUNDERS. Because of the inspections, Lieutenant. There's a contradiction in the Army, and it's never more clear than in a situation like this. First of all, we're expected to run a crackerjack prison. No leniency. No compromise. Then, as soon as we get tough one of these damned fools gets out of hand or tries to escape. Then the inspectors come asking, "Why, Why?" We're told to be tough. We *are* tough. And then we must apologize for it. You're just in time for our most important inspection, Lieutenant. I'm afraid we're in for difficulty. You see, we don't get commended for our marksmanship. Sometimes I'm tempted to let them get away.

LANSING. The old man, sir. The one in the cage. Is he one of them?

SAUNDERS. Ah yes. The biggest thorn of all. Our genius. We specialize in sub-intellects but Lionel Jackson is our extravagant exception. While the others, small minds that they be, committed crimes that benefitted only themselves, Jackson benefitted the enemy—in the name of ideals.

LANSING. I'm sorry to see him here. I know who he is.

SAUNDERS. I suspected that you read poetry. I used to read it, too. I'm afraid, however, that we're less impressed with his poetry than we are with his activities as traitor. That is, so to say, the government's feeling. My gripe against the old bastard is that he's placed in our responsibility. You know Lieutenant, there's just one function you can perform around here. If you manage it I'll not only be surprised, but grateful. With this pile up of investigations and the pending inspection, I want you to come up with some ideas on how we can continue our duty and at the same time discourage the frequency of incidents. I know that's a vague order for someone who hasn't even observed the operation, but it is one that, frankly, I don't see any solution for. It is necessary, however, to be able to say that a conscientious effort has been made. Perhaps your fresh eyes on this tired scene will discover something. As for your routine duties, it will be a pleasure having you relieve me, the Sergeant and the supernumeraries on that all-night vigil known as Charge of Quarters. As for any others, I'll let Sergeant Heath— You've met Sergeant Heath?

LANSING. Yes.

SAUNDERS. He's in charge of executing most of the orders and he can fill you in on details. He's a good man. He's tough. He's according to the book. Well, you'd better get billeted. I have a corpse to dispose of. A function that should not take you unawares sometime, perhaps. Any questions?

LANSING. I'm sure there will be—

SAUNDERS. Very well, then. (*going into Orderly Room*) Sergeant, will you see that the Lieutenant gets an escort to his billet, gets settled and takes a look around? (*To* LANSING) I'm interested in seeing your more refined reaction. (*To* HEATH) I want those reports this afternoon, Sergeant. Now where did this thing take place last night?

HEATH. South Gate, sir. I'll get the Captain of the Guard—

SAUNDERS. Never mind, I'll get him.

(*The* COLONEL *exits up right, hesitating briefly as he critically examines* JACKSON'S *cage.*)

HEATH. Your billet, Lieutenant, will be behind the Dispensary. The Colonel lives off post but requested that the junior officer reside on. The view is not bad. Did the Colonel outline your duties for you?

LANSING. He gave me a general impression of what they might be. He didn't glorify the situation.

HEATH. There's little to glorify here, Lieutenant. Nothing but cut-throats here. Every man's a criminal.

LANSING. I'm aware that it is a prison, Sergeant.

HEATH. That's half the battle isn't it?

LANSING. You know better than I, Sergeant.

HEATH. Yes—

(*The* DRILL PLATOON *marches back into the Quad, drum banging, the* DRILL SERGEANT *shouting commands. It marches once around* JACKSON'S *cage and halts. The* DRILL SERGEANT *put the* PLATOON *at "Dress Right Dress" and begins to examine the alignment of columns.* JACKSON *comes forward in his cage, observing.*)

JACKSON (*mockingly*). There's one missing from the ranks, Sergeant. One of your party is missing, Sergeant. Now how could he have gotten away? Where did he go?

(*The* PLATOON *shows a slight tremor of reaction. The* DRILL SERGEANT *warns them to "straighten up."*)

Which one was he? Mannion? No. Alvarez? No. Darby? Darby! It was Darby, Sergeant. Darby's missing! (*calling*) Darby! Oh, Darby! Where are you, Darby!

(*The* PLATOON *moves restlessly.* HEATH *rushes to the door and down the steps as* GUARDS *enter Quad.* DRILL SERGEANT *attempts to order* PLATOON *back into order.*)

HEATH (*to* GUARDS). Bring that bastard out here!

(*The* GUARDS *unlock padlock on entrance to cage.* JACKSON *has shrunk back into corner but* GUARDS *drag him out by arms into Quad. The* PLATOON *is frozen at Dress Right position, their eyes straining at the corners to see.* LIEUTENANT LANSING *has come to the steps leading into Quad as* HEATH *approaches* JACKSON *who kneels, arms held by* GUARDS.)

HEATH. I warned you, Jackson. I said one more disturbance and I'll break your neck.

JACKSON. Don't touch me! You touch me and so help me God, I'll see you ruined.

HEATH (*striking* JACKSON *across the face*). You dirty Fascist! Don't threaten me! You'll get your neck twisted off before they ever put a rope around it—

LANSING (*coming forward from off steps*). That's enough, Sergeant! Stop it!

(HEATH, *one hand raised for a blow, stops surprised. He turns, incredulously, to the* LIEUTENANT. JACKSON *is crying softly.*)

LANSING. That will be all, Sergeant. (*To* DRILL SERGEANT:) Move these men out of here.

(*The* DRILL SERGEANT *salutes, calls* PLATOON *to "Ready Front" and marches them off.* GUARDS *release* JACKSON's *arms.* HEATH *stands dumfounded and furious facing* LIEUTENANT LANSING.)

HEATH (*after sound of marching platoon has faded*). Lieutenant! I was performing a legal punishment!

LANSING. I am assuming that duty, Sergeant.

HEATH. Lieutenant, I don't think you understand. This sort of thing happens every day. It's necessary to keep discipline—

LANSING. I'm sorry if you feel that I have interfered, Sergeant, but now that I have, please leave it in my hands. (*To* GUARDS:) Is he hurt?

GUARD. Don't think so, sir.

LANSING. That will be all.

HEATH (*to* GUARDS). Put him back.

LANSING (*to* GUARDS). Leave him where he is. That will be all.

HEATH. You can't leave him out, Lieutenant.

LANSING. Sergeant, I don't think that we should prolong this argument in front of the prisoner.

(HEATH, *nonplussed with rage, stares hard at* JACKSON *and then at*

LIEUTENANT LANSING *before exiting into the Administration Building.*)

LANSING. Mr. Jackson, stand up. Please.

(JACKSON's *head lifts alertly upon being addressed in this manner. He contemplates the* LIEUTENANT *and then stands.*)

Are you hurt?

JACKSON. Do you mean physically, Lieutenant?

LANSING. Yes.

JACKSON. No. This old skin is calloused with the buffeting. (*tapping his chest*) Inside the bruises linger.

LANSING (*reciting*). "But not this cage of iron shall they harm
                     Beware the fragile heart. . . ."

JACKSON. Where—where did you get that?

LANSING. I've read it many times.

JACKSON. My things? You've read my things?

LANSING. All of them.

JACKSON. "But not this cage of iron shall they harm
          Beware the fragile heart."
It's not one of my best. Early stuff. So you've read my things.

LANSING. You have not changed your sentiments?

JACKSON. Everything changes. If not apparently so—well, look at me now.

LANSING. You continue to write?

JACKSON (*nodding*). I'm a writer. I do nothing but write and when I don't have paper to write on I select and arrange words in my mind. Like a linotypist. I'm not a has-been, my boy. Those things you children read in senior seminars are but the flexing of the muscles. The old man is trying to survive so that he can write the big thing.

LANSING. You're working on it here, now?

JACKSON. Here! Now! Not likely! There's an anti-intellectual movement in command here. The monkey house is manned by apes. I hope, Lieutenant, that you are not just *visiting* the zoo?

LANSING. No.

JACKSON (*suddenly confidential*). Help me, Lieutenant. I'm just an old man and I'm losing my mind. I've been here eight weeks. Eight weeks! They lock me up. They took all my belongings—all. They hate me here, Lieutenant. I've begged them for some books. It wouldn't matter if I could have some books. But they refuse. They say they'll look into it but they never come back. I've asked for paper, but no. It's horrible to be put in the care of men who have cut off their ears and closed their eyes because they've been told to hate me. Hate me! And what have I done to them? Nothing! Lieutenant, I'm going to die here in this cage unless I can get out. They'll be sorry. I've got friends. The Colonel will suffer if I die here.

LANSING. What do you want, Mr. Jackson?

JACKSON. Lieutenant, there's a hospital in Pisa. I should be there. They say I'm well but it's not true. I'm an old man. They've no right to keep me here like an animal. They'd send me to that hospital if I got hurt. I know a way. Lye. I've seen the others do it. They put lye inside their shoes. They have to take them into Pisa. Lieutenant, get me some lye. It won't take much.

LANSING. You know that I cannot do that.

JACKSON. No. Well no matter. I have another way. They took everything. Belts, shoelaces, everything. They always do. But I've been collecting. I've got some laces. I'll get more. Enough to make me a rope. They'll be sorry. The fools threw me in here. They don't know why. They never asked.

LANSING. I asked.

JACKSON. And they told you what they had been told and you think it's true. Put me back and let me finish it. When this is over you can tell your professors that you saw me in the withered flesh. That you not only saw me, you locked me up in a cage!

LANSING. I admire your work very much, Mr. Jackson. I have read all of it, but even if I hadn't, even if I had read only the short piece, the one about "sparrows braving prismed skies," I should find it difficult to hate you.

JACKSON (*after a long look at* LIEUTENANT LANSING *raises gaze to sky and points*). There! Four and twenty blackbirds etched upon a sky. Memorable interruptions on the surface of the eye. Watch them! When they light on the wires—they always do—we'll see a Bach cantata spread out before us like some incongruous lantern-slide. There, you see! Not so much Bach perhaps as Brahms. They can do them all— those little birds.

LANSING. I always look for the One among them. I assign him a name and wonder how he fares once he leaves the wire and disappears in a black clump with the others. I never look at them as a composition. (*smiling*) Perhaps I'm not musically inclined.

JACKSON. Sentiment.

LANSING. I suppose. Not the highest of emotions.

JACKSON. It has its uses. (*He begins to examine his hands.*)

LANSING. What's wrong?

JACKSON. Just vanity. You see I've been visited twice today by Sergeant Heath. Unfortunately I had no rescue earlier. You had not arrived.

LANSING. What did he do?

JACKSON. I suppose Heath is a good man for this work. It takes a sadist to operate a place like this.

LANSING. Has he beaten you before?

JACKSON. No. Just crushed my hands against the wires there. They cut a little. I wouldn't mind being struck on the mouth or kicked in the groin to help pacify the brutes, but my hands, my hands. They can take away my paper but they can't take away my hands. They might, of course. Heath might. I shouldn't be surprised. If he thought that he'd left me with an instrument to write with. . . . He's denied me paper.

LANSING. What are you working on?

JACKSON. An epic! I'm afraid any artistic epic will, of course, prove puny compared to our worldly holocaust. But it will perhaps be more comprehensible and meaningful than all (*waving about prison*) this. It's outgrowing my mind though. I need to start putting it down.

LANSING. Perhaps I could get the paper for you.

JACKSON. Could you? Could you? (*pause*) I would be grateful.

LANSING. Only paper? Is that all you need?

JACKSON. And pencils. Lots of pencils. Some books, too. Anything to read. Newspapers, trash, anything. Just let me see something in print again. I've never been without these things. Do you know that Heath and the Colonel pretend not to know who I am? They're not the sort to read anything, but my name at least—I'm not boasting, but I am a man of repute am I not? And they've taken my things away.

LANSING. Are you eating well?

JACKSON. Not like a king. But they refuse to starve me. They want to keep me alive. Fatten me up for the kill. You will get me the paper, won't you, Lieutenant? You won't let them dissuade you? Sometimes I think that when I am finally allowed some paper my time will be too short. It will be too late.

LANSING. Are you able to live in there comfortably?

JACKSON. I am not an elegant person. I don't complain. (*suddenly bowing head*) Why does a man have to be so humiliated? At night— I'm an old man and I have to use the latrine at night. But the guards won't let me out. It's not so far. . . . At first I could manage, but now —now. In the morning, Lieutenant, I wake with my humiliation—

LANSING. I'm sorry, Mr. Jackson. I'll ask the Colonel about the necessity for the lock.

JACKSON. There's always someone that needs to be asked! (*pause*) You'd better put me back now.

LANSING. Whenever you are ready, Mr. Jackson, you may go in. Leave the door open behind you. (*pause*) May I have the shoelaces, Mr. Jackson?

JACKSON (*he hands* LIEUTENANT LANSING *the laces from his pocket*). So you are to be the one. So you are to be the one. (*Starts back into cage and then turns, pointing to the sky.*) Look at them! Ironic that birds should demonstrate their freedom atop our fences. There they go! There's always one that guides them into flight.

(LANSING *watches the flight pass as* JACKSON *retreats into cage. The* COLONEL *enters, observes his gaze.*)

SAUNDERS. Observing the grounds, Lieutenant?

LANSING (*startled to find* JACKSON *replaced by the* COLONEL). Oh, yes sir.

SAUNDERS. Your gaze was a little high. Were you measuring the fence?

LANSING. No sir. Just admiring the sky.

SAUNDERS. The sky? It's not bad today, but it changes. Soon now, when the rains come, there's no sky at all. (*The* COLONEL *enters the Administration Building. The* LIEUTENANT *follows. Noticing the* LIEUTENANT's *bag:*) You haven't gone to your quarters yet?

HEATH. No sir. There was another disturbance in the Quad. Jackson heckling the drill and—

LANSING. And I interrupted.

SAUNDERS. What do you mean?

LANSING. I understood that Lionel Jackson is a civilian detained here under arrest, not punishment.

SAUNDERS. Yes.

LANSING. So I prevented what I thought might be an error on Sergeant Heath's part.

HEATH. It was the third disturbance today, sir—

SAUNDERS. What were you doing?

HEATH. The usual sedative, sir. Jackson was making a fool of the Drill Sergeant just like the Lieutenant did by interrupting me in front of the platoon.

LANSING. Sir, you asked me to help reduce incidents. I was afraid

that the beating of a civilian in our custody in front of a platoon of
witnesses might prove awkward regardless of the disturbance being
caused. I have spoken with Mr. Jackson and I think with a few
reasonable concessions we can count on his cooperation. (*putting laces
on desk*) I got these from Mr. Jackson. He was planning to kill himself.

SAUNDERS. That's all we'd need, Sergeant. Well, Lieutenant, I'm
impressed. I had no idea you would plunge in so immediately. Sergeant have you got those reports yet?

HEATH. No sir.

SAUNDERS. Perhaps if you had not taken time out for the
fracas. . . . You've had too much to do, Sergeant, to be able to do
it gracefully. We've got the Lieutenant to help us now. Lieutenant, I
suggest you get billeted. Sergeant, get someone to take him over. (*To
LANSING:*) I am interested in these "concessions." We rarely bargain
with our prisoners, Lieutenant. I trust that you have been discreet. I
am pleased with your grasp of the situation. (*The* COLONEL *exits into
his office.*)

LANSING (*to* HEATH). Can you get Oriole to take me over to the
billets?

HEATH. Oriole?

LANSING. The one up for clemency. Another unimportant mission.
We might as well give him the opportunity to help himself.

(HEATH *stares at* LANSING *for a moment, then uses the telephone to
place request for Oriole.* LANSING *opens his bag and removes several
books.*)

HEATH. I don't want to get out of line, Lieutenant, but maybe you'll
allow me to point out some things.

LANSING. I'd appreciate that, Sergeant.

HEATH. This, Lieutenant, is not a unit. We're responsible to these
bastards only to keep them confined and to keep them alive—until
we can get rid of them. We do this by any means we can.

LANSING. I understand.

HEATH. I'm not sure you do, Lieutenant. Out there with Jackson. I
staged that deliberately. You complain about witnesses. Lieutenant,
I intended for there to be witnesses. Jackson is an agitator. He needs
to be taken down in front of the others. You didn't understand. I
don't blame you, you didn't know. But my job's not easy. It's hard
as hell to stay on top of 197 cutthroats. And that's what I have to do.
You've messed up my job, Lieutenant. I brought Jackson out there
to take him down and you know what you did? You took me down in
front of them!

LANSING. I wouldn't have acted. The man is old—

HEATH. And he's a genius. Isn't that what you're saying? Maybe so. But just between you and me this world don't need no geniuses. Jackson's the kind that writes books with one hand and stabs us in the back with the other. The smart guys always want to run everything. And why should they get their way? They're no better than anybody else. You know, if it weren't for him and his friends all these bastards wouldn't be rammed down my throat. They might be in jail someplace, but they wouldn't be in this hole and I wouldn't have to beat the drum or see the rocks get hauled. Ol' Jackson kept busy when he wasn't writing poems. I say he gets what the rest gets. Spit.

LANSING. Don't you suppose a man like Mr. Jackson might suffer considerably from his mistakes?

HEATH. Him? Suffer? I don't know what you're talking about, Lieutenant.

LANSING. I have said that I am sorry, Sergeant, but I don't regret my action. You said that we're to confine and sustain these men by any means we can. I'll do that. My means may differ from yours, but in the end I shall be doing what's expected.

HEATH. I don't think your way is going to work, Lieutenant.

LANSING. I would have said the same for yours if I had not tried it.

(ORIOLE *comes across Quad to door.*)

HEATH (*to* ORIOLE). Come in here. Take the Lieutenant over to the officer's billets. Take his bag.

LANSING. Oriole, do me a favor first. Take these books to Mr. Jackson out there, will you? (ORIOLE *hesitates before* HEATH.) Go ahead, Oriole. (ORIOLE *takes books and leaves Administration Building, walking cautiously toward* JACKSON'S *cage.*)

HEATH. You don't ask them to do favors, Lieutenant. You tell them.

LANSING (*calling to* ORIOLE *from door*). The door, Oriole. It's open.

(ORIOLE *extends the books inside.* JACKSON *comes forward, seizes them, holds them to his breast.*)

HEATH. I wouldn't do him no favors, Lieutenant.

LANSING (*coming down steps*). Come on, Oriole. Let's go to the billets.

(ORIOLE *takes the* LIEUTENANT'S *bag and leads him off up right as* JACKSON *watches.*)

HEATH (*going into* COLONEL'*s office*). Sir, the Lieutenant has taken on Oriole as an escort!

SAUNDERS. So?

HEATH. Sir, I don't think he realizes that we don't just drag a trainee in off detail to point out the landmarks around here.

SAUNDERS. He's not sending him off post is he?

HEATH. No.

SAUNDERS. Well now, it seems as if the Lieutenant is at least exercising more discretion than was exercised earlier today.

HEATH. And he's sent Jackson some books.

SAUNDERS. What sort of books?

HEATH. Reading books. Stories, I suppose.

SAUNDERS (*chuckling*). "Reading books"? I see, Sergeant. That is probably one of the Lieutenant's concessions to the old man. Don't worry about it yet, Sergeant. Let's see how it works. I'll keep the Lieutenant in line, don't you worry about that. You worry about those incident reports. I want them now. If they're not here I suggest you go after them.

HEATH. Yes sir.

(HEATH, *furious, storms out of Administration Building and starts across Quad.* JACKSON, *watching him, begins to sing softly.*)

JACKSON. "Glory, glory, hallelujah!
         Glory, glory, hallelujah!
         They are trampling out the vintage
         Where the grapes of wrath are stored"—

(HEATH *stops, looking at him.* JACKSON *stops singing.*)

JACKSON (*pause, then smiles*). It's been a busy day so far, hasn't it, Sergeant? A busy day.

(HEATH *turns and exits off up left.* JACKSON, *still smiling, watches him leave. Then, humming, he begins to turn the pages of a book as:*)

THE CURTAIN FALLS

ACT TWO

SCENE ONE

It is a month later. An early September morning, grey with chill. LIONEL JACKSON *sits in the Orderly Room of the Administration*

Building at HEATH'S *desk. He is typing rapidly, using the index finger of each hand.* ORIOLE *is sweeping the floor and performing the house-keeping duties of an Orderly. A* GUARD, *acting as Charge of Quarters, sits in a chair near the door. After a moment, the* GUARD *looks at his watch, gets up and goes into the* COLONEL'S *office where he begins to write his duty report.*

JACKSON (*typing*). And merrda for the brutes! (*He apparently types this phrase, then stops, thinking.*)

ORIOLE. Did you say something, Mr. Jackson?

JACKSON (*preoccupied*). To you, no. Or, perhaps yes, to you, among others.

ORIOLE. I sure do wish I could write on one of them machines. Wouldn't my daddy be surprised to see a letter from me all writ out like a newspaper!

JACKSON. Why don't you be quiet and sweep the floor?

ORIOLE. Yes sir, Mr. Jackson.

(ORIOLE *resumes sweeping.* JACKSON *resumes typing.* HEATH *enters the Administration Building from up right.*)

HEATH (*to* JACKSON). Get out from behind my desk.

JACKSON. I have the Lieutenant's permission—

HEATH. I don't give a damn whose permission you've got. It's my desk and you move out when I move in. (*turning to* ORIOLE) You! Get that broom out of here! (ORIOLE *exits.*) Where the hell's the C.Q.?

GUARD (*emerging from* COLONEL'S *office*). Right here, Sergeant.

HEATH. How come I have to wade through half the god-damned jail-birds around here before I find you? (*meaning* JACKSON) This one write poems all night?

GUARD. Guess so.

HEATH. What do you mean, "Guess so"?

GUARD. He's been typing steady most of the night.

HEATH. That must be some poem, Jackson. (*taking sheet from typewriter*) I'd like to read this poem—

JACKSON (*snatching it from him*). No! You wouldn't understand it, Sergeant.

HEATH. Think it's too highbrow for me? (*deliberately sweeping* JACKSON'S *papers off the desk onto floor*) Nobody's going to read this poem. They're going to bury your scribbles with you, Jackson.

JACKSON (*anxiously collecting the papers*). Nobody's going to bury me.

HEATH. Oh? I suppose you think they'll stuff you and put you up in some museum.

JACKSON. Nobody's going to touch me!

HEATH. Want to bet? They're just stalling to think of all the things they want to do to you. They're going to put you on the rack, Jackson. They're going to bust you this way and that. Nothing's too good for a traitor. A dirty Fascist.

JACKSON. Can you prove it? Can you?

HEATH. I don't have to. I'll let them prove it. It won't take them half an hour to put the rope around your lousy neck.

JACKSON. And if they could prove it they wouldn't do anything. They wouldn't dare.

HEATH. Like hell!

JACKSON. I have friends in this world.

HEATH. Nothing compared to your enemies, Jackson.

JACKSON. In numbers or intentions, Sergeant? Well, no matter. I shall continue to write.

HEATH. Not here you don't. Not at my desk.

JACKSON. The Lieutenant has gotten permission from the Colonel for the use of this machine.

HEATH. And I'm telling you you're not using it.

JACKSON. Aren't you bucking your superiors, Sergeant? Or has even the invincible Army turned upside down?

HEATH. I say you're not going to use my desk, Jackson. I have my ways.

JACKSON. To be sure. And I have mine. If you get the machine, Sergeant, I shall not be inconvenienced. I'll continue work in the "bungalow." I may have to have some repairs made, a roof perhaps, but I'll continue.

HEATH. You're not going to get no roof or anything else, Jackson, except a good hanging.

JACKSON. No one is going to hang me.

HEATH (*pause*). If I thought that, Jackson, I'd get you before you got out of here.

JACKSON. Is that a threat?

HEATH. You going to run and tell the Lieutenant? Go on, tell him I threatened you.

JACKSON. Sergeant, you have always flattered yourself that you could frighten me with beatings and threats. I don't scare easily. I'm not only too intelligent for you, I'm too tough for you.

HEATH (*long pause, then, tapping his forehead*). You're getting soft in the head, Jackson. You better take care you don't bump it. It's so soft.

(*The* COLONEL *enters the Administration Building.*)

SAUNDERS. Good morning, Sergeant, Jackson. (*To* JACKSON:) You're getting ahead on that book, I see.

JACKSON. Yes, Colonel, thanks to your generosity.

SAUNDERS. I'd like to read it sometime.

(JACKSON *nods, smiles and sidles past the* COLONEL *and* HEATH, *holding his papers guardedly. He exits Administration Building and crosses toward Quad. The* THREE ITALIANS *pass outside the fence.* JACKSON *and the* THREE ITALIANS *contemplate one another for a moment and then continue on their ways.*)

I hardly expected to find creativeness in our desert. Where's the Lieutenant?

HEATH. He's out inspecting morning mess.

SAUNDERS. Good. (*Turns to go into office.*)

HEATH. Colonel, I'd like to say something about Jackson.

SAUNDERS. Jackson again? He hasn't created another disturbance has he?

HEATH. No, but I don't like his using the office to write poems in. It isn't right.

SAUNDERS. Now Sergeant, you know the reason for that. The Lieutenant suggested it and I've agreed to Jackson's using the room and typewriter when it was available. There are times when, of course, he can't use it, but I see no difficulty.—particularly when it is keeping him quiet. Are there any difficulties?

HEATH. I just don't think it looks good for him—

SAUNDERS. You let me decide that, Sergeant. (*Starts for office.*)

HEATH. Colonel, there's something else, if it's convenient.

SAUNDERS. What is it?

HEATH. Personal request, sir.

SAUNDERS. Something wrong, Sergeant? If so, you'd better tell me.

HEATH. Nothing wrong, sir. Except I don't think that I am fulfilling my duty. I'd like your permission, sir, to request transfer.

SAUNDERS. Now slow down, Heath. I know the grass is always

greener. . . . It's certainly greener almost anywhere but here, but this place has got compensations, Sergeant. Stick it out here and you're on top for promotion. What assignment have you got your eye on?

HEATH. I don't have any assignment in mind, sir. I simply find it difficult to fulfill my requirements as Provost Sergeant and I want to leave.

SAUNDERS. Difficult to fulfill requirements? What do you mean, Heath? You've been doing a splendid job. You were recommended for this post because you're thorough, you're efficient, you're tough. What do you mean, "difficult to fulfill requirements"? I haven't any complaints.

HEATH. Everything that was once my duty seems to be wrong now. Seems that we are getting softer—I just don't know what's expected of me.

SAUNDERS. Still stinging from that episode out there? Heath, as one professional soldier to another, I know that it's difficult to tolerate a youngster coming in and taking over. Well, the Lieutenant is *not* taking over. So far his suggestions have worked—so far. At the moment I'm interested less in means than in ends. After the inspection we'll re-examine the Lieutenant's concessions. But, so far, they've worked. You've got to admit that.

HEATH. It doesn't seem right to have the prisoners making themselves at home here in the office, using my desk, my typewriter. Free to come and go.

SAUNDERS. Jackson. Well, Heath, if that's all it is, we'll retract our favors. The understanding was that he used the typewriter if it was available. We'll simply have to make it unavailable. That's simple. But let him know it's not spite, Sergeant. He may be with us for some time. Rumor has it that he may never be brought to trial.

HEATH. Never brought to trial? Do you mean that they'd let him go?

SAUNDERS. Only rumor, Sergeant. But while we have him let's keep him quiet. It wouldn't surprise me if they hoped he'd die here with us. It would save them the embarrassment of a controversial trial. They've stalled for some time as it is and he's an elderly man. . . . At any rate, Sergeant, stick it out. At least until after the inspection. Things are looking up. I can't afford to lose you now. You know that.

(*The* THREE ITALIANS, *arms raised above them, are marched into Quad by* GUARDS *at "Ready Arms."* JACKSON *comes forward in cage. The* THREE *are halted in front of Administration Building.* HEATH *and the* COLONEL *come outside. The* LIEUTENANT *comes from up left.*)

Who are these men?

GUARD. Don't know, sir. They were loitering around outside.

SAUNDERS (*speaking to* FIRST ITALIAN). Who are you? What is your name? (*The* FIRST ITALIAN *shakes his head, uncomprehending. To* GUARDS:) Where were they?

GUARD. Outside, walking along the fence. They had picks and a shovel.

SAUNDERS. Did they run?

GUARD. No sir. They didn't put up any fuss when we took them.

SAUNDERS (*returning to the* ITALIANS). English? Do any of you speak English? (*The* THREE ITALIANS *shake their heads.*)

FIRST ITALIAN. Lavoratori, signore, lavoratori.

SECOND ITALIAN. Lavoratori di qualita, signore.

THIRD ITALIAN. Lavoro ben fatto, signore, per un po' di pane. Soltanto pane, signore.

SAUNDERS. One at a time! One at a time!

LANSING. Sir, I think they want work.

SAUNDERS. What do they mean, work?

LANSING. In exchange for food, they said.

SAUNDERS. All our work is done gratis by the inmates. You can tell them that. (*To* GUARDS:) Take them over to South Gate. Find out who they are and don't release them until I hear from you.

GUARD. Yes sir.

(*The* GUARDS *march the* THREE ITALIANS *off.*)

SAUNDERS (*to* LANSING). You speak Italian, Lieutenant?

LANSING. No sir. Just a few words. All they wanted was food for work.

SAUNDERS. I presume that's all they wanted. Well, we'll find out who they are first. Check on them.

LANSING. Yes sir.

(*The* COLONEL *and* HEATH *exit into the Administration Building. The* LIEUTENANT *turns to follow the* GUARDS.)

JACKSON. Good morning, Lieutenant.

LANSING. Good morning. How's the work coming?

JACKSON. Oh, so-so. Can't type too well. Fingers getting stiff at night now. That time of year. There was a thin slice of frost on the ground last night. Imagine that, Lieutenant, winter comes here too.

LANSING. Do you need another blanket?

JACKSON. I need a house with a roof, that's what I need. No blanket is going to keep this world outside.

LANSING. Perhaps I can have you moved into the Dispensary.

JACKSON. No, oh no. I prefer even this to that disinfected shack. Just something over the top would do it. Keep the winter out.

LANSING. I'm not sure—

JACKSON. Winters always haunt old men. Never any snow here but the rain—worse than snow. In Rome, I could always tell autumn's approach. Old men are wily. Their bodies always reminding them of the future. I remember the hottest days in August, sitting on the Via Veneto, watching the fat jew-merchants, oozing sweat, sitting, drinking. Ah, how little did they know compared to me! I could feel the autumn in my bones, see it, like a small faraway mist approaching over the hot leaves in the Borghese Gardens. Coming to wash the sweat off the arrogant merchants, sitting there in the cafes, beating the tabletops for service, demanding pounds of flesh. I could see the day when the table-tops would be left empty— Only rain beating on them now. And not a gentle rain, Lieutenant, not a gentle rain. They all ran for cover, if they had one. The rain makes the ground grow soft. It's a bad time for old men.

LANSING. And anyone without a roof.

JACKSON. Especially old men.

LANSING (*looking at top of cage*). Perhaps a tarpaulin— Why did you say that about the merchants?

JACKSON. The world is full of Shylocks. Not on the Via Veneto anymore. We're rid of them there. But everywhere, every street, every alley in the so-called democracies is filled with their slippery eyes. The moneylenders! (*mimicking*) Two will get you three and three will get you four— Step right up and we'll bleed you to death. We'll buy your ten-cent souls out from under your skin. (*stopping suddenly*) Ah, but you mustn't listen to an old man. Especially an old man with ache in his bones. Old men like to fabricate. Only this morning I was told I was getting soft in the head. Dumb. (*chuckling*) Like a fox.

LANSING. Looks like rain.

JACKSON. Yes. Gently at first and then whoosh—

LANSING. Would you like me to keep your papers? They would stay dry in the office.

JACKSON. Oh no. That's very kind, very kind, but I mustn't let them go until it's done. Just a roof perhaps. I'll see that nothing happens to them.

LANSING. I'll see—

JACKSON. Fabrication, Lieutenant, fabrication. That about the merchants. Just impressions. Spur of the moment sort of thing. It's all I have—the mind's eye. Nothing for me to see here except my crisscrossed house and the unreliable moon. But that's enough.

LANSING. How can you mean—enough?

JACKSON. My mind's eye is rich! Imagination, my good Lieutenant, and sensitivity. They're the things which make life excruciating but bearable. The rest of them here, nothing! They're dead. They die so easily when the glare of their lightbulb world is turned off and the moon substitutes. They're being punished, true. But at least they are out from that puny gaze of electricity that hangs above them in their whorehouses and their saloons. The moon's too much for them now. They hang their heads and lift their rocks. The existing dead!

LANSING. Not everyone. I know that they move like robots, they lift the stones with their eyes shut, but I have heard some of them crying at night. It must be difficult to care about anything, moving from a war to a prison. Do you suppose that, individually, each one of them is innocent? Only when packed in together in the world they become guilty?

JACKSON. No. You are a romantic aren't you? A man doesn't wait for the guilty world. The world doesn't care unless he makes it care.

LANSING. Why should he want to make it care?

JACKSON. Am I to be your tutor?

LANSING. That would be an honor, Mr. Jackson. I'm willing to be your student. But there's not a single tree in our quadrangle, the dormitories have no vines—

JACKSON. All the world's a gymnasium. You are different from the rest. You can see and benefit from the moon. My keeper, my scholar, what is it you wish to know?

LANSING. Shouldn't my innocent man have some humility?

JACKSON. Humility? Those three men dragged in here just now. Humble peasants begging for bread. Begging for work in order to feed their bellies. And the bellies of their enormous families, waiting in a cold house with the roof blown off. And where does their humility get them? Hands in the air and a rifle butt in the backbone. Humility gets abuse. They'll slap them around over there out of sight and send them off with broken fingers to complement their empty bellies. And the humble peasants will bury their emaciated infants one by one, stupidly insisting that it's "God's way." If they want bread in this world they've got to scheme and steal.

LANSING. They won't be hurt. We have only to find out who they are, why they're here.

JACKSON. Perhaps. But the military brute is impatient and stupid. He'll twist their arms to make them speak English. Pain, the universal language.

LANSING. I'll give them some rations before they leave.

JACKSON. That's charity, Lieutenant. They came to bargain. Work for bread. Bread for work. Don't give somebody something for nothing. It creates softness and breeds rot. Give them bread, Lieutenant, but allow them the dignity of working for it.

LANSING. I didn't mean to deny them that.

JACKSON. Of course not. Remember that there is greater dignity in stealing than in begging for one's existence. To beg suggests indifference toward oneself. Let them work for their bread.

LANSING. But if my innocent man schemes and steals he is no longer innocent.

JACKSON. Innocence! Only the innocent cherish it. It has its charm. Like old Valentines and babies. But it's something that is inevitably got rid of. A nice thing, an enviable thing, but its value is mostly nostalgic. It's something to remember, but in the end it inhibits.

LANSING. But surely it has a value?

JACKSON. That's doubtful. Innocence is usually too busy comparing itself to the so-called evils not to have some wear off on it.

LANSING. And so it's lost?

JACKSON. Like childhood. You can't work at innocence. It's unnatural. Innocence is never aware of itself until it's lost.

LANSING. You paint a bleak world, Mr. Jackson. It wasn't always like this was it?

JACKSON. I don't remember. Perhaps not, but I don't remember. There are exceptions still, of course. Like you. You've been most kind, Lieutenant. If it weren't for you I might not be writing again. I shall have to stop soon. The rain will be stiffening my fingers.

LANSING. I'll see about the roof.

JACKSON. Thank you, Lieutenant, thank you. If I finish the poem in time you will have been responsible.

LANSING. I would like to read it when it's ready.

JACKSON. You will be the first.

LANSING (*going*). I'll see about the roof.

JACKSON. Oh, Lieutenant, and the men—

LANSING. The Italians?

JACKSON. They're harmless. Give them some bread—but let them work for it.

SAUNDERS (*calling from inside Administration Building*). Lieutenant, will you come in here, please? (LANSING *enters the Administration Building.*) Would you make arrangements for those Italians to be escorted off the grounds?

LANSING. Have they been cleared?

SAUNDERS. Yes. Apparently local farmers, too old to fight and fairly stupid.

LANSING. They're all right, then?

SAUNDERS. What do you mean?

LANSING. They weren't hurt were they?

SAUNDERS. I was interested only in identifying them. I didn't prescribe any methods.

LANSING (*pause*). We could use them, sir, if they're all right.

SAUNDERS. Use them?

LANSING. They could help bury the old latrines.

SAUNDERS. We don't have to hire help for that.

LANSING. I thought it might speed things up. Our men could dig the new ones while these men buried the old. It would save time in getting ready.

SAUNDERS. Five days. The General will be here in five days. It would help, you think, to use them?

LANSING. Yes, sir.

SAUNDERS. What arrangements?

LANSING. Just some food— That's all they asked.

SAUNDERS. Very well, Lieutenant. I'll leave them to you. Any complaints over at the mess?

LANSING. No sir, everything seems to be going smoothly.

SAUNDERS. Yes it does. Not that we ever had any trouble—real trouble. Nothing has ever really gotten out of hand around here. But, nonetheless, in spite of all the efficiency, we always had evidence of unrest among the individuals. That seems to have eased for a time now. Perhaps it's the weather getting cooler. But also, Lieutenant, I think you deserve a little credit. Your duty here has perhaps not always been wholly military in its executions, but it has in its own way accounted perhaps for removing that unrest. At least it has enabled Jackson to become so occupied as to relieve us of his demonstrations.

LANSING. It seemed a waste not to—

SAUNDERS. Yes. You see it's not the deed but the result that counts. Not the action taken but the ability to foresee its result. It's abilities of that caliber that separate the officer class from the others.

LANSING. It seemed only humane—

SAUNDERS. Perhaps. But it's best to gauge humanitarian deeds by the results one gains from them. It never helps, I think, to put pennies in a blind man's cup, if you know what I mean. Nonetheless, I am pleased. Results so far have been good. No more escape attempts. No more demonstrations. Everything going smoothly. I hope it continues. At least for the next five days. There is one ruffle, however. Lieutenant, I shall have to discontinue Jackson's privileges in the Orderly Room. He can write longhand out there if it's so important. Also, he is to be advised that he must not circulate without an escort. That is to say, if he needs the latrine at night he's to summon a guard to see him to and from. Sergeant Heath has pointed out the difficulty of the guards distinguishing Jackson at night. He shouldn't take it amiss. It is a courtesy we extended, it is a courtesy we retract. Let him know we are not doing this out of spite but for his own protection. I don't want him acting up again.

LANSING. It will make it difficult for him to continue his work, sir. Do you suggest that we billet Mr. Jackson somewhere else now that cold weather is setting in?

SAUNDERS. No. Hadn't thought about it.

LANSING. There was a frost last night. The rain and the cold might affect his health.

SAUNDERS. We're pinched for space. It's difficult enough keeping him separated from the others.

LANSING. Perhaps a roof. Something over the top of the cage. Something to keep the rain from him. The inspectors will probably take notice of it.

SAUNDERS. Very well. Nothing elaborate. See what can be drawn from the supply depot and detail someone to do whatever's necessary. Keep it down to essentials. No need to baby him.

LANSING. No sir.

SAUNDERS. That's all, Lieutenant. Just a word to say keep up the good work. Oh, and also a word of caution. Give Heath as much lee-way as possible. I think he feels a little left out. He's proud, but he's good. I don't want him to become dissatisfied here. He's indispensable.

LANSING. I'm afraid that he has not forgiven my interference that first day. I know that he does not agree with my point of view.

SAUNDERS. Points of view are secondary to getting the job done. Despite all the rules and regulations we sometimes have to innovate.

LANSING. Yes sir.

(*The* COLONEL *returns to papers on desk. The* LIEUTENANT *goes into Orderly Room where* ORIOLE *is polishing boots. Observing him for a moment—*)

Oriole, how are you with a hammer and nails? Could you, do you think, build a sheltering roof?

(HEATH *looks up from his work.* ORIOLE *nods "Yes."*)

CURTAIN

SCENE TWO

Four days later. Late afternoon.

JACKSON, *wearing an old overcoat and scarf, is seated at a table within his cage, writing.*

ORIOLE *kneels overhead, putting the final nails in a makeshift roof. He fastens the last nail, sits back on his haunches and observes the sky from his vantage point.*

JACKSON. You finished up there? Hey, nigger, you got that roof fastened?

ORIOLE. Oh, yes sir, Mr. Jackson. She on good now. No rain is going to get into your house.

(JACKSON *comes outside cage to survey the roof.*)

JACKSON. Ah! Now my little bungalow is complete. Too bad it wasn't done sooner. Now I must move on.

ORIOLE. They coming to get you, Mr. Jackson?

JACKSON. Yes. They're coming to get me. (ORIOLE *starts down off roof.*) No, no. Stay up there. That's it. Stand right there. Oriole, Oriole. How did you come by a name like that?

ORIOLE. I don't know. My daddy called me a blackbird. He says I was a blackbird, always singing, movin' about.

JACKSON. Poetic! There you are, Oriole, perched atop a roof, ready to fly. Fly! There's nothing above you, no fences, nothing but clouds to hide you. No, no stay there, Oriole. (*pointing to sky*) Look. Think of yourself as one of them. Fellow blackbirds sailing through the air. Nothing to stop them. What keeps you here, blackbird?

ORIOLE. You mean me?

JACKSON. Yes, I mean you.

ORIOLE. Fences. Fences keep me. But I'm going soon now, too. I been good. Like the Lieutenant say, I been doing good work, toeing the mark. I bet just putting this roof over your head I'm going to get my walking papers. They going to say, nigger, get on out ahere!

JACKSON. You don't really believe that do you?

ORIOLE. The Lieutenant say so. The Lieutenant say so.

(LANSING, *followed by the* THREE ITALIANS, *enters the Quad.*)

LANSING. Have you finished it, Oriole?

ORIOLE. Yes sir. No rain going to get Mr. Jackson.

(LANSING *comes down into Quad to look at roof.* HEATH *rises from his desk and watches from the Administration Building door.*)

LANSING. It looks good, Oriole. What do you think of it, Mr. Jackson?

(JACKSON *is staring at the* ITALIANS. HEATH *notices this and comes out on the steps, watching.*)

Mr. Jackson—?

JACKSON. Oh, the roof. It'll do nicely.

LANSING. It should help. Perhaps you'll be able to work out here awhile yet. The noon sun is still warm.

JACKSON. It won't be long now. It'll soon be finished.

LANSING. Oh, I didn't know you were able to make so much progress. I was afraid that once you didn't have the typewriter—

JACKSON. I have no need for the machine. They think they can stop me simply by denying—

LANSING. Come down, Oriole. You've done a good job. We thank you.

(ORIOLE *hesitates, looking once more at the sky.*)

What's the matter, Oriole?

ORIOLE. It ain't true is it, Lieutenant? They not lying to me about me getting out, are they?

LANSING. What do you mean?

ORIOLE. I been good, ain't I, Lieutenant? They not teasing about me being good and maybe not let go?

LANSING. No, they're not teasing. Your chances for clemency are very good. What makes you think they're teasing?

ORIOLE (*looking at sky*). I don't know. I just worry. I think my poor daddy, he wonder about me. About what's going to happen to me.

LANSING. Does he know where you are?

ORIOLE. I don't know. I don't know. I never wrote him no letter.

LANSING. Come down, Oriole. I'll let you know what the chances are.

JACKSON. One favor deserves another, Oriole. Would you like to send a letter to your daddy?

ORIOLE. I would like that, Mr. Jackson.

LANSING (*rejoining the* ITALIANS). It's all right, Oriole. Tell Mr. Jackson what to write. Go ahead. (*To* ITALIANS:) Venite!

JACKSON. No, no Lieutenant. It's "Sequitemi!" "Sequitemi!"

LANSING. Thank you. They are very good. They seem to know what I mean whatever I say. Perhaps I shall learn Italian.

JACKSON (*to* ITALIANS). Sta studiando l'italiano.

ITALIANS. Ah!

JACKSON. Attenzione, professori, perche e' un bravo studente.

ITALIANS. Bene!

LANSING. What did they say?

JACKSON. They like you, of course.

LANSING (*to* ITALIANS). Sequitemi!

JACKSON. That's right, that's right.

(LANSING *and* ITALIANS *exit. To* ORIOLE:)

Come on, blackbird. You ever write a letter before?

ORIOLE. No sir. I never had no need—

JACKSON. That's right, no need. You have little needs, don't you? Well, need or no need, tell me what I'm to put down.

ORIOLE. I don't know what to say. It's like talking out loud and nobody there.

JACKSON (*going into cage, sitting at table, prepared to write*). That's so. That's the trouble with writing. Except there *is* somebody there. At least we hope so. Well, now, blackbird, what do you call your daddy?

ORIOLE. How do you mean?

JACKSON. Come in here and watch, Oriole. Let's write a letter. Now watch. (*writing*) "Dear Daddy Oriole—"

ORIOLE. That's not his name.

JACKSON. He'll know what you mean— "Dear Daddy Oriole, I'm tired of my stay in sunny Italy and I want—" What do you want, Oriole?

ORIOLE. How do you mean?

JACKSON. What I said. What would you like most of all if you had a wish?

ORIOLE. I would like for everybody to leave me alone and let me rest.

JACKSON (*writing*). "—to be left to rest." Now, what do you want to tell him Oriole?

ORIOLE. I don't know. Tell him I'm going to be free of here soon. Tell him the Lieutenant says he going to see to my papers. I'm going to leave here soon.

JACKSON. Why don't you tell him about what you've been doing here?

ORIOLE. No. That's not what he wants to hear. It's the same thing like what he does. Sweeping out floors, nailing things to keep the rain out. There's no need to tell him what he knows.

JACKSON (*writing*). "Today I stood atop a roof and watched blackbirds flying by. I'm going to fly soon, too. No more fences for this blackbird." Now what?

ORIOLE. Tell him it don't snow here either. Just rain like at home. But they's no cottonwoods here. Except for the rain, tell him it's nothing like home.

JACKSON (*writing*). "It doesn't snow here either. Just rain—" Where does this letter go?

ORIOLE. My daddy. Mr. Carver Williams in Louisville.

JACKSON. Street address?

ORIOLE. I don't remember. It's been a long time now.

JACKSON. How do you expect to mail it if you don't have the address?

ORIOLE. The Lieutenant will help me. The Lieutenant will mail it for me.

JACKSON. Ah, yes, the good Lieutenant. He does everything, doesn't he?

ORIOLE. He's going to see to my papers—

JACKSON. What else goes in here?

ORIOLE. What else?

JACKSON. What else do you want in the letter?

ORIOLE. I don't know. What have I said in it so far?

JACKSON. Very little— But enough. Why not just sign it? (*writing*) "Blackbird."

ORIOLE. Is that enough for a letter?

JACKSON. That's the best letter you ever wrote, Oriole. It's compact and to the point. Says everything there is to say. Like poetry.

ORIOLE. I sure do thank you, Mr. Jackson.

JACKSON. Don't mention it. You might do me a favor sometime. Tell your daddy to hang onto that letter. It'll be worth something someday. If they believe it.

ORIOLE. Yes sir. I'll tell him.

JACKSON. You tell him a bona-fide poet wrote that letter.

ORIOLE. Yes, sir. I'll tell him.

JACKSON. You be sure now.

ORIOLE. I will, sir. I will.

(ORIOLE *begins exit.* JACKSON *is chuckling to himself.*)

HEATH (*coming out of door, Administration Building—to* ORIOLE). Get in here and start pushing that broom!

(ORIOLE *goes into Administration Building.* HEATH *comes into the Quad, appraising the roof.*)

JACKSON. How do you like it, Sergeant? It's an improvement to the grounds, don't you think? This place might become choice real estate if it weren't for the neighbors. (HEATH *remains silent, looking at the roof.*) Want to buy it, Sergeant?

HEATH. I don't have to. I'll get my hands on it soon enough.

JACKSON. Soon enough. Yes, my lease is about to run out.

HEATH. Yeah? And where do you think you're going?

JACKSON. They're coming for me.

HEATH. Oh. We haven't heard.

JACKSON. Premonition, Sergeant. Men with soft heads are frequently afflicted with premonitions. That doesn't interest you, does it?

HEATH. You know I care very much what happens to you, Jackson.

JACKSON. But you have so little to say about it, don't you? You're better off controlling the fate of fellow brutes, Sergeant. Rascals like me are something else again.

HEATH. I'm beginning to see clear through you, Jackson. Better than most around here.

JACKSON. Perhaps you do. Perhaps you do. It doesn't seem to get you anywhere does it?

HEATH. Wait and see, Jackson. I'm going to keep a personal watch on you. When I pass this cage I want to find you in it. 'Cause I can get you, Jackson, when you're out of it. Once and for all I can get you and there'll be no questions asked. Wait and see.

JACKSON. I'll wait if it's not too long.

HEATH. You're like an old dog straining at the rope. Always barking. You're going to choke yourself barking.

JACKSON. When the old dog gets loose, Sergeant, he'll tear the behind out of you.

HEATH (*sauntering back to Administration Building*). They shoot mad dogs, Jackson. They shoot mad dogs.

JACKSON (*calling after him*). Only after they bite, Sergeant. Only after they bite.

(HEATH *enters the Administration Building.* ORIOLE *is sweeping vigorously, whistling.*)

HEATH. Shut up. Did you sweep out under the desk? And the chair? Get under that. Now, what are you so slap-happy about?

ORIOLE. I'm going to leave here soon.

HEATH. Oh you are?

ORIOLE. The Lieutenant says he going to see to my papers and he say I been good. I been doing good things. He says I built a fine roof over Mr. Jackson's head.

HEATH. You're becoming quite a buddy with Jackson aren't you?

ORIOLE. Mr. Jackson is a good man. He wrote me a letter to send to my old daddy in Louisville.

HEATH. Well let me tell you, Oriole, Mr. Jackson would just as soon shoot your daddy as write a letter to him. That's how stupid you are being sucked in by him. Mr. Jackson don't think niggers are fit.

ORIOLE. Oh no, Mr. Jackson don't say that. You shouldn't talk like that—

(HEATH *takes* ORIOLE *by the shirt front.*)

HEATH. Who are you telling how to talk! Ah, ah, ah. (*holding his hand out*) What do we have here? A button! Came off without even being asked. That button couldn't have been on very tight. I wonder if they're all loose. (*Backs* ORIOLE *against wall.*) I'll tear every button off you. You, out there playing games with Jackson! Coming in here and being sassy! You aren't smart enough to know who you're supposed to be nice to and who you're not. Not smart enough to be let out of here. You better stay with us and dig holes and sew buttons, Oriole. You're getting out of line. You're going to lose points. Now you get on your knees in here. I want this floor scrubbed. Don't you step out of here until it shines. Don't move out of here if it takes you all night!

(ORIOLE *kneels and brings bucket from around behind desk. He begins scrubbing. The* COLONEL *enters from his office.*)

SAUNDERS. Well, Heath, tomorrow is the day.

HEATH. Yes sir.

SAUNDERS. The sun quits early now. It's cold without it.

(*The* LIEUTENANT *enters the Administration Building.*)

LANSING. Good evening, sir.

SAUNDERS. Your duty tonight?

LANSING. Yes sir. Is there anything that you wish me to work on?

SAUNDERS. I hope that it is all done. Our time is up. The General will be here first thing in the morning. This place going to be all ready by then?

HEATH. When he finishes scrubbing, sir.

SAUNDERS. Then we're ready. Thank god, we're ready. Sergeant, will you take retreat with the guards tonight?

HEATH. Yes sir.

SAUNDERS. And Sergeant, tell them to start using the storm flag tomorrow. The wind is getting strong.

HEATH. Yes sir. Is there anything else?

SAUNDERS. I hope not. Unless the Lieutenant. . . .

LANSING. No sir.

SAUNDERS. Good night, Sergeant.

HEATH. Good night, sir. (*Exits across the darkening Quad.*)

SAUNDERS. Tomorrow. What a petty thing to attach one's reputation to, an inspection. And how can one hope to succeed at the impossible? But we have, haven't we, Lieutenant? I can't help succumbing to a certain pride in doing that. And who would have suspected success in this place? Sunny Italy gone sour. Nothing here to stop the wind once it begins. Nothing visible for miles once those leaves have left those trees off there. Dust of course. Dust in waves. On a good day before the rains you can drown in dust and then—mud. You know, Lieutenant, I've discovered something. We're not too unalike, you and I. Perhaps, like you, I should never have been a soldier, and yet I wonder if sometimes we don't succeed best at what we're not. Perhaps a little bit of poetry helps. I don't know. We'll know tomorrow.

LANSING. We're ready for them.

SAUNDERS. Good night, Lieutenant. Tomorrow.

LANSING. Good night, sir.

(*The* COLONEL *exits across the Quad, pausing to look up as the lights on pole are illuminated. He exits.*)

LANSING (*to* ORIOLE *who is scrubbing*). How long is this going to take you, Oriole?

ORIOLE. I don't know, Lieutenant. It's got to shine and I got to make it shine.

LANSING. What do you mean, "shine?"

ORIOLE. The Sergeant says it got to shine and he mean it. Lieutenant, I'm never going to get out of this place. I've lost my chance now for sure.

LANSING. What do you mean?

ORIOLE. I'm never going to get this floor as clean as the Sergeant says and I'm never going to get out of this place. Every time I think I'm going to go, something goes wrong. I'm going to stay here forever. I'm going to die in this place.

LANSING. What makes you say that, Oriole?

ORIOLE. First Mr. Jackson says they fooling me when they say I going to get out and then the Sergeant, he found my button. It come off. I forgot. I thought they was all on tight but the Sergeant got it. He says he going to get them all if I don't stay away from that Mr. Jackson and toe the mark.

LANSING. Get up, Oriole.

ORIOLE. No, Lieutenant, I ain't going to get up until this here floor shine or I'm dead trying.

LANSING. I said get up, Oriole. (ORIOLE *gets up slowly.*) I told you I'd look into your clemency papers. Well, I have. I don't like your mooning around as if all your chances were gone. You're eligible to come before the board next month.

ORIOLE. No, I lost it. Sergeant Heath—

LANSING. Oriole, shut up! There's nothing to be afraid of. You haven't lost your chances. If you don't give up now, I promise you that everything will be all right. I promise you. Now, get back to whatever Sergeant Heath asked you to do. I'll tell you when the floor shines, Oriole. It won't take forever.

(LANSING *sits at* HEATH'*s desk.* ORIOLE *returns to scrubbing. Outside, several soft whistles are heard.* JACKSON *comes forward in his cage. He whistles in return.*)

Oriole, why did you kill a man?

ORIOLE (*after considering*). He lied. I believed him. I believed what he told me and he lied.

(*The* THREE ITALIANS *enter the Quad. They scatter past the cage, looking into the darkness. They beckon to* JACKSON.)

LANSING. Are you sorry?

ORIOLE. He shouldn't of lied to me. I didn't mean to kill him. I didn't mean for me to come to this place. But he didn't have to lie to me, either. (*As* ORIOLE *speaks* JACKSON *opens the cage door and joins them, moving up left.*)

LANSING. What will you do, Oriole, when you are free?

ORIOLE. Oh, they'll send me back to the Infantry. They'll tell me what to do. But it'll be different than here.

LANSING. And after the Infantry?

(*As* ORIOLE *begins to speak* JACKSON *and the* ITALIANS *stop and begin to retreat.*)

ORIOLE. Then I'll go back to Louisville, I s'pose. Get me some kind of job. Some nights, visit with my daddy, some nights go down on Cleveland Avenue, drink beer, watch the showlights chase around on front of the moviehouse. Jus' relax, not be worry all the time.

(*As* LANSING *begins to speak* HEATH *enters the Quad.* JACKSON *darts back toward the Administration Building, standing quietly on the steps. The* THREE ITALIANS *disappear behind the building.*)

LANSING. There's nothing to worry about now, Oriole. I promise.

ORIOLE. I worry till it comes true.

(*As* HEATH *approaches center Quad,* JACKSON *darts into the Orderly Room.*)

LANSING (*rising, startled*). Mr. Jackson! What are you doing here?

JACKSON. I know, Lieutenant, I know. Regulations. I've got a chill and I felt—I felt as if I needed someone to talk to.

LANSING. I'll call the Dispensary.

JACKSON. No, no. They can't help me. It's not sickness, it's old age. Their pills won't change that and they won't change the weather. It's cold again tonight. It's nice here, Lieutenant. May I stay awhile, please? Just for a bit?

(*Outside,* HEATH, *having circled the cage, saunters off.*)

LANSING. You shouldn't have left your cage—

JACKSON. I know, I know. I am so tired of requesting.

LANSING. It's dangerous. The guards might not have recognized you.

JACKSON. Just as well. If they had they would have shot me. I'm not well liked, Lieutenant. Except by you, perhaps. Just an old man on his last legs. I think they thought they'd bury me here. They're waiting for the weather to get me. Won't be long now. I'm beholden to you for the roof.

LANSING. Oriole built it.

JACKSON. It's not the carpenters but the enterpreneurs who matter in this world. I'm beholden to *you*, Lieutenant.

LANSING. I can see that you get more blankets if that is what you want. I'll take you back now, Mr. Jackson.

JACKSON. Oh no, not now. I've got a surprise. This is a very special night! Don't send me back, Lieutenant. I've finished the poem!

LANSING (*eagerly*). When may I see it?

JACKSON. That's why I came. You have been most kind, Lieutenant. I wanted to thank you for all you've done. I told you that you should be the first to see it.

LANSING. Tonight?

JACKSON. Tonight!

LANSING. Did you bring it with you?

JACKSON. No. I left it out there. I wasn't sure that you'd let me in.

LANSING. Perhaps in the morning then.

JACKSON. No. Please. I want you to have it tonight. I may not be here in the morning.

LANSING. What do you mean?

JACKSON. I told you about old men and premonitions. The wind has an ominous sound. It has been a hard year of fighting and now that I've finished what I wanted, it doesn't matter that I fight any longer.

LANSING. Are you sure that you're feeling well? I'll call the Dispensary. You'll spend the night there.

JACKSON (*chuckling*). No, no, Lieutenant. I promise you that I will not die tonight. But there is that in the air. The innocent die young. Old rascals like myself fear only damnation and I'm not convinced. Let's get the poem!

LANSING (*pause*). No. You should have brought it with you.

JACKSON. I was afraid that you'd be angry—

LANSING. But I don't want you stopped out there. You'd lose all the privileges you've gained.

JACKSON. Oriole. Send Oriole.

LANSING. No. I don't think we should. I'll see it tomorrow.

JACKSON. Please, Lieutenant. I've worked very hard to finish it. Don't disappoint me. We have defied them so far. Now that the deed has been accomplished, we deserve our celebration—tonight! What better time than now when the world sleeps. Say yes, Lieutenant. Send Oriole. Oriole can get it.

LANSING. Mr. Jackson—

JACKSON. Oh my god, Lieutenant! You have done so much for me, don't deny me my success—*our* success. The poem is yours. I've done it for you. I want you to have it now. Please. It's for you, Lieutenant, for you. Send Oriole. (*Low whistles are heard in the darkness outside.*) It's for you, Lieutenant, for you.

LANSING (*pause*). Where is it?

JACKSON. On the table—with a rock on top of it. It's light enough there. He can find it.

LANSING. Oriole—

ORIOLE. Please, no, sir. Don't make me go.

LANSING. What's the matter with you?

ORIOLE. Don't make me go. I'll never get out of here.

LANSING. Quiet! How many times, Oriole, do I have to tell you to do as you're told. That's the only way you'll ever get out of here. Don't be belligerent.

JACKSON. I'll get it myself.

LANSING. No. Oriole, you heard what Mr. Jackson said. There are papers on his table in the cage—

ORIOLE. Please—

LANSING. Oriole, go out there and get those papers and bring them to me.

ORIOLE. Yes sir.

(ORIOLE *goes to door hesitantly, goes out and down steps to cage.*)

JACKSON. The children are difficult aren't they?

LANSING. It's difficult. . . . When did you finish it?

JACKSON. Only today. Early this evening. And I am pleased with it. It's my best.

LANSING. Then it must be very great.

(ORIOLE *gets papers and is just leaving cage when* HEATH *returns.* ORIOLE *shrinks to rear of cage. Subsequent action in the Quad is simultaneous with conversation between* JACKSON *and* LIEUTENANT LANSING.)

JACKSON. You shall be the judge of that.

(HEATH *continues across the Quad when the sound of whistles stops him. He listens intently for a moment—*)

LANSING. Oh no, the world will have its say.

(HEATH *walks toward the upstage fence, causing* ORIOLE *to retreat around the cage.*)

JACKSON. Yes, I suppose it will insist on it. But still it's yours.

HEATH. Who's there!

LANSING. You've never told me what it's about.

(HEATH *draws his pistol and begins to circle the cage.* ORIOLE *circles round front, climbs on top of the cage, hugging the roof.*)

JACKSON. Ah, but you shall see—

(*The whistles become more insistent.*)

LANSING. Was that a whistle? Are you sure that Oriole can find it?

JACKSON. Oh yes, it's there. Clear in the moonlight. He'll find it. He'll find it.

(HEATH *has circled the cage and found no one. He stands quietly beside the cage.* ORIOLE *begins to get up cautiously. Finally he stands. The movement startles* HEATH *who stands just below him.*)

LANSING. I shouldn't have sent him. He's frightened.

JACKSON. They always are.

(HEATH *whirls and fires once.* ORIOLE *falls to the roof,* JACKSON's *papers fluttering to the ground.*

LANSING *has leaped to the door while* JACKSON *rushes to the far side of the room.*

GUARDS' *voices are heard calling post to post. A siren begins in the distance.*)

LANSING (*on steps*). What is it, Sergeant?

(HEATH *is dragging* ORIOLE's *body from off the roof, laying it on the ground in front of the cage.*)

HEATH. I thought it was Jackson! I thought it was Jackson!

(LANSING *crosses slowly to the body.* JACKSON *exits through the* COLONEL's *office. More sirens have begun to sound.*)

I thought it was Jackson, Lieutenant. I thought it was Jackson!

(LANSING *kneels beside the body.* GUARDS *rush across upstage.*)

Where *is* Jackson, Lieutenant?

(LANSING *gestures absently toward Administration Building.* HEATH *dashes to it, searching both offices. He returns to the steps.*)

HEATH. Jackson's not here. Where is he, Lieutenant? Where is Jackson?

(LANSING, *holding* ORIOLE's *head, looks up slowly, staring straight before him. Machine guns begin to fire, sirens rise, and the search-lights collide as:*)

THE CURTAIN FALLS

ACT THREE

The following morning. Heavy rain can be heard falling at first and then wanes as the Act progresses.

In the Administration Building the COLONEL *stands, facing the door expectantly.* HEATH *sits at his desk.*

On the Quad between the Administration Building and the cage are the bodies of ORIOLE *and the* THREE ITALIANS. *The* CAPTAIN, *Graves Registration Officer, stands over* ORIOLE's *body, writing on a clipboard. A* GUARD *draws a cover over the body as the* CAPTAIN *finishes.*

CAPTAIN (*turning to the other bodies*). These the wops?

GUARD. Yes sir.

CAPTAIN. Wonder what they thought they were going to get out of it.

GUARD. Don't know sir.

CAPTAIN. Better cover them.

(GENERAL DUNCAN, *accompanied by his* ENTOURAGE, *enters across Quad. He stops long enough to scan the bodies and return the salute of the* CAPTAIN *and* GUARD *before entering the Administration Building. Upon his entrance the* COLONEL *calls "Attention!"* HEATH *stands beside his desk.*)

DUNCAN. There was to have been an inspection here this morning, Colonel.

SAUNDERS. Yes, General.

DUNCAN. This inspection has been announced for some time. The usual directives have been explicit, outlining what was to be expected.

SAUNDERS. Yes, General.

DUNCAN. I have made every effort, officially and directly, to impress upon you the importance of this inspection. The importance not only to this installation but to you, professionally. And, Colonel, what do I find? It would seem that any preparation you have made, any control you have exercised has run amuck. Your most valuable prisoner has fled. A quarter of your guards runs frantically through the countryside searching for an old man. The path to your door is piled high with bodies. It is as if *no one* had been in charge.

SAUNDERS. My men will find Jackson.

DUNCAN. Again, you are laggard. Lionel Jackson was taken this morning. He will be returned here shortly to be shipped to the States immediately, under escort. I suggest that his papers be gotten ready. I have sent everything else. (*pause*) Well, it would be a sham to hold an inspection this morning, Colonel. What I have seen has revealed more than I expected. You had better make whatever repairs you can and make them suddenly. I shall expect to hear from you within twenty-four hours.

(GENERAL DUNCAN *and* ENTOURAGE *leave the Administration Building, meeting* LIEUTENANT LANSING *on the steps, coming in. They pause, exchange salutes. The* GENERAL *and* ENTOURAGE *exit across Quad. The* LIEUTENANT *enters Administration Building.*)

SAUNDERS (*in his office*). Come in, Lieutenant. The inspection is over. Everything is over. I have learned something from this, from you. You and I, Lieutenant, are human beings and it was not required of us. Not asked of us. I have received orders, perhaps my last, to correct "the errors." I must begin with you. Yours was less wrong than mine, but it was the gravest. Not an error of duty or performance, but an individual error of—shall we say, "the heart"? I won't put it in your file. It would be difficult to explain that kind of error in a military file. But you must go. And so, for reasons explained only as "misplacement of officer strength" I have arranged for you to go south—Sorrento. You will leave immediately. I know a colonel there in charge of a Rest and Rehabilitation Center. It's a choice assignment—Sorrento. You'll like it. Sympathy, compassion are welcomed there. You'll be more at home.

LANSING. There will be nothing for me to do at Sorrento. Sir, isn't it possible that I stay here?

SAUNDERS. No. I cannot afford your natural charity. It does not correspond with what is asked of me here. It is not needed.

LANSING. Sir—

SAUNDERS. It is not *wanted* here!

LANSING. What was the first mistake? The day I stopped Heath?

SAUNDERS. I cannot and will not argue that with you, Lieutenant. Sorrento it is.

LANSING. Hospitals. Bandages. Soft voices. Wounds need only to bleed to receive care. But they've got to bleed or no one will believe it. They'll have no need for me in Sorrento. Surface wounds are always looked after, comforted.

SAUNDERS. In this world of wars, Lieutenant, the effort is to keep the heart beating, not comforted. You had better get your things together. You will leave the RTO this afternoon. Should I not see you before you leave—farewells are as superfluous as welcomes at this place—I say goodbye to you. Your error was decent enough, Lieutenant, but that does not protect it from being wrong. We know that now. Now. Wisdom shouldn't come so late.

LANSING. Goodbye, Colonel.

(LANSING *salutes. The* COLONEL *returns the salute.* LANSING *exits into Orderly Room as the* CAPTAIN *enters.*)

CAPTAIN (*to* HEATH, *who is finishing signing papers at his desk*). Now, we have all the witness reports, have we not? Everything that needs to be reported has been put down, has it not?

LANSING (*to* CAPTAIN). No. I noticed, Captain, on the form that I filled in—there was no way of explaining why Oriole died.

CAPTAIN. I have answered that in my report. "Death instantaneous. Cause: single fire, pistol, U. S. Army, Model M-1911-A2." If you wished any additions in your report, Lieutenant, there was space provided under the heading, "Further Comments."

LANSING. Three lines. I wouldn't have been able to explain it on those three lines. It's not really enough is it, Captain?

(*The* LIEUTENANT *turns and exits into the Quad just as two* GUARDS *enter with* JACKSON. *The* LIEUTENANT *and* JACKSON *stop, facing one another across the bodies.*)

JACKSON (*after a long moment he chuckles*). Well, the old man didn't make it. But for an old rascal it was a pretty good try. Now that they see how spry I am they're finally bundling me off to the States. America the beautiful. Land of well-scrubbed justice.

LANSING. I'm leaving too. Sorrento.

JACKSON. Ah, Sorrento! You'll like Sorrento! It's much warmer and when it rains it's gentle. Much better than here.

LANSING. Goodbye, Mr. Jackson.

JACKSON. Wait Lieutenant! Your books. I haven't returned your books.

LANSING. I won't need them. Do with them as you please.

JACKSON. But Lieutenant, I wish to thank you for your kindness. I'm a lost man now. I've wanted to live so much, so much. There's nothing without it—life. It's the only thing we're slave to. And I could have gone on, Lieutenant, I could have. Out there, running through the dark, cold blades of grass, lashing these old legs on, my breath like a ghost puffing about my whiskers and the moon, ah, my moon, slipping in and out of clouds, arranging shadows here, showing me the way there. It was so good to be running with those alive things. I was so close to succeeding, so close! I shan't forget your help, Lieutenant.

LANSING. I wish, Mr. Jackson, that I could forget. You mustn't forget that Oriole helped. Your friends helped.

JACKSON. Yes, yes they did. But not without you. There has to be the thinker and the guide and the others do as told. Some men are gods—some are tools. They say that's not right. I don't argue. All I say is that's the way it is. You'd be a god, Lieutenant, except you're selfless. Me, I'm self*ish,* and the world knows who I am because of it. And you, what's your reward, Lieutenant? I'll wager the world doesn't even comprehend you.

LANSING. I would have cut the fences for you, Mr. Jackson, rather than have you do what you did. I had unlocked one door, I would have cut the fences to save you from disgrace!

JACKSON. No. No, you wouldn't have cut the fences. Your sense of propriety would have stopped you short of cutting fences for me. And Oriole? My friends? I didn't kill Oriole. You didn't kill Oriole. Heath. Heath did it. No romantic complexes. Heath. Heath did it.

LANSING. And we saw to it that he did.

JACKSON. The world is a mysterious place. Who knows the hunter from the hunted? Who could tell that by crossing that threshold, stepping down those steps into the moonlight that death was inevitable? Killers pass casually in the night and death is a coincidence. One never knows. One never knows.

LANSING. You knew, didn't you, Mr. Jackson?

JACKSON. I?

LANSING. Some are gods and some are tools. Surely you are a god, Mr. Jackson.

JACKSON. Yes, surely I am. But do not blame me for it. Don't become petty and self-righteous like the rest of them. Who are they, who are you, to condemn me? You, who have done nothing.

LANSING. I did nothing? Some are gods and some are tools. Surely I was the tool. Surely I was the one who defied the regulations, who unlocked your cage, let you roam about, pointing at the heavens and the blackbirds. Surely it was I who provided this roof, provided you with paper— And it was I, too late, but knowing, *knowing,* who said, "Oriole go." And even when he tried to tell me, I insisted and it was not my military bearing, I have no military bearing, but I said, "Go" because I wanted that poetry. I wanted that poetry because I adored you. Yes, I adored you because you were a god and I wished to share your godliness! But if you were a god, Mr. Jackson, you should not have been so afraid of dying. You should not have stooped. You're just a man like the others aren't you?

JACKSON (*after pause*). I shall remember you, Lieutenant. I shall remember that charity is found among those who do not observe regulations.

LANSING. And I shall become *fastidious* about regulations.

JACKSON. Oh, please, not you! I have written about innocence and I have written about all the things you have ever dreamed of and admired. All the things which make this life, this world so unbearably marvelous. The world will see my words and understand. What will the world ever learn from you?

LANSING. Only what it teaches me.

JACKSON. Perhaps. (*reaching under his coat*) But it is all here. The poem, Lieutenant. Would you read it?

LANSING. I was to have read it last night. The papers you sent for were blank.

JACKSON. I had taken it with me, of course. No sense in leaving valuables behind. But now, before I die, I don't need it. I need for you to have it. (*stretching out his arm, offering the poem to* LANSING) I promised you'd be the first. It is for you.

LANSING. For me?

JACKSON. You wished to share and you have. It is yours. It is yours.

(LANSING *hesitates, then raises his hand to take the poem.*)

If it had not been for you—

(LANSING *withdraws his hand abruptly.*)

LANSING. No. I'm sorry. I have wanted this poem very much, but it has cost so much. I'm sorry, Mr. Jackson, it's not enough. Goodbye.

(LANSING *turns and begins to exit up right.*)

JACKSON. Lieutenant! You shan't regret that you have helped me. (*desperately*) They shall hang me! They shall hang me!

LANSING (*turning, shaking his head*). Surely, Mr. Jackson, you will think of something.

(LANSING *exits up right.*

JACKSON *reluctantly puts the papers under his coat. The* GUARDS *lead him to his cage and lock door behind him.*

The COLONEL *comes out of office into the Orderly Room.*)

SAUNDERS. Now, Sergeant, we must make repairs. The General will return. If only this all could have waited— It won't be easy, but you can do it. I want you to be ruthless, Sergeant. I want the trainees worked within an inch of their lives so that when the inspectors see them this place will—shine! I want them to stand at attention, exhausted and serene. Take up the reins, Heath, where they've gone slack. (*Goes to door, looking over Quad, where* GUARDS *begin to remove the bodies, then, almost wistfully*:) Compassion is an anachronism here.

(COLONEL SAUNDERS *goes out and begins to cross Quad.* HEATH *stands in door watching him. The* COLONEL *pauses, indicating the cage.*)

SAUNDERS (*calling back to* HEATH). We should see that this gets out of the way.

HEATH. Yes sir.

(COLONEL SAUNDERS *exits.* HEATH *remains standing, filling the door. A young officer,* LIEUTENANT SAWYER, *accompanied by two* GUARDS *enters the Quad. The* GUARDS *remain down left.*

SAWYER, *looking about him, crosses to the Administration Building.*)

HEATH. Have you come for Jackson, Lieutenant?

SAWYER. Yes—yes I have, Sergeant. I'm Lieutenant Sawyer. I'm going to escort Lionel Jackson back to the States. Is that him?

HEATH. Yeah, that's him.

SAWYER. Is he ready to go? I've got a sedan waiting outside.

HEATH. Yes, he's ready to go. Here's a file for you. Everything else has been forwarded by mail.

SAWYER (*observing* JACKSON). He's much older looking than I thought he would be. Did you keep him in that cage?

HEATH. Some of us did.

SAWYER. It's a shame to treat a man that way. The man's a genius, you know. It must have been very interesting having him here.

HEATH. We're not sorry to see him go.

SAWYER. Oh?

HEATH (*impatiently*). You can take him to the hangman now.

SAWYER. I don't think they'll consider hanging him, Sergeant. Talent like his is so rare in this world. He deserves a little respect.

HEATH. If you think he deserves so much respect, Lieutenant, don't keep him waiting.

(SAWYER *goes to the cage. The* GUARD *salutes him, unlocks the gate.* LANSING *comes with his bag to the Administration Building.* JACKSON *stands, walks out of the cage. The two* GUARDS *come forward from down left, one taking* JACKSON'S *duffel bag.* SAWYER *and* JACKSON *begin to cross Quad down left followed by* GUARDS. HEATH *and* LANSING *stand watching from the Administration Building.*)

SAWYER. I've read some of your things, sir. I think they're very good.

JACKSON (*stopping*). Ah, you like poetry?

SAWYER. Yes, I think I do. I like yours.

JACKSON. That's very kind of you to say, Lieutenant. Very kind. (JACKSON *and* SAWYER *move a few steps further down left.* JACKSON *stops suddenly and points up into the sky.*) Look, Lieutenant, look! Graceful aren't they? Many's the day I've watched them fly overhead. I shall miss them.

SAWYER (*looking up*). They're blackbirds, sir. You can find those everywhere.

JACKSON (*looking at him for a moment, then smiling*). Yes, yes, indeed. (*They begin to move off down left.*) So you like my poems, Lieutenant? (JACKSON, SAWYER *and* GUARDS *exit.*)

LANSING (*standing at the foot of the steps,* HEATH *still standing above, in the doorway*). You've won, Sergeant.

HEATH. I'm used to winning.

LANSING. I suppose so.

HEATH. The sedan is waiting for you, Lieutenant.

LANSING (*taking look around the Quad*). Yes. Goodbye, Sergeant Heath.

(LANSING *picks up his bag. The* COLONEL *enters.*)

SAUNDERS. Now, Sergeant, let's get down to business!

(*Immediately a whistle sounds, the drum begins its cadence and the* DRILL PLATOON *marches in loudly.*

The DRILL SERGEANT *marches them in front of the cage and calls* "Halt!" *He holds the* PLATOON *at* "Attention."

HEATH *comes down the steps into the Quad slowly. He goes to the cage. He surveys it. He climbs to the roof quickly, stands there, tapping it with his foot for a moment as if testing its strength, then stoops quickly and wrenches a plank from it. He throws the board to the ground.*)

HEATH (*to the* DRILL SERGEANT). Let's get this eyesore out of here!

(*The* DRILL SERGEANT *blows his whistle. The drum begins beating a soft cadence. The* PLATOON *falls out and converges on the cage.* LIEUTENANT LANSING *begins to cross Quad slowly as the* PLATOON *begins dismantling the cage.* GUARDS *move in, surrounding the action.* LIEUTENANT LANSING *exits.* HEATH, *still on the roof, standing proudly, looks up into the sky, then looks down. He spits.*)

THE FINAL CURTAIN FALLS